PETER CUSHING
The Reluctant Globetrotter

PETER CUSHING
The Reluctant Globetrotter
Mark Iveson

First published in 2025 by Telos Publishing Ltd
139 Whitstable Road, Canterbury, Kent CT2 8EQ

www.telos.co.uk

Telos Publishing Ltd values feedback. Please e-mail us with any comments you may have about this book to: feedback@telos.co.uk

Peter Cushing: The Reluctant Globetrotter © 2025 Mark Iveson

ISBN: 978-1-84583-241-4

Cover Art: © 2024 Mark Maddox

The moral right of the author has been asserted.

British Library Cataloguing in Publication Data. A catalogue record for this book is available from the British Library.

This book is sold subject to the condition that it shall not by way of trade or otherwise, be lent, resold, hired out or otherwise circulated without the publisher's prior written consent in any form of binding or cover other than that in which it is published and without a similar condition including this condition being imposed on the subsequent purchaser.

Contents

Introduction   9

1. The Early Years   11
2. Hollywood Beckons   19
3. One-Way Ticket to Hollywood   24
4. *The Man In The Iron Mask* (1939)   28
5. *A Chump At Oxford* (1939)   35
6. *Vigil In The Night* (1940)   42
7. *Women In War* (1940)   49
8. The Passing Parade Shorts   52
9. *Laddie* (1940)   55
10. *The Howards Of Virginia* (1940)   58
11. *They Dare Not Love* (1941)   61
12. One-Way Ticket to Blighty   66
13. Cushing Down Under   75
14. Homegrown Television   90
15. *The Black Knight* (1954)   94
16. *Magic Fire* (1955)   99
17. *Alexander The Great* (1956)   103
18. Homegrown Star   107
19. *John Paul Jones* (1959)   113
20. *Sword Of Sherwood Forest* (1960)   118
21. *She* (1965)   126
22. Marking Time in Blighty   137
23. *Horror Express* (1972)   161
24. Back to Blighty   173
25. *Legend Of The 7 Golden Vampires* (1974)   185
26. *Shatter* (1975)   195
27. *Tender Dracula* (1975)   199
28. *Shock Waves* (1976)   204
29. *The Devil's Men* (1976)   211
30. *Star Wars* (1977)   215
31. *Battleflag* (1977)   219
32. *The Uncanny* (1977)   223
33. *Hitler's Son* (1978)   227
34. *A Touch Of The Sun* (1978)   230
35. *Mystery On Monster Island* (1980)   234
36. *Black Jack* (1981)   238

37. The Final Years	240
38. Epilogue: *Rogue One* (2016)	248
Bibliography	250
Title Index	251
Name Index	254
About the Author	256

Dedication

*Dedicated to the Memory of Peter Cushing.
Brilliant actor, gracious gentleman and boyhood hero.*

*And to the memory of Reece Williams and Gwyn Eklund.
Two wonderful friends who were taken too soon by Covid-19.*

Acknowledgements

I feel so lucky to be blessed by so many friends who have supported me with completing this book and my previous books. I would like to claim a long list but will have to limit my gratitude to the chosen few.

To my mother Inga, especially when she was looking after me when I had health problems. To dear Carolyn Eastgate, my resident Girl Friday. To the wonderfully supportive Sally Franz, who remains a great influence with her guidance, and the Swanwick Writers Retreat.

To Daniela Norris, Ema Daggett and Marcus Brooks, and new friends Pauline Peart, Peter Fuller, Selene Paxton-Brooks, Eric McNaughton, Darrell Buxton and Raven Dane, all of whom have been so supportive in one way or another.

Special thanks to my talented friend Lucy Dawlish, who co-organised our book launch/art exhibition, *Meet the Author, Meet the Artist*, held in Newcastle in June 2022. It was a blast!

My amazing thanks to Steve Walker and David Howe at Telos. They are two excellent people who have been so good to me. I'm eternally grateful to you both, especially David and his amazing wife Samantha when you got me involved in the 2022 *Sci-Fi Weekender*, which was so much fun and the 2022 *Hulloween Festival*.

I reserve my greatest thanks to my wonderful lady Heather Powell, who has been the ultimate inspiration in my life. I cannot imagine life without you and your support.

Introduction

Ever since I watched *Dr Who and the Daleks* (1965) when I was a kid, Peter Cushing has remained my boyhood hero. As I learnt more about him growing up, I was amazed by his versatility and his ability to tackle all kinds of roles during his long and distinguished career.

What made him fascinating was his essential Britishness. His love and devotion for his country is something that seems rare nowadays, but for Cushing, he lived it. So much so, that his reluctance to travel overseas limited his career options, even when the British film industry went into meltdown during the seventies.

And yet he did work abroad and even travelled to Hollywood with dreams of movie stardom.

When I was writing *Vincent Price: The British Connection*, my focus was on Price's career in England. For this book, I went to the opposite end by focussing on Cushing's foreign output, from his glory days in Hollywood to the increasingly strange Euro-puddings produced in the seventies.

Peter Cushing: The Reluctant Globetrotter looks at the overseas period of his career. It has been a hard book to write during a difficult period with Covid-19 running rampant, along with my own health problems. But I made it through in one piece!

Enjoy!

Mark Iveson
12/04/2024

1: The Early Years

An early photograph of Peter Cushing.

What can one say about a man whose life has been written about by so many biographers over the years without repeating oneself?

Hollywood's future film star was born Peter Wilton Cushing on 26 May 1913 in Kenley, Surrey. His father, George Edward Cushing, who was born in 1881, came from a strict and conventional upper class Victorian family, and as a result, his upbringing made him a reserved individual. 'I always had the impression his childhood had not been a happy one,' Cushing said of his father, 'although he didn't ever admit it.' The relationship between father and son remained a distant one.

'My father was a practical man. He was a quantity surveyor which is all to do with mathematics. I can't add up two and three and get it right.' George Cushing followed in his father's professional footsteps, working for Selby and Saunders until his retirement.

Born in 1882, Cushing's mother, Nellie Maria King, was the daughter of a successful carpet merchant. They married on 3 July 1907. Cushing's brother David was born in 1910.

The brothers enjoyed a happy family life. 'We were by no means a rich family,' the younger brother recalled. 'I should think very middle class with just enough to get by. No more than "just enough", because tax wasn't a problem in those days. Looking back, we always had what was to me a very nice house, and always a very nice garden.' A year after his birth, the family moved to Dulwich. It was the beginning of World War One, and the actor's earliest memory was seeing Zeppelins flying overhead.

Cushing's immediate family didn't have a strong connection to the theatre, and George Cushing had scant regard for the acting profession, typical of his Victorian upbringing. According to his son, 'It was still a period when they regarded all actors as rogues and vagabonds.' Several family members had successful stage careers, enough to influence Peter's future endeavours.

The most influential was George Cushing's sister Maude, who acted under the stage name Maude Ashton. She had a reasonably successful career and prior to her early retirement, Peter saw her in a one-act drama where she played a lady of easy virtue. The youngster wasn't aware of the character she was playing, but he was thrilled to watch her on stage. One actor who knew Aunt Maude professionally was Ronald Squire, who unsuccessfully persuaded her to return to the stage. Cushing and Squire later worked together in the 1946 London production of *The Rivals*.

Aunt Maude was of haughty mien and felt her brother married beneath him. She also provided her nephew with an interesting fact regarding his grandfather, Henry William Cushing.

A quantity surveyor by trade, Henry Cushing was a stern figure who never encouraged any artistic pursuits. Aunt Maude often gave her nephew souvenir programmes of Sir Henry Irving's famous Lyceum Theatre productions. This included Shakespeare's *Henry VIII*, where the cast included Henry Cushing in a supporting role.

Henry Cushing pursued a chequered career, working in a variety of jobs, none of which included quantity surveyor. He had spells as a vocalist before rounding things off as a tragic actor. In addition to touring England, Canada and the USA with Sir Henry Irving's company, he worked with theatre greats Ellen Terry, William Terriss and Forbes Robertson.

Another family member was Cushing's step-uncle Wilton Herriot, an actor, playwright and stage manager of some repute. A tragic actor by profession, Herriot wrote several music hall sketches and stage-managed the original production of *Charley's Aunt* in 1892. He died shortly before his nephew was born.

The most mysterious figure in the Cushing family tree is Albert Cushing, or Uncle Bertie. In 1948, Cushing told his father he would be touring Australia and New Zealand with the RSC, and George Cushing let slip that, 'Your Uncle Bertie was banished to Australia in 1901, we've never heard of him since.'

Such a bolt out of the blue prompted the inquisitive Cushing to find out more information about Uncle Bertie, only to be told by his father that he was 'of artistic temperament', and, 'a wanderer'. To this day the gentleman's whereabouts remain unknown, but it was clear from George Cushing's vague description, that Uncle Bertie was a stage performer.

Nellie Cushing desperately wanted a girl, and to hide her disappointment at Peter's arrival, dressed her youngest accordingly until he was two years old, by which time Mother's Little Girl went missing!

George Cushing notified the police and was later informed by a police sergeant that a missing girl had just been found. Much to the embarrassment of his father and the police sergeant who found out the hard way that 'she' was a 'he', it was decided that the boy should now be dressed in accordance with his own sex.

That didn't stop the youngster from dressing up and performing puppet shows for his family. 'I did these terrible performances in a high squealing voice,' he admitted.

This odd start to his life didn't have any impact on Cushing's sexual preferences, especially, when he admitted after watching a stage production of *Peter Pan* as a child, that he fell madly in love with Peter, which wasn't so odd since the part was played by an actress, which was always the case in pantomimes of that era.

'I'm surprised you did not become another Oscar Wilde,' was the comment from Aunt Maude, 'not in the poetic sense, but most certainly in the other.' Actor John Fraser, who worked with Cushing in *Fury at Smuggler's Bay* (1961) was equally surprised. 'He told me his mother brought him up almost as a girl, and it's a miracle he didn't grow up gay, which of course he didn't.'

As a boy, Cushing loved his toy soldiers and comic books and enjoyed acting out make-believe adventures. His love for toys made him an avid collector of military figures in later life; he often re-enacted famous battles at his Whitstable home.

'He was always busy with his hands,' said Christopher Lee, 'making row upon row of lead soldiers and painting them, so you'd talk to them amid set pieces he contrived for battles, and planes dangling from the ceiling. Or he'd make mock-ups in cardboard of theatrical productions.'

One of his comic book heroes was schoolboy adventurer Tom Merry, and Cushing always followed the character's principles of 'No cribbing and no smoking', which he maintained until he became an actor and started smoking to prepare for a stage role.

Cushing had a happy childhood, but he was a solitary boy living in his own fantasy world. Three near fatal bouts of double pneumonia made his mother overprotective of him. The youngster was best described as Peter Pan, the boy who never grew up.

Cushing's only link to reality was his brother David, who also joined in with Peter's love of theatrics, but had a more mature outlook on life and often put his sibling wise to the outside world. David's nickname for Peter was Brighteyes.

Cushing was also a movie fan, especially westerns. Long before John Wayne, Tom Mix and his loyal horse Tony ruled the cinematic Wild West, and Cushing watched his films at the local Picture Palace. 'I thought that all Americans were cowboys. Mix was the Clint Eastwood of my youth, so I always wanted to go to Hollywood.'

Cushing was so in awe of Mix's big screen heroics, he took to re-enacting them, and this almost ended in tragedy on one occasion. The long garden of the family home represented the open range while mother's bike acted as his horse. As the prairie sloped down to a railway embankment, Cowboy Cushing, mounting his steed, came barrelling down the slope and crashed his bike. 'I took encore after encore, until either the bike, or I, or both, needed running repairs.'

Cushing also recreated a lynching scene by dangling from a clothesline attached to a tree in the garden. 'I hanged myself from mother's washing line but fortunately she didn't see me. I suppose it's all to do with imagination and trying to copy what one's hero did.' He further added that, 'dangling grotesquely for long stretches of time perhaps assisted my efforts to add to my stature.' Thanks to these dangerous Wild West exploits, Cushing became immune to physical damage.

'Anything that didn't interest me had no chance of going in one ear, let alone coming out the other. Even that passage denied it.' Cushing wasn't a good student. His first seat of learning was Dulwich Kindergarten, where he made his acting debut as a green hobgoblin in a school play. The family then moved to Purley in Surrey.

Unlike his brother, Cushing didn't inherit his father's mathematical skills. 'I have always found it easier to draw, paint or mime something than to present it in words.' Veering his talents towards art, his other boyhood passion was ornithology.

At 11, Cushing was sent to a boarding school in Shoreham-by-the-Sea in Sussex. He lasted one miserable term before returning to Purley where he attended Purley County Secondary School, not far from the family home, and developed into an accomplished sportsman, especially with rugby and swimming. 'Academically, I was no great shakes, but the athletic pursuits have served me well because I'm rarely in a film in which I don't either fall or get knocked out.'

Thanks to a massive appetite and his sporting prowess, Cushing grew into a handsome, well-built teenager, towering at 6ft tall. He remained a hopeless case in other school subjects, to the frustration of his teachers and his father, whose annual reading of the boy's school report didn't inspire confidence.

Cushing's physics master Mr P D Davies saw him in a different light.

'He needed no gift of insight to conclude that I was no budding Einstein. He was very keen on the theatre, always producing the school plays. Having detected in me some acting potential he did much to foster my development in the field, and deciding – as his colleagues had done – it was a waste of time and mine to attempt to instil my mind with any gems of scientific phenomena, he allowed me to be *absens* from his allocated hour, so that I could be more usefully employed in painting the scenery for our forthcoming presentation.'

Cushing enjoyed this assignment, which took place in the main hall, where he performed a bit of Fred Karno slapstick to the delight of the children in attendance and to the annoyance of the teacher in charge.

Thanks to Mr Davies, Cushing played the lead in nearly every school production. 'I think it was Mr Davies more than anyone else who encouraged me to take up acting professionally.' His evenings were spent studying painting and drawing at the Croydon College of Art, which he continued after leaving school.

With the brothers approaching adulthood, George Cushing was eager for them to go make a living for themselves in the adult world. David was better prepared for a business career, and his father used his influence in the city to secure him a position of employment with an insurance company in London.

David's ambition was farming, but his father had no connections with the agricultural industry. 'It is nice to record that we both achieved our youthful ambitions in the long run,' Cushing observed, 'his much shorter than mine.' David detested his job and London, and after several unhappy months, his father arranged for an apprenticeship at a farm in Pulborough in Sussex, and then helped David purchase a smallholding in Norwood Hill in Leigh, Surrey.

Despite being close as children, the brothers never stayed in touch as adults. 'He was reticent about his family life and never discussed his parents,' said Christopher Lee, 'though he always wanted to know all about mine. On one occasion, he told me he had a brother. "This was forty years ago," he added. "Still alive?" I wondered. "Oh yes, yes, he farms." "Do you ever see him, Peter?" "Very seldom." I risked pushing on: "Any reason for that? Don't you get on?" He sighed. "We get on very well," he replied. "I'm quite fond of him, but you see, his wife doesn't approve of what I do." Apparently, she was one of those who consider an actor a rogue and a vagabond, not suitable company for solid citizens, an opinion not confined to starchy members of certain golf clubs.'

Then came Peter's turn. Thanks to his drawing skills, his father secured Cushing a position in the Drawing Office of the Surveyor's Department at the Coulsdon and Purley Urban District Council.

Cushing's position was Surveyor's Assistant, but he was little more than a glorified office boy. Nor did he make any effort to advance within the council, his job being a paid distraction from his goal to make a career in the theatre. He did as little work as possible, tried to leave the office as early as possible (his timekeeping was dreadful) and stretched out whatever duties he did. The only job he enjoyed was drawing proposed buildings and architectural designs. 'It was said of my plans, that any resemblance to a real building was entirely coincidental.'

Thanks to former teacher Mr Davies, Cushing continued acting in the school plays, and later joined a couple of local drama groups. While at work, he suggested to his colleagues that he could put the ordinance survey maps in order. They were situated in a large attic room, but instead of doing the job, he rehearsed the lines for a forthcoming play to an audience of mice and spiders.

During the weekends, Cushing travelled to London's West End to watch a theatre production and, 'to revel in that intoxicating atmosphere and heady odour – a combination of dust, size, distemper and greasepaint.' Every week he bought a copy of *The Stage*, and answered countless advertisements, without any success, his lack of professional experience being a hindrance. He adopted the stage name Peter Ling, only to be mistaken for a Chinese actor when he did get a reply from a repertory company.

Friday nights at the cinema also kept his artistic mind busy, and although he died in 1926, Rudolph Valentino was still an influence on men's fashions and hairstyles of 1933. Cushing looked every inch the handsome well-dressed young man about town, attending tea dances and having a girlfriend.

By 1935 he had grown depressed at his unsuccessful attempts to break into acting. After spending a small fortune on postage to no avail, and being considered hopeless by everybody around him, it began to affect his mindset, making him decide to end it all.

While his parents were spending the weekend bank holiday at David's farm, Cushing travelled to Exmouth where he planned to throw himself off a cliff. Instead, he got distracted by a friendly Wheatear bird and followed it to the coastal resort of Budleigh Salterton. Staring out at the sea, he decided to follow his dream.

The gods were smiling on the train home. After finding an article about scholarships at the Guildhall School of Music and Drama, he realised a course was a step in the right direction and applied. To his delight, he received a reply asking him to attend an interview with one of the adjudicators.

Arriving for his interview, Cushing met Allan Aynesworth, who, 'belonged to the Old School of Thespians'. The moment he opened his mouth, the distinguished gentleman recoiled in horror at his accent and appalling diction and was promptly thrown out of the office. 'I didn't know what a dreadful accent I had until I got rid of it,' he later admitted.

After seeing the other applicants, Cushing was ushered back into Mr Aynesworth's office, his body language giving the impression that the young man should remain silent. Telling Cushing that, 'Your diction, which I can only liken unto that of a coaster-monger, will not do for the theatre,' he was then given a sheet of paper showing the basic vowels he needed to master if he had any chance of acceptance. He was also given a booklet on how to speak the correct way using his lips.

Cushing slowly mastered his speech pronunciation, the office attic being the perfect place to practise. With the assistance of James Cairns-James, formerly of the D'Oyly Carte Opera House, he took countryside walks. 'To improve my diction and practice voice projection, I used to go for long walks over the nearby downs, bawling such lines as: "How now brown cow?" "The Moon in June is full of beauty." I became known as "the Madman of Purley."'

After achieving some improvement, Cushing returned to the Guildhall, and was accepted. 'Never did a more ardent and punctual pupil attend these classes, so different from the slackers at those other schools. Happy times they were, too: I felt I was at last making some headway towards my ultimate goal.' Travelling into town twice a week, Cushing was also taught the rudiments of make-up and poise.

Cushing appeared in two end-of-term plays, *The Red Umbrella* by Brenda Girvin and Monica Cosens, and *The Torch-Bearers* by George Kelly. It wasn't the required acting experience he needed, but he used his London appearances to re-double his efforts in contacting the various provincial repertory companies. He even included a photo, which he admitted, 'made me look like a glass eyed juvenile delinquent in the last stages of degeneracy.'

The Connaught Theatre in Worthing, Sussex received the heaviest bombardment. Run by W Simpson Fraser (better known as actor Bill Fraser), Cushing received a reply inviting him to what he thought was an interview.

Cushing was so ecstatic, he handed in his notice, and headed down to Worthing to meet the formidable Mr Fraser.

Walking into Fraser's office, Cushing was greeted with a stern 'Who are you?' from the man himself. When Cushing introduced himself, Fraser told him in no uncertain terms to, 'Please, please stop writing to me!'

The aspiring and sensitive young actor was shattered at the response. 'The sun that shone so brightly clouded over, and all was grey again. Tears of frustration stung my eyes.'

Fraser went from stern to compassionate at Cushing's reaction and saw something of himself in the young man. He forsook a banking career to become an actor and experienced his own hardships when work was scarce, often sleeping rough on the Embankment in London. He offered Cushing a walk-on part in his production of J B Priestley's *Cornelius*, which was being presented that evening. '(Fraser) took pity on me and put me on the stage that very night.'

The next day, Cushing acquired some digs and reported for work the next day, although Fraser thought he had seen the back of him, he knew the young man wouldn't disappear and offered him the job of Assistant Stage Manager at 15 shillings a week, which was half the salary he had received at the local council.

The door was now open to a new life in the theatre. 'Thus, in June 1936, after almost five years of blood, toil, tears and sweat, I entered the ranks of the profession – with a fifty per cent drop in salary, but a five hundred per cent rise in morale.'

2: Hollywood Beckons

Cushing playing King Rat in *Dick Whittington*, 1937.

Any doubts Bill Fraser had about hiring an inexperienced newcomer were soon dispelled as Cushing vindicated his position in his company. The one-time local government slacker became a hard-working Assistant Stage Manager.

'An Assistant Stage Manager's job in weekly rep is excellent training for any would-be actor. It is a gruelling occupation, especially when you are called upon to play parts as well – so many lines to be committed to memory before turning in for the night, rehearsing during the day, and performing the current production in the evening.' His duties included preparing for each production, meaning he had to beg, borrow or steal furniture and props, and return them in good condition. This made him both an expert with props and a compulsive note-maker.

Cushing's weekly salary of 15 shillings went on room, board and breakfast, leaving him foraging for food the rest of the day. Following a large breakfast every morning, he arrived at the theatre at 8:00 am and remained there staving off hunger until midnight. At least the food used in some of the theatre productions was real and provided by Sainsbury's and other local outlets in exchange for free advertising. 'I made a point of scanning advance scripts for eating scenes.'

'I was always delighted when a script needed food to be served, because it meant I could have a jolly good tuck-in from the leftovers after each performance. Noel Coward's *Hay Fever* was a great favourite of mine; all those lovely tea and breakfast scenes!' Cushing also loved 'North country plays,' because, 'they often featured a high tea. Whatever its dramatic merits, I did not care!'

Cushing was able to 'invent' food instead of using the real thing, which didn't go down well with the cast. He had to suffer during a production of St John Ervine's *Anthony and Anna*, where the main character was a disabled American millionaire who lived solely on charcoal biscuits. 'By the end of the week I felt I could portray the invalid with more conviction than the leading actor.'

Impressed by Cushing's commitment, Fraser cast him in several small roles. His earliest stage credits included *It Pays to Advertise* by Rue Cooper Megrue and Walter Hackett, and Jack Celestin's *The Man at Six*, a comedy about a butler found murdered in a stately home (Cushing played a police surgeon). Continuing his links with J B Priestley, Cushing played Mr Tooke in the murder mystery *The Bees on the Boatdeck*.

Towards the end of the summer season, Bill Fraser took a short holiday and Peter Coleman stepped in as guest producer and lead actor. He cast Cushing in Montague Glass and Charles Klein's three-act play *Potash and Permutter*, and F McGrew Wills' *The Midshipman*.

Coleman ran the Southampton Repertory Company and, impressed by Cushing's hard work, hired him as his ASM when he returned to Southampton. 'He was a dear person, and I was delighted to accept his offer, but ever grateful to Bill Fraser for giving me my first opportunity.'

The Grand Theatre in Southampton was a big improvement on the Connaught Theatre and Cushing's salary was higher. The acting roles, though small, were better too, ranging from juvenile leads to character parts, and the ever-enthusiastic actor did everything to stand out in each production. Bill Fraser gave him the tools to begin his career, but it was working with Coleman that taught him the ropes.

'For the next four years I played repertory all over the country and it was a marvellous experience, apart from being a great training ground. You're literally involved with three plays at one time: you're playing one, rehearsing the next and learning the lines of the third. It demanded great concentration not to come out with the wrong part when you got on stage.'

Cushing now had the experience and the range to play character parts, which included his first stab at villainy as King Rat in *Dick Whittington*; he even worked out an acrobatic routine that almost killed the actor portraying the cat! Other credits included an elderly English traveller in *Winter Sunshine* and a Chinese servant in Hsiung Shih-I's *Lady Precious Stream*.

With a year's acting experience behind him, Cushing left Peter Coleman's company and joined The William Brookfield Players in Rochdale. The company toured Scarborough, Burnley and other northern provinces. Week-long special engagements were popular in Burnley and the surrounding areas.

Being a handsome and dashing young man, Cushing fell in love and out of love with every actress he worked with. 'I did, with unfailing regularity, but never had the time to pursue these romances.' Moving away from the childhood antics of Tom Mix, Cushing's new Hollywood idol was Loretta Young.

In 1937, Cushing was invited to join Harry Hanson's Court Players, a prestigious repertory company based at Nottingham's Theatre Royal which toured the UK with scaled down versions of classic West End hits. On his way to Nottingham, he met an actor who was to become his oldest friend, Peter Gray.

'We first met at Euston, on a train bound to Nottingham,' recalled Gray. 'I was travelling to take up an engagement with Harry Hanson's Court Players for a long season of weekly, twice nightly repertory at the Theatre Royal. Having settled myself gracefully into the corner seat of an empty compartment, I was hoping to remain undisturbed. I had just been jilted.'

Gray's solitary journey was soon interrupted by, 'a substantial hunk of masculine brawn and muscle that would have graced an international rugby team.' Unhappy with the new arrival, Gray had no choice but to welcome the man and soon found out they had something in common. 'It transpired that he, too, was joining the Court Players, having just finished his first full season of rep at Southampton. Sandwiches were swopped and one of us had a Guinness which we shared.'

The two men became friends, and according to Gray, 'My resistance began to crumble, eroded by a torrent of bonhomie from my companion and his disarming candour.'

The 'Two Peters', as they were called by their colleagues, arrived in Nottingham and acquired digs near the theatre. With Gray's influence, Cushing moved away from comics to adult literature. 'We spent many happy Sundays on the River Trent,' said Cushing, 'pulling ashore to partake of tea in some sequestered inn and to hear each other's lines.'

Peter Gray saw a childlike innocence in Cushing that made him perfect for acting. 'Make-believe, that childhood propensity had more attraction to him than reality, and it was this total suspension of disbelief in the far-fetched phantasies of his horror films that enabled him to make, for his audiences, "the incredible credible", to quote one of his thousands of fan letters.'

Cushing was so wrapped up in his work, he was unaware of the increasing political tensions in Europe. '[I was] so engrossed in what I was doing, I had become oblivious to what was going on in world affairs, and scarcely aware that war was not only inevitable, but also imminent.' He watched a cinema newsreel of Prime Minister Neville Chamberlain stepping out from the Munich Agreement holding up the infamous piece of paper declaring, 'My good friends, for the second time in our history, a British Prime Minister has returned from Germany bringing peace with honor. I believe it is peace for our time...' 'In my ignorance, I took his word for it and got on with the job in hand.'

Joining the Court Players was financially lucrative and his £2.10 per week salary enabled Cushing to open his first Post Office savings account, which allowed him to plan his next career move. Still an avid film fan, the voice of Hollywood began calling him, and this was fuelled by a chance meeting with the actor who inspired his death defying stunts on his mother's bike.

Tom Mix was making a personal appearance in Nottingham, and never one to miss out on an opportunity, Cushing paid him a visit and thanked the cowboy star for the pleasure his screen antics had given him as a child. 'That's real nice of you,' replied a gracious Mix, who then asked Cushing to read aloud a contract he had been offered and act as witness (apparently Mix could not read). Since this was 1937, the whereabouts of the contract remains unknown.

The Two Peters travelled extensively with the Court Players. In March 1938, they appeared in Zoe Akins' *The Greeks Had A Word For It* at the Penge Theatre, near London and remained there the following month for a production of Ivor Novello's *Fresh Fields* before returning to Nottingham's Theatre Royal for Cyril Campion's *Monkey Business*. 'We mostly appeared as dashing juveniles during those unsophisticated days,' said Gray, 'all eyes and teeth with lines like, "Who's for tennis?" and bouncing about off sofas with our adorable pretty young female counterparts.' When the Court Players went to Peterborough, the friends parted company with

2: Hollywood Beckons

Gray joining the Royal Navy.

Despite the threat of war, Cushing wanted to give Hollywood a try, much to Gray's surprise. 'Peter confided to me about having a bash at Hollywood. My wits reeled! Hollywood in those days was a glittering world of film stars and entertainment, as remote from weekly rep as sky from earth! I think I must have exuded doubts about his chances; he had no contacts over there, had never been inside a film studio, was relatively inexperienced and virtually penniless. How wrong was I!'

'Peter had a vision,' Gray continued. 'Hollywood and its films had been to him more – much more – than mere entertainment; they had transported him from suburbia and a surveyor's office into a world infinitely more glamorous, more adventurous, more romantic – and yet, because of his addiction to make-believe, infinitely more real than reality! Given his indomitable will, it wasn't an irresponsible decision.'

Cushing also felt restricted by his work in repertory theatre. 'I got tired of this and realised that if I wanted to further my career I would have to go elsewhere. I recalled those Tom Mix epics that delighted my childhood and decided the answer lay in Hollywood.'

It was also personal. During his time in rep, Cushing was engaged to 18-year-old actress Doreen Lawrence (who he only mentions as a colleague in his autobiography). She broke it off because he always brought his parents on their dates and was too easily moved to tears. When the relationship ended, Cushing felt the need to prove his worth by going to Hollywood.

Cushing wasn't completely penniless. His work with the Court Players enabled him to save £50 in his Post Office account. Further financial assistance came from his American half-cousin Wilton Haley, who agreed to sponsor the move to America.

'Having saved a small sum during my time in Rep, I asked Father if he would assist with my passage to the States. He did so, presenting me with a ticket. I noticed it was only one-way.

'It bothered me at the time. I think he thought I could swim home.'

Cushing had nothing to lose. 'If I landed film parts, fine! If I didn't, well, I was young and would be able to come back to Britain to try again.'

The family Christmas of 1938 was spent in preparation for Cushing's departure. On 18 January 1939 he boarded the *SS Champlain* in Southampton, 'full of high hopes and the abounding impetuosity of youth.'

3: One-Way Ticket To Hollywood

Robert Morley as Oscar Wilde at the Fulton Theatre, 1939.

'I had this great passion to go where Tom Mix lived, he was my hero you see. So, I went to America. My dad, bless him, bought me a one-way ticket. No one knew me as an actor so when I went to Hollywood it was really a case of a fool stepping where angels feared to tread. But I was frightfully lucky, and I did remarkably well.'

As the *SS Champlain* set sail from Southampton, Cushing began a new phase in his career, and one that could go either way – success or failure!

The journey was uneventful, which made things frustrating for someone who was 'agog with excited anticipation.' And the situation didn't improve because Cushing's roommate spoke only Afrikaans, and all attempts at communicating proved disastrous. At least his parents had written a batch of letters that were left in the care of the purser, who provided one each day to help lift the tedium as he worked out his plan of action.

Arriving in New York in February, the *Champlain* entered the Hudson River and approached Manhattan Island where Cushing saw the great silhouette of New York City, and quickly felt in awe of his new surroundings. 'It really was a superb and breath-taking sight. I felt a trifle insignificant when we slipped into our berth, standing beneath all those towering blocks of skyscrapers, but I soon became accustomed to these strange surroundings, and stimulated by the electric atmosphere.'

Disembarking, Cushing set his campaign in motion. 'I knew it was imperative to live as frugally as possible and to start earning as soon as I could. My decision was to stay for seven days in the city, making the rounds of all the film company offices, which I would look up in a telephone directory, and ask if they could oblige me with letters of introduction to the casting directors in the corresponding studios on the coast.'

He needed a roof over his head first. 'I settled into the YMCA, paying a week in advance, also buying a train ticket to Los Angeles, although this expenditure made quite a nasty dent in my capital.'

Despite the money problems, he had help from his cousin and sponsor Wilton Haley, who lived in New Jersey, and where Cushing would spend his weekends, charming the ladies with unfailing regularity. 'All the girls thought he was wonderful,' observed Wilton Haley's daughter Phyllis, who was a college student when she first met Cushing. 'He was also very outgoing and a good sport. He was a charmer.' Another cousin, Marjorie Zeliff, was only 15 when she met Cushing and was taken by his good looks and charm. 'It was exciting to have a family member who wanted to be a movie star. I mean, you can imagine how a teenage girl felt at that point.'

Romantic liaisons were the last thing on Cushing's mind. He contacted all Hollywood studios' East Coast offices and 'met a great number of polite but unforthcoming individuals during my tramping of the "Great White Way".' After several rejections, Cushing met a representative from Columbia Pictures called Larney Goodkind. 'He knew someone connected with Edward Small Productions who might be useful to know and gave me a note as requested.'

Handing the letter of introduction over, Goodkind gave Cushing a friendly word of warning that his chances were slim. 'According to him, about one in five of the whole population of the USA wanted to get into the industry, but my English accent could be an asset, and give me some slight advantage over the host of other hopefuls.' His theatre experience and positive work ethic would also work to his advantage. The letter didn't carry much weight, but it was an encouraging step in the right direction.

Prior to leaving New York, Cushing bought an economy ticket for the Broadway show *The Gentle People*, starring Franchot Tone and Sylvia Sydney. This was the first time Cushing watched two Hollywood stars in a theatre production, and he was in awe of the experience.

Cushing remained on Broadway seeking out a few more helpful contacts. He decided to meet Robert Morley, who was making his Broadway debut as Oscar Wilde at the Fulton Theatre. 'Nothing ventured, nothing gained,' thought Cushing when he met Morley backstage.

Cushing found Morley 'most kind and hospitable,' but when he told the actor of his intentions, the reaction wasn't positive. 'It's very crowded, you know, dear boy. Why don't you go there for a holiday? Have you brought your bathing costume with you?' Morley also pointed out that Cushing wasn't alone in achieving the Hollywood dream.

On 6 February 1939, Cushing boarded *The Challenger* at Grand Central Station, departing from New York, and passing through New Jersey, Pennsylvania, Ohio, Indiana, Illinois, Iowa, Nebraska, Wyoming, Utah, and Nevada, before arriving in California on 10 February.

The journey on *The Challenger* was uncomfortable. Cushing accepted a pillow from a train attendant, only to return it immediately when the attendant asked for $3! Sharing his compartment were three college students who went up and down the train entertaining fellow passengers with barber-shop songs while one of them played ukulele. Cushing joined the trio for their train tour, his job was to carry the hat and collect all the tips. He got an equal share-out with the others.

'After the stuffiness of New York and the days of being cooped up on the train, the crisp California air and the scent of the orange groves quite went to my head. I began to feel like a film star before I had set foot in a studio.' As intoxicating as the citrus was, when the train arrived in Los Angeles, Cushing was in for a shock. 'Having always heard of "Sunny California", I was a little dismayed when I stepped out into the teaming rain!'

Rain aside, and forever keeping a tight grip on the purse strings, Cushing walked from the LA train station to Hollywood – dressed in a thick tweed suit and lugging two heavy suitcases. 'It was a four-mile trudge, and very sultry. Quite soon I was perspiring like a packhorse.'

Arriving soaking wet at the YMCA at North Hudson Avenue, Cushing presented himself to a shocked receptionist and delivered his well-

3: One-Way Ticket To Hollywood

rehearsed speech to the clerk.

'I've come from England to get into films. I have $16 and an Ingersoll watch, cheap but reliable. Would you please accept these as a deposit until I am in a position to settle the bill for my room and board?'

Without saying a word, the receptionist handed Cushing a room key. A few weeks later when the two of them got to know each other better, Cushing asked him why he accepted such a small deposit for a room.

The receptionist replied, 'You were so plumb British, and so honest, I just hadn't the heart to refuse.'

Fifteen days after his 'wet' arrival in Hollywood, Cushing went to visit Edward Small Productions. 'I armed myself with two addresses and just went to Edward Small's studios where I heard they were making a picture.' Brimming with naive enthusiasm, he presented himself at the gate of the studio entrance.

'At the gate, I was immediately confronted by a policeman bristling with guns. I told him boldly that I was going into pictures, and he looked at me absolutely dumbfounded.

'I handed him my precious entrée, waited patiently, and presently he led me to the casting director's office.'

Cushing was at the right place at the right time. 'I deliberately took myself to the very centre of the film industry, Hollywood, and asked for a part, and much to my surprise, and that of everyone else, I got one!'

'I learned that it was apparently my Englishness and obvious innocence that opened the doors to me. The policeman, and the others in the studio, were all so amazed that they thought, "This man's an idiot or he's very honest," and they let me in to see the casting director.'

Cushing then signed on for a picture currently in production, on a salary of $75 a week, 'which represented a small fortune in my present circumstances,' and a guarantee of two months' work. 'I could hardly believe it, as I signed on the dotted line at the foot of my contract.' With so many newcomers often hanging around a studio waiting to be discovered, all Cushing did was walk into one and was hired on the spot.

The movie that Cushing signed up for was *The Man In The Iron Mask* (1939).

4: The Man In The Iron Mask (1939)

Cushing (right) in *The Man In The Iron Mask*.

The Man In The Iron Mask was the third film in a five-picture deal that Edward Small had made with United Artists, and it was Small's most ambitious picture to date. Based on part of the book by Alexandre Dumas (published in 1850), pre-production began in September 1938 with Douglas Fairbanks Jr set to play the royal twins.

Signing up as director (on Small's insistence) was a man who had an indirect impact on Cushing's future horror career, James Whale.

Whale defined Hollywood horror in the thirties. A complex, sensitive individual, resentful of his working-class roots, he worked hard to establish himself as a director of note.

By 1935, Whale was one of Universal's top directors. He dabbled with a wide variety of genres with considerable success and reached his peak with the musical *Showboat* (1936). An eccentric who wore thick tweed suits even in the hot sunshine, Whale was openly homosexual at a time when it was unacceptable. By 1936, his aloof behaviour quickly blotted his copybook with Universal.

By the time he directed *The Man In The Iron Mask*, the disenchanted

4: The Man In The Iron Mask (1939)

Whale was just a gun for hire. At least it was a high-profile picture for a big studio.

Edward Small arranged a meeting with Whale and Douglas Fairbanks Jr, who had returned to Hollywood after a few years working as an actor-producer in Britain. Fairbanks was set to play the dual role of King Louis XIV and his twin brother Phillippe, but Small insisted that Louis Hayward play the part instead, having previously worked with the actor on *The Duke Of West Point* (1938). Impressed by his performance, Small signed Hayward to a multi-picture deal.

It was Small's intention to make Hayward Hollywood's newest swashbuckling star and *The Man In The Iron Mask* was considered the perfect vehicle. However, despite being a fine actor, Hayward didn't have the athletic presence and suffered badly in comparison to Errol Flynn in *The Adventures Of Robin Hood* (1938).

With Hayward and Whale on board, the rest of the casting followed. Playing Princess Maria Theresa was Joan Bennett. After playing winsome blonde *ingénues* during the silent era, she changed her image (and hair) to play slinky brunette *film noir* femme fatales, often in films for Fritz Lang. Her appearance in *The Man In The Iron Mask* started that phase of her career.

Playing D'Artagnan was Warren William. Now all but forgotten, William was a top Broadway star of the thirties. In films he was often cast as a ruthless businessman, a corrupt official or an assortment of cads and charlatans that reflected the hardships of the Great Depression. Despite the 'man you loved to hate' image, William was a shy and private man who kept out of the limelight throughout his career.

William enjoyed sympathetic roles, playing Perry Mason, The Lone Wolf and Detective Philo Vance in several movies as well as private eye Sam Spade in *Satan Met A Lady* (1936). As an older D'Artagnan (he was 43 at the time), playing an action hero, albeit an ageing one, made a welcome change.

Playing D'Artagnan's loyal musketeers Porthos, Aramis and Athos, Alan Hale, Miles Mander and Bert Roach all had long careers in supporting roles. Hale is best known for his work with Errol Flynn, most memorably Little John in *The Adventures Of Robin Hood*. A suave British actor specialising in oily villains, Mander is best known as creepy Giles Conniver opposite Basil Rathbone's Sherlock Holmes in *The Pearl Of Death* (1944). Roach was a popular silent comedian who made a partially successful transition to sound. *The Man In The Iron Mask* was one of his last films in a leading role, after which he was reduced to uncredited bit parts for the remainder of his career.

With Austrian actor Joseph Schildkraut playing the villain, other familiar faces included Montagu Love and Albert Dekker. Playing

Cardinal Richelieu was British actor Nigel de Brulier, who had previously played the role *The Three Musketeers* (1921), *The Iron Mask* (1929) and *The Three Musketeers* (1935).

After getting over the shock of being hired, Cushing now had to learn a new style of acting. 'Here was a Heaven-sent opportunity for someone who had never set foot in a film studio before, to observe and learn from old hands as Joseph Schildkraut and the rest of the distinguished cast set about the method of acting in this very technical medium, so different from giving a live performance in the theatre. Furthermore, I would be able to see the rushes, and correct the many faults I was bound to commit, and so gradually improve.'

Louis Hayward was playing twins in this film, and James Whale was looking for someone who could play opposite Hayward for the split-screen scenes. 'Luckily, I convinced them I was their man – though all my experience had been on the stage – and so I went into films. Because of the nature of the part I played, I was literally snipped off in the cutting room and Louis Hayward ended up talking to himself!'

Cushing wore full costume when playing his scenes with Hayward. 'I'm afraid the story that I actually played the man in the iron mask is not true, Louis Hayward played them all himself!' From the surviving photos of the pre-splicing scenes between Cushing and Hayward, the young actor looks comfortable in period costume and clearly took his work seriously.

'I dislike the word "technique", but that was where I learned the technique of screen acting. I was on the picture for three months, playing all these scenes with Louis. I played both parts and was able, on so doing, to learn a great deal about filming. I don't really like the word, but it's a very technical medium. Why I say I don't like the word – I don't think there's a technique in acting because to me there isn't, you either can or you can't.

'The greatest compliment is that it all looks so easy. But as a medium it is very technical. You've got not only to remember your lines and the character but also where you're standing, whether your foot's on a mark, and getting your key light and trying to keep your shoulder out of the leading lady's light – there's a great deal on your mind for those few seconds that you're filming. That's where the mental strain comes in. You've got to remember a lot at very short notice, and you get little rehearsal time in films.

'Nevertheless, it was a marvellous experience because it gave me a chance to study the great Hollywood stars at first hand – and earned me $75 a week which was an absolute fortune because I had nothing!'

Watching the daily rushes helped Cushing evaluate and refine his performance, although he wasn't impressed with his work. 'I nearly fainted when I saw myself for the first time. I was dreadful! My voice

4: The Man In The Iron Mask (1939)

sounded awful, and I was as round as a dumpling. However, as the weeks passed, I got better, and I even ended up with a one-line part.

'It was really a wonderful break. You can never give a stage performance on film because it's just so overdone. In the theatre you have to arouse the people at the back of the guards as well as those in the front row of the stalls, so you have to overdo things; but in films you only have to raise an eyebrow and it tells everything. You don't have to do much more than that.'

Cushing developed a close bond with his 'twin'. 'I got to know Louis Hayward very well while we were working, and we were firm friends. He struck me as a sad and lonely soul, disenchanted with the film business, who seemed glad to have someone to talk about "the Old Country" with. He was married to Ida Lupino, and living in a delightful villa on the Brentwood Heights, about half-way between the film capital and Santa Monica. I spent many enjoyable weekends there, and finally they kindly invited me to stay with them for as long as I wished. Like *The Man Who Came To Dinner*, I did.'

Being the daughter of music hall legend Stanley Lupino, Ida Lupino inherited her father's sense of humour. According to writer and Cushing biographer David Miller, 'Lupino, a practical joker, started a story about her "adopted son" coming to stay. A puzzled columnist followed up the story "Ida Lupino is always talking about her adopted son who lives with her. People are always surprised when they meet him, because he's 6ft 2in Peter Cushing, the RKO actor."' The publicity his 'mother' provided to the press helped boost Cushing's profile.

The Man In The Iron Mask was a troubled shoot. Working hard on his performance and enjoying himself in the process, Cushing scarcely noticed the internal conflicts between James Whale and Edward Small. Small distrusted directors, and disliked Whale, who found his creative control being taken away from him following the extensive re-writes of George Brice's overlong script. A difficult man at the best of times, Louis Hayward and his fellow actors found him aloof on the set. Whale did his best to annoy Small by lighting a cigar and allowing the smoke to drift onto the set during a scene, prompting expensive reshoots. Small eventually fired Whale from the picture.

Cushing had no problems with the director during filming. 'Whale was an incredibly patient and tolerant man with a beginner like me.' And Whale was happy enough with Cushing's hard work to give him a tiny role with one line of dialogue.

'My confidence grew day by day, and to compensate for all my footage which lay on the cutting room floor, I was given a small part, The King's Messenger, which involved me and my attendants in a sword fight with D'Artagnan.'

Whale asked Cushing if he had ever done any fencing before. 'Oh yes,' he lied. 'I fenced all my life.' 'Good,' replied Whale. 'Go along to see Monsieur Cavens – first class swordsman. He'll take you through the routine that's been mapped out.'

The film's fencing master was Fred Cavens, who had taught many Hollywood greats how to use the sword and had previously worked on the 1935 version of *The Three Musketeers*.

The formidable Cavens smelt a rat the minute he laid his rapier over his left forearm for Cushing to take hold of. 'You have fenced before?' he asked his new pupil.

'No, dear fellow, never,' replied Cushing, 'but I had to say yes to get the job.' Cavens was pleased with his honesty. 'So!' he exclaimed in his strong Belgian accent. 'If you had said yes to me, you would have insulted my intelligence as well as my art. Now that you've been truthful, I will teach you to be one of the best swordsmen in Hollywood.'

'I didn't attain that dazzling peak of perfection, but he taught me enough to hold my own against Warren William when the time came.' As the years went on, Cushing became a first-class fencer, drawing a rapier several times during his career.

Next came the wardrobe fitting. 'I did have the chance to dress in period costume, though, which was a delight. The film was set in the period of Louis XIV, and they wore lovely big hats with feathers and spurs. So, when I went to get costumed, I remembered the marvellous sound Tom Mix's spurs made, and got myself a huge pair.'

'They were very large, and made the most satisfying jingle as I proudly strode about in my fancy dress.'

All that was to change.

'I was given a splendid steed, with a saddle resembling a small armchair, and stirrups like backless clogs. I had to ride into the courtyard of an inn, and say to one of the Musketeers, "The King wants to see you."'

When Cushing mounted the horse, he dug the spurs into the animal sending it on a mini rampage around the studio. 'The beast took off like a thunderbolt,' he said, 'leapt over an oak table, scattering extras and their pewter tankards of ale in all directions, charged into a section of scenery which came crashing down, stampeded wildly around and around, my sword-sheath swinging of its own free will like a flail, thwacking its side which encouraged even greater displays of frenzied rodeo-like acrobatics.

'Suddenly it jerked to an abrupt four-hoofed stop, depositing me in a dazed heap on the studio floor. As I lay there, befuddled and dusty, it began to paw the sawdust and straw, then bent over to nuzzle my neck. For one horrible moment, I thought he was going to eat me!'

Once the commotion died down, James Whale asked, 'Is the horse okay?'

4: The Man In The Iron Mask (1939)

'What a come down for a cowboy!' exclaimed Cushing. 'In any event I was de-spurred on the spot and told that I would cost the production several hours delay, not to mention several thousand dollars.'

Cushing should have got his marching orders after such a disastrous incident, but Whale, knowing it wasn't the actor's fault (no one on the production queried his horsemanship), and aware of his hard work on the film, gave him a second chance. The following day, with the scenery restored, the de-spurred Cushing repeated his scene, on the same horse, and without further mishap. 'During the coffee break, I gave my now docile charger a lump of sugar and I could swear that animal winked at me! It had given me an extra day's work while the set was being rebuilt!'

The Man In The Iron Mask got its cinema release in July 1939, performing well at the box office. While it suffers in comparison to *The Adventures Of Robin Hood*, it is still a rollicking yarn that incorporates enough action, adventure and swordplay to keep everyone happy. Whale retains some of his trademark homoerotic tones, with Hayward's effeminate, eye-rolling performance as the sadistic twin, and Joseph Schildkraut's Ernest Thesiger-inspired Fouquet. Thanks to Whale's eccentric touches, the film avoids becoming a routine potboiler.

Away from the swordplay, the film sags, and Louis Hayward and Warren William look too heavy to pass themselves off as action heroes. The performances are decent, and the period settings and costumes retain the typical high standard that one expects from a high-profile movie.

Peter Cushing's film debut amounts to 17 seconds of screen time and two lines of dialogue. Arriving in the courtyard of D'Artagnan's home with the King's men, the commanding officer asks Cushing if he knows the place. 'How could I mistake it?' he replies, his voice much lighter than fans are used to. 'I've been here before.' Hardly an acting performance, but Cushing looks good in costume, and despite the horse issues, seems comfortable on his mount.

Then comes the swordplay between the King's goons and the Musketeers. Cushing doesn't do much fencing as D'Artagnan runs him through almost immediately.

Critical evaluation towards *The Man In The Iron Mask* was mixed. *Variety* found it, 'highly entertaining adventure melodrama for general appeal and satisfaction with excellent direction,' while critic Leslie Halliwell said it was an 'exhilarating swashbuckler based on a classic novel with a complex plot, good acting and the three musketeers in full cry.'

The positive reviews continued with Richard Mallett from *Punch* calling the film, 'A sort of combination of *The Prisoner Of Zenda* and *The Three Musketeers*, with a few Wild West chases thrown in. Not unentertaining.' *Film Daily* singled out Louis Hayward for his, 'best screen work to date.'

The New York Times wasn't so impressed: 'Not quite the swashbuckler tale we expected.' *The New Yorker* felt the same. 'The piece belongs to the old school of things and the Douglas Fairbanks of 1929, but Fairbanks is not here, and the swordplay, the hard riding, and the desperate escapees seem to demand him. Louis Hayward can give a modern effete touch when that is needed in the double role he has, but he can't compete with his rapier or his acrobatics.'

Not surprisingly, the critics gave no special mention to Cushing's performance, not that he was bothered. 'All in all, I learnt a great deal from my first steps into the world of Motion Pictures.'

5: A Chump At Oxford (1939)

Cushing (left) in *A Chump At Oxford*.

'Hollywood was like a small town back then,' Cushing said about his time in California. 'Everyone knew everyone else, so when news came out that a new actor had arrived, word spread and soon enough I was getting a fair bit of work.'

After his three months on *The Man In The Iron Mask*, Cushing was financially better off to settle his bill at the YMCA, where he remained until he was 'adopted' by Louis Hayward and Ida Lupino.

While he waited patiently for his next role, Cushing hung out at Schwab's Pharmacy on Sunset Boulevard, described as 'a home away from home, an office for the office-less, and a place where thousands of actors could get a free meal and a warm hello.'

'A few days after the completion of *The Man In The Iron Mask*, I was at that rendezvous again, enjoying a milkshake, and it was there that I heard Hal Roach was needing English-type actors for a Laurel and Hardy film, *A Chump At Oxford*. I lost no time in making contact with his studios and was accepted.

'The fact that I had worked on [*The Man In The Iron Mask*], and that I had an English accent, undoubtedly helped me get a much better role in the Laurel and Hardy film.' Professionally and personally, *A Chump At Oxford* meant so much to Cushing. 'My part was little more than an extra's, but I was so proud to be with two of the greatest comedians the cinema has ever produced.'

Stan Laurel was born Arthur Stanley Jefferson on 16 June 1890 in Ulverston, Lancashire, and greasepaint flowed through this young man's veins. Inspired by his boyhood hero, Dan Leno, Laurel made his theatre debut aged 16, and honed his comic skills in a variety of pantomimes and music hall sketches.

In 1910, Laurel joined Fred Karno's comedy troupe as understudy to Charlie Chaplin. Karno was the master of slapstick and a massive influence on Laurel's future career. The troupe, known as 'Fred Karno's Army', toured the United States, where Laurel and Chaplin remained.

Making inroads into films, he first worked with Oliver Hardy in *The Lucky Dog* (1921). In 1926, he joined Hal Roach Studios as a writer and director, and teamed up with Hardy again in *Yes, Yes, Nanette* (1926).

Oliver Hardy was born Norvell Hardy in Harlem, Georgia on 18 January 1892 (he took his father's name Oliver when he became a performer). He took a great interest in the fledgling motion picture industry, and after working in vaudeville as a singer, made his film debut in *Outwitting Dad* (1914). Originally billed as 'Babe' Hardy, he often played heavies due to his large frame, and starred in several comedy shorts opposite Charlie Chase, James Finlayson and Larry Semon; he was the Tin Man in the Semon-directed *Wizard of Oz* (1925).

Laurel and Hardy did not become a partnership until 1927, creating the famous bowler hatted image of the amiable losers forever getting into mishaps made by their own stupidity. Although Hardy was (arguably) the straight man, he got just as many laughs as his more creative partner.

Being a visual double-act, Laurel and Hardy made a successful transition to sound. They continued making shorts, including the legendary *The Music Box* (1932) and made their feature film debut in *Pardon Us* (1931). As a partnership, Laurel was the gag writer and (uncredited) director, with Hardy happy to let his friend do most of the work.

The pair hit their peak with *Way Out West* (1937), but behind the scenes Laurel had a difficult relationship with Hal Roach. The ultra-conservative Roach was not happy with the free-spirited Laurel living out of wedlock with a married woman. Contractual disputes also got Laurel fired several times. By the time the duo filmed *A Chump At Oxford* (1939) Laurel tried to sue Roach over breach of contract. The case was dropped, and Laurel returned to the studio. *A Chump At Oxford* was the penultimate movie the duo made for Roach.

5: A Chump At Oxford (1939)

Cushing was unaware of these problems when filming began in June 1939; he was simply mesmerised by the presence of two brilliant comedians. 'Both were perfectionists, Stan thinking up most of the gags and routines, and then discussing them in detail with Oliver Hardy and the director, Alfred Golding.'

Laurel always had full control of his movies regardless of who was in charge. 'Laurel bossed the production,' said Hal Roach. 'With any director, if Laurel said, "I don't like this idea," the director didn't say "Well, you're going to do it anyway." That was understood. As Laurel made so many suggestions there was not much left for the director to do.'

Cushing saw Laurel's work first hand during the filming of the maze scene. '(Alfred) Golding wanted a birds-eye view of the famous pair, staggering about carrying a vast portmanteau, seeking the exit from Hampton Court Maze. As their faces would not be seen, he used doubles. When Laurel and Hardy saw the rushes, Stan said, not unkindly, "Olly and I must do that ourselves. Those two are trying to be funny, and it shows." Such was their professionalism.'

Another incident was the classic scene where Cushing and his fellow Oxford students set out to try to lynch Stan and Olly. When they confront Stan, who in a past life was the ear-wiggling Lord Paddington, and had just regained his memory, the students are all thrown out of a nearby window and into a fountain, along with Olly and the Dean.

According to Cushing, 'Daytime was extremely hot, but there was no twilight, the sun sinking swiftly below the horizon, making the temperature drop considerably. There was an evening sequence where several undergraduates had to fall fully clothed into a swimming pool. Both the stars made sure there were towels, blankets and hot drinks available for all of us when we climbed out of the water, shivering in the chilly air. Such was their thought for others.'

Hardy was doubly concerned for the cast and personally brought in a large tray of doughnuts for the soaked students.

While Laurel worked on the film, Cushing got to know Hardy and found him charming. 'Oliver Hardy was a very intelligent man, but he left the working out of all the gags to Laurel. Then they would get together and sort of improvise on them. Stan was the brains of the team in that way.

'Olly was a key-chain swinger,' he added, 'twirling it round his forefinger until it formed a huge ring, and then reversing the process, all this while humming a little tune. He was followed everywhere by a small black boy, who pushed a trolley groaning with coffee and doughnuts. "I have to keep eating these things," he once enlightened me, "in order to keep my weight up. Try one?"'

Production wrapped in June 1939 with the final cut completed at the end of August as a 42-minute streamliner featurette intended as a double bill with a bigger movie for its American release.

In October 1939, Roach re-edited the film, adding a further 20 minutes footage to bring it up to six reels for European distribution. Cushing was not involved in this footage, directed by Gordon Douglas, who is uncredited in the final cut. The scenes are unrelated to the boy's Oxford antics and features them checking into an employment agency looking for work.

The footage, which was later added for American distribution, features the duo recreating their butler and maid routine from the silent classic *From Soup To Nuts* (1928), with the climax taken from another silent *Slipping Wives* (1927). Appearing uncredited in the new footage were two of the duo's best known members of their stock company – James Finlayson, whose walrus moustache and twisty faced expressions of outrage, made him a perfect foil for Stan and Olly, and the tall, stunning and statuesque comedienne Anita Garvin, best known as Stan's shotgun shooting wife in *Blotto* (1930), who came out of retirement to appear in the film at Laurel's request.

In the original 43-minute version, the name of the president of the bank where Stan and Olly foiled the robbery is James Finlayson! The scene was removed once the new footage with that actor was added on.

The final 63-minute cut was released through United Artists in February 1940, and was paired off with two inappropriate films. New York's Rialto Theatre had the film supporting *The Siege At Warsaw* (1940), a controversial documentary about Nazi Germany's bombing of Poland, and Boston's Trans-Lux released it as a second feature to the Bela Lugosi chiller *Human Monster* (1940).

Critical reaction was positive. *Time Out* felt the film was, 'Not so much a parody of the nonsensically moralising *A Yank At Oxford* (1938) as an amiably shaggy-dog romp through the usual Laurel and Hardy routines. The best moments see Stan and Olly chaotically in service as butler and maid, and Stan's marvellous transformation, by amnesia, into an aristocratic twit.' Leslie Halliwell agreed, finding it a 'Patchy, but endearing romp, starting with an irrelevant two-reel about their playing butler and maid, but later including Stan's burlesque impersonation of Lord Paddington.'

Novelist and critic Graham Greene enjoyed the film immensely. He wrote in *The Spectator*, 'Ranks with their best pictures, which, to one heretic, are more agreeable than Chaplin's. Their clowning is purer; they aren't out to better an unbeatable world; they never wanted to play *Hamlet*.'

While it remains one of their most endearing comedies, *A Chump At Oxford* is half-hearted at times. With the additional material, it looks like two unrelated shorts shoehorned together to make a feature length movie.

5: A Chump At Oxford (1939)

Another fault is the scene in the maze where Stan and Olly are duped by the students, resulting in them staying there all night and being harassed by a ghost. It's a funny scene, but overlong. The film also cries out for a classroom scene like the boys' prison short *Pardon Us* (1931), where Stan and Olly could make fools of themselves among their new schoolmates. It would allow Cushing and co to carry out further pranks as well as having James Finlayson back twisting his face as the bombastic and ineffectual teacher.

But even with these faults, *A Chump At Oxford* is a funny film. The butler and maid scene is brilliantly orchestrated ('Serve the salad undressed!'), with Stan and Olly performing their famous routine with total aplomb, while Finlayson remains as outraged as ever.

The second half is a departure from their usual comic personas. Forever the losers with their failed businesses and nagging wives, Stan and Olly become painfully aware of their lack of prospects, realising that an education is the only way forward. They get a chance when they go to Oxford University, only to arrive inappropriately attired. 'You're dressed for Eton,' says one of the students, to which Stan exclaims, 'Well, that's swell! We haven't eaten since breakfast.' Groan worthy, but still a classic!

Stan's portrayal of the 'legendary' Lord Paddington provides a great deal of interest. Since their teaming, Stan has always been Olly's clueless one-man fan club, forever at his friend's beck and call. His transformation to Lord Paddington is the first time since 1927 that he is playing a different character. He puts Olly in his place by turning him into a lackey and calling him 'Fatty!' Who's the boss now? It's a performance of some distinction even if his upper-class accent occasionally slips into his Lancashire/Geordie twang.

Although Cushing said he was just an extra, he has a reasonable amount of screen time, and some priceless dialogue. 'What is it?' he asks, in reaction to seeing Stan in his Eton uniform. It is Cushing who says to his fellow classmates, 'I think they're entitled to the royal initiation; don't you think?' Later, the students dupe the chumps further by donning false walrus moustaches and posing as senior faculty members.

These comic moments are memorable because Cushing stands out from his co-stars. While they all adopt affected accents, Cushing keeps his voice natural, making his performance more effective. Immaculately dressed, with waved hair and a pencil thin moustache, he *is* the handsome Hollywood star on the rise.

Cushing was also being noticed behind the scenes. According to the film's press publicity, 'Numbered among the real-life Oxonians are Peter Cushing.' Considering his lack of formal education, being part of the Oxford elite, even on film, must have surprised and amused the actor.

Cushing regarded his time with Laurel and Hardy as one of the highlights of his career, 'I was only with them for a week. It is one that I treasure.' The Sons of the Desert, the most famous of the Stan and Olly appreciation societies presented Cushing with an award in 1971.

Around the time *A Chump At Oxford* was being made, Cushing quickly became well known in Hollywood circles. According to Cushing biographer Deborah Del Vecchio, 'Louis Hayward and his wife Ida Lupino provided Peter with not only a place to live, but almost certainly with introductions to others in the film industry. As two of Hollywood's up and coming young stars, the Haywards were capable of opening doors to which Peter Cushing lacked the key.'

With war in Europe being a reality, the timing was perfect. 'As a young man with a proper British accent,' Del Vecchio added, 'Peter filled a type that often need filling as many English actors were being called home to fight. Since Peter was exempted from military service due to athletic injuries from his school days, he was able to fill the void.'

'I count myself very fortunate to have been domiciled in Hollywood during the golden days of its zenith,' recalled Cushing. Now in the world of big film stars, he acted like a trainspotter, ticking off the names of any famous actor he met or encountered.

And the stars were equally taken by his charm. 'The hospitality of our American cousins and British expatriates was overwhelming. I was a guest at many tennis parties, and swimming gatherings in private garden pools of cerulean blue, and every imaginable shape or size, or on the beaches at Santa Monica and off Catalina Island, which meant trips in various sea-going craft finishing the day with a barbecue.'

There were plenty of places to visit in Hollywood. 'Ida and Louis took me to dinner one evening to Ella Campbell's restaurant on Sunset Boulevard, which was run by that very English lady, who specialised in the traditional fare of her homeland.' During dinner, Cushing and the Haywards autographed their names on a piece of plywood fixed onto the wall. By the time he left Hollywood, the wall was completely covered in autographs from some of the biggest stars of the time.

Later that evening at a party, Cushing was introduced to his heartthrob Loretta Young. 'She was as gracious and beautiful off the screen as on. I kissed her hand in greeting, which was more than I ever hoped for or expected.'

Cushing didn't neglect his sporting duties as Hollywood was full of cricket fans. In 1932 C Aubrey Smith (described by Cushing as 'That grand old man of the British Theatre, Empire and Cricket') formed the Hollywood Cricket Club. According to writer Cynthia Lindsay, 'The Cricket Club boasted a roster which, on a marquee, would have filled any theatre in the land. Ronald Colman, Clive Brook, Basil Rathbone, Nigel Bruce, R C Sherriff, H B Warner, Noel Maddison, Claude King, and later

5: A Chump At Oxford (1939)

younger boys, Frankie Lawton, Errol Flynn, Cary Grant and David Niven, as well as other distinguished gentlemen in fields other than the theatre. Pretty ladies like Merle Oberon and Vivien Leigh watched their countrymen (and stray Americans, including Douglas Fairbanks Jr) from the sidelines. It was all very exciting, particularly if one understood the game. I didn't!'

Boris Karloff was an avid cricketer as was Louis Hayward, and through Hayward, Cushing was invited to play. 'I was bowled out first ball,' he lamented, 'and missed several easy catches when fielding mid-on, being so distracted by all those luminaries surrounding me. My services were not called upon again, but I attended several matches as an onlooker from the pavilion.'

Peter Gray was surprised and impressed by Cushing's adventures. 'Soon I was receiving snaps of him looking utterly at home with stars in Hollywood who were to me mere gods on Olympus. Nothing ventured, nothing wins, indeed!'

If Cushing's cricketing skills disappointed C Aubrey Smith, a meeting with British actor and fellow cricket enthusiast Robert Coote, led to his biggest Hollywood role to date.

6: Vigil In The Night (1940)

Cushing and Anne Shirley in *Vigil In The Night*.

From a tiny part in *The Man In The Iron Mask* to lead role in *Vigil In The Night* (1940), and in the space of a year! Not bad going for a young actor who stepped out into the unknown.

Even with stardom just around the corner, Cushing continued to live frugally at the YMCA, and thanks to his previous assignments, he bought a car ('on the never-never'), a 1940 Hudson which enabled him to travel more.

After mixing with so many big names with the Haywards, he got the chance to meet a real Hollywood legend.

'Louis and I went to visit Ida on location at Big Bear Lake, when she was making *High Sierra* (1941) with Humphrey Bogart.'

Although Bogart was known for being difficult, Cushing found him, 'a most charming and intelligent person. Bogart was simply wonderful, very unsure of himself, not a bit like the tough sort of character he played. It goes for all actors really. They were all absolute bags of nerves, really and truly. He just tried not to let it show.'

6: Vigil In The Night (1940)

Bogart was an ace marksman, and, according to Cushing, 'he demonstrated his superb marksmanship and quick draw with a revolver, tossing coins high up into the air, nine times out of ten scoring a bull's eye before they reached the ground!'

Returning to LA, Cushing found out that Robert Coote, who was working as dialogue director for a new RKO production, had recommended him for a film role in *Vigil In The Night*.

'He thought I would be good casting for Joe Shand, a lad from the North Country who worked as a motor mechanic. He suggested this to director, George Stevens, I was given a screen test, and to my delight, it was successful.

'I got the part because I could manage the Lancashire accent required. The war was in full spate and there was an enormous shortage of young actors. The film was based on a story by A J Cronin about hospitals, and the producers wanted someone who could assume a North Country accent that the Americans could understand and would be acceptable in England as well. So, I was to immerse myself in an important part.'

It was Cushing's most important Hollywood role to date. 'The second male lead, and to have landed it in such a comparatively short time was most satisfying.'

A J Cronin's novella was published as a serial in the British magazine *Good Housekeeping* in 1938. The following year *The Hollywood Reporter* announced that RKO had purchased the rights to the story as a vehicle for Carole Lombard.

An actress since she was a child, Lombard had worked for Mack Sennett in several shorts before signing to Paramount Studios where she acted in several dramas during the silent era. With the coming of sound, she found her niche in comedy after starring in Howard Hawks' *Twentieth Century* (1934).

By 1937 Lombard was one of Hollywood's most popular and highest paid actresses, her profile further increased by her marriage to Clark Gable in 1939. Leaving Paramount to choose her own projects, her strong desire to perform more dramatic work prompted her to accept the lead in *Vigil In The Night*.

Alongside Carole Lombard, the film also starred Brian Aherne, with Anne Shirley and Julien Mitchell playing the other main characters.

Shooting began at RKO Radio Studios in July 1939, but after three days, production stopped when Lombard was rushed to hospital. According to Cushing, 'Miss Lombard had to undergo surgery for an acute appendicitis. This delayed commencement for about six weeks, but it helped her a great deal with her part as a nurse, as she was able to observe closely the daily routine of a hospital ward.' Hollywood rumours claimed that Lombard suffered a miscarriage and that the press covered up the incident by reporting it as an appendectomy.

During the six-week hiatus, Cushing was offered two films. The titles are unknown, but out of loyalty to Carole Lombard, he turned both down. 'This was quite a show of dedication,' said Deborah Del Vecchio. 'As a lifelong movie fan, he was in awe of Carole Lombard and valued the opportunity to work with her.'

Journalist Elizabeth Copeland wrote an article entitled *Peter Cushing, by Skimpy Living, Manages to Wait for Carole Lombard Film*, in which she wrote, 'Peter Cushing's long-standing admiration for Carole Lombard has cost him a number of good roles and a sizable addition to his bank account. During his London stage career, Cushing conceived his admiration for the blonde actress. When he decided to come to Hollywood, one of the motivating factors was the hope that he might have a chance to play in a picture with her.'

Copeland's article ends on a high note. 'Cushing had arrived in the country almost flat broke, and he could weather this production delay only by the most skimpy living. During the six-week interim, he was offered substantial parts in two other pictures but the acceptance of them would have caused him to abandon his part in the Lombard film. It was a temptation, but he struggled through and at length realised his ambition in scenes before the camera with Miss Lombard.'

The article was enough to build up Cushing's burgeoning Hollywood reputation.

Cushing wasn't idle during the interim. 'I drove to Palm Springs, where the Haywards were taking a vacation. I was delighted to discover a summer stock theatre there, and to learn they wanted someone to play Bruce Lovell, the leading part in *Love From A Stranger* by Frank Vospers, for two weeks. Ever hopeful, I asked if I could oblige, and was surprised and gratified when they said, "yes please."'

Adapted from the Agatha Christie story *Philomel Cottage*, Cushing had taken a supporting role in the play a year earlier with the Court Players in Nottingham.

Love From A Stranger also starred Ida Lupino, who clearly used her influence to get Cushing the lead in his American theatre debut. This gives an interesting insight into Cushing's relationship with his adopted 'mother', which runs on similar lines to his future relationship with his wife Helen.

As a shy, introverted and insecure actor, Cushing wasn't one to make decisions; his trip to Hollywood having more to do with the madness of youth. 'At the time, he had nothing else [except] time and [personal] drive,' said Marcus Brooks, founder of the *Peter Cushing Appreciation Society*, who also makes an interesting point about Cushing's relationship with both women, 'Helen stepped in when Ida stepped out.'

6: Vigil In The Night (1940)

It was a golden opportunity for Cushing to play a villain, and he took full advantage of the beautiful scenery around Laguna as he prepared for his role. 'Taking the script to study my lines, I walked up into the mountains, and enjoyed a swim in a natural pool amongst the rocks. I made my way down again, by leaping from boulder to boulder in the middle of a gushing stream.'

Cushing was required to play the part with blond hair, so he bought some gold lustre from an art shop. 'It was most effective. It also turned my scalp bright green.'

The living quarters provided by the producers consisted of small, primitive wooden huts. According to Cushing, 'the inside walls (were) made of whitewashed plywood, with nails driven in to hang your clothes on. Mine were constantly working loose, depositing my wardrobe on the dusty floor, so in the end I left it there, neatly folded.

'The furniture consisted of an iron bedstead with questionable sheets, a handy jerry underneath, except the handle had been broken off, an upright rickety wicker chair which I imagined had seen better days, and a marble-topped washstand complete with china basin and jug, plus a cracked, fly-blown mirror. Any water required was drawn from an artesian well in the centre of the compound.

'No charge was made for this accommodation,' he added, 'it was considered part of my salary.'

The uncomfortable living quarters didn't help Cushing's mood and the threat of war also troubled him. 'I felt homesick for the first time, and I was also worried about what was happening in England.' Had things been different, he would have battled homesickness long enough to establish himself in Hollywood.

There was a serious incident that occurred which had the following news report, 'It was a close call for Ida Lupino the other day when she slipped off the rocks at Laguna, fell into the briny, and was unconscious when rescued by Peter Cushing, a house guest.' Saving a Hollywood star from drowning was definitely enough to boost the actor's profile for life.

After his two miserable weeks on stage, Cushing returned to Hollywood to resume work on *Vigil In The Night*. On 3 September 1939, Britain officially declared war on Germany, and with typical British patriotism, Cushing was ready to forgo his movie contract by reporting for duty. 'I wasn't all that keen to kill anyone in conflict, or to be killed for that matter, but I did want to get home, back to England.'

Due to torn knee ligaments and a perforated eardrum, Cushing was classified 4C and told to stand by, leaving the actor deflated. 'It wasn't because I wanted to fight, or anything, I'm not really a fighting man – I'm sure hundreds of people weren't – but I did want to be home. It's a strange thing but I think it's a natural instinct. There was quite an exodus of British actors from Hollywood at that time. We all had our medicals, and my results were pretty low because of some old wounds I sustained at rugger. Those of us who were not 100% were told to stand by, but I couldn't wait for that, and I decided to get back home on my own.'

With Carole Lombard out of hospital, filming resumed at the end of September 1939. Cushing's scenes alongside Lombard and Anne Shirley were enough to temporarily lift his spirits.

After previously seeing both actresses at his local cinema, Cushing was completely in awe of them. 'I was mesmerised in the presence of these fabulous creatures, regarding all film stars as not of this world, and verging on the sacrosanct.' When he was ready to shoot his first scene with Lombard, he asked George Stevens, 'Am I allowed to touch her?' Giving him a look of astonishment, Stevens replied, 'You can do what you like with her, so long as you cause no bodily harm!'

'They were wonderful to work with,' Cushing said of the actresses, 'and George Stevens was most helpful, encouraging and complimentary.'

Stevens was so impressed with Cushing's performance, he gave him a specially written scene towards the end where a distraught Joe Shand blames Anne (Lombard) for the death of his wife Lucy (Shirley). Stevens' faith in Cushing was a further indication of the actor's growing reputation.

One morning Cushing spotted a propman carrying a large slice of bacon into the operating theatre set and enquired if it was lunch. 'Nope,' replied the propman. 'Operation,' and placed the bacon on an extra's stomach so that Brian Aherne could insert a scalpel into it to make it look like a real operation!

Filming wrapped on 30 November 1939, and as was the normal practice for any Hollywood production, there was a wrap party for the cast and crew. The food and drink were served in hospital utensils by waiters wearing clinical gowns and rubber gloves, and they provided toilet rolls instead of serviettes. 'Suffice to say,' recalled Cushing, 'it rather took the edge off my appetite.'

Cushing was not alone regarding the party. One of the visitors on the set was Carole Lombard's husband Clark Gable, who took one look at the buffet and exclaimed, 'Gee! I am glad I'm slimming!'

Vigil In The Night got its New York premier on 4 February 1940 before gaining a general release on 9 February; the UK premier took place in April. Critical reaction was favourable, if unspectacular, *The Times* stating that the film, 'has been made with a painstaking sincerity and both acting and directing are level-headed and restrained, but inspiration is lacking, and the film never touches the heights.' Leslie Halliwell was less impressed, saying it was a 'Dull, downbeat melodrama with a miscast lead.'

Cushing also got his first critical notice. According to Kit Cameron of

6: Vigil In The Night (1940)

The New York Daily News, 'Peter Cushing dominates two dramatic scenes. His acting has the same forceful quality that distinguishes Spencer Tracy's performance.' Such a positive review not only vindicated George Stevens' faith in Cushing's abilities, it also showed Hollywood that there was a promising new talent on the rise. So much so, Cushing signed with the George Ullman and Hallam Cooley Agency.

Shortly after the film's release, Cushing was interviewed by the *New York Journal American*. When the reporter enquired if he had now gone Hollywood, he replied that his home had a swimming pool, tennis court and gym. 'I merely rent a room there, I live at the YMCA!' By that time Cushing had moved in with the Haywards but valued their privacy enough not to mention them in the interview.

Budgeted at $920,000, *Vigil In The Night* made $1,004,000 at the box office – a slight profit although it did much better overseas. The commercial disappointment had a lot to do with audiences not being keen on Carole Lombard being dramatic in a film that was gloomy for cinematic tastes, a situation not helped by the outbreak of war in Europe.

Although decently made and acted, *Vigil In The Night* is dull. In an earnest attempt to make a good movie, George Stevens succeeds in making something with an average feel to it, and this is not helped by a miscast Lombard. Anne Shirley fairs better in the smaller role.

Brian Aherne gives a bland performance and his lack of chemistry with Lombard is evident. The rest of the cast is solid but forgettable – except for one actor.

Despite his inexperience, Peter Cushing steals the acting honours. With his slight Lancashire accent, he gives a sensitive portrayal of a young working-class man with so much love to give, and his first scene with Carole Lombard generates more chemistry than she has with Brian Aherne.

Cushing's second scene where Joe tells Anne of his intention to marry Lucy evokes a great deal of sadness because he knows he's marrying the wrong woman but desires the happiness that is supposed to come with marriage.

Cushing's next two scenes are stand-outs. The first sees a despondent Joe after Lucy has left him, and in his final scene, he is devastated at Lucy's passing. One can see why George Stevens wrote that additional scene. He knew Cushing had the talent and star quality to make it work. Had he remained in Hollywood, Stevens would undoubtedly have used him in more films.

With *Vigil In The Night* behind him, Cushing succumbed to melancholia once more.

'As all the boats were being commandeered for the war effort,' he said, 'I thought that the only way I could get home would be at the expense of the British government so I must head for Canada. I decided to go by way of New York earning what money I could on the way.'

Cushing's plans were put on hold due to a serious leg infection. 'A blister on my heel had burst and turned septic, coinciding with a severe case of athlete's foot caused by contact with contaminated water in the shower bath. The infection increased rapidly causing considerable discomfort, so I went to a clinic for treatment.'

The infection was so bad, Cushing came close to losing his leg. 'A scalpel-happy surgeon was all for amputation, but after seeking a second opinion, I'm glad to say some less drastic measures were taken, the poison being drained away by a system of rubber tubes.'

The second option saved both his leg and career. 'Although infinitely preferable, it was a lengthy and uncomfortable process, and also very costly. When I was discharged, I returned my car, as I was unable to keep up with the monthly instalments.'

Back to square one, Cushing spent Christmas with the Haywards. With little money to his name, he had to continue working while planning his return to the UK.

7: Women In War (1940)

Cushing in *Women In War*.

To promote the British war effort, Hollywood did their bit with films like *Women In War* (1940). Production began in January 1940, a month after the defeat of the German cruiser *Graf Spee* during the Battle of the River Plate. Having Wendy Barrie playing an American socialite drafted into the

British army made it one of Hollywood's first 'British' war films; it would be another year before America joined the allies in Europe following the Japanese attack on Pearl Harbour in December 1941.

Women In War made some impact on its release because it marked the big screen return of respected stage actress and former silent movie star Elsie Janis. As 'The Sweetheart of the American Expeditionary Force' Janis entertained British and American servicemen in France during World War I.

Another actress making a comeback was Mae Clarke. Best known for having a half-grapefruit pushed in her face by James Cagney in *Public Enemy* (1931), she earned horror immortality as Elizabeth Frankenstein in *Frankenstein* (1931), a role she never cared for and one that haunted her for the rest of her career. *Women In War* was her first film in three years.

Cushing's involvement consists of a two-minute uncredited appearance as an RAF flyer. Resplendent in his uniform, he looks every inch the dashing, fun-loving British officer. Appearing 13 minutes into the film, he smokes, drinks and flirts with the nurses, before vanishing altogether. Not surprisingly, he made no impression on critics and audiences despite giving an enthusiastic performance.

Produced by Republic Pictures, *Woman In War* was directed by Budapest born John M Auer, who specialised in crime thrillers for the studio, so this was a departure from his normal output.

Founded by Herbert J Yates in 1935 following the acquisition of six poverty row studios (all of whom owed money to Yates for unpaid lab bills), Yates put together a seasoned team of professional actors and technicians under the Republic banner, and thanks to the advanced technical facilities and established crew at Republic, filming went smoothly.

Women In War premiered in May 1940, and went on general release in the following month before arriving in Britain in February 1942, by which time America was fighting with the Allies. Exploitation being the order of the day, the outer lobby of one theatre featured a machine gun pit surrounded by sandbags, with bomb explosions and gun fire blaring out from the loudspeakers. The publicity worked well enough, but it hardly made *Women In War* great entertainment.

The attempt at realism pulls no punches, especially during a brief but violent bombing of a French village by British forces, which received an Academy Award nomination for the special effects team, but the film buckled under a flimsy story, not helped by the lack of star power and a better-known director. There were no stand-out performances, giving the impression that the cast came on set, did their job, and returned home. Janis' lack of acting experience with talking pictures shows, and this is not helped by the stolid casting of Wendy Barrie, Patric Knowles and Mae Clarke.

7: Women in War (1940)

The American critics weren't enamoured by this 'uplifting' propaganda effort. While praising the special effects and miniature work, *Variety* said the film 'unfolded in an episodic manner, skimming over the thin story structure at a fast pace.' *The New York Daily News* felt 'it packs too much punch.'

The worst review, which came from an unknown source, said, 'If this is the best the war can inspire, let's do without war pictures.'

Women In War boosted Republic's profile, especially with the Oscar nomination, which was rare for a B movie. Considered 'lost' for many years, it eventually surfaced on VHS video, and the overall evaluation on IMDB is more positive than that of the critics of the day. Nitrate prints of the film survive in the UCLA Film and Television Archives but it is not listed for preservation.

Women In War is for Cushing completists only. The actor never spoke about the movie in his autobiography, and probably had little recollection of his time on the set. It was a case of the producers hiring a British actor who just happened to be around.

In any case Cushing was past caring about his Hollywood career. 'I really wanted to get home. Of course, even if I had the money, you couldn't just buy a ticket on an aeroplane or a boat because everything was commandeered for the war effort.'

Had he focused on his career and less on his homesickness, he could have built on *Vigil In The Night* and held out for better roles instead of taking bread-and-butter efforts like *Women In War*. He had the motherly support of Ida Lupino, the various friendships of his fellow actors and the admiration of directors George Stevens and James Whale. There was no way he could have failed, especially when there were better wartime propaganda movies which could have made good use of an English actor.

Cushing remained on standby.

8: The Passing Parade Shorts

Cushing in 'Dreams', part of the *Passing Parade*.

'The Hidden Master' and 'Dreams' were both part of an MGM series entitled *Passing Parade*. This was the brainchild of Canadian actor, writer, producer and radio announcer John Nesbitt, who first presented the series on NBC radio in 1937. *Passing Parade* focused on strange but true historical events, both famous and obscure: he conceived the idea after his father left him a trunk containing news clippings of weird stories from around the world.

Other than Nesbitt's stirring narration, the series did not use music or sound effects. According to producer Joseph Koehler, 'There was a time when no one could be sold the idea that one man, without much musical help, could fill a half hour and hold his audience. Nesbitt has disproved the bromide because he's Nesbitt and spins a yarn that's as tight as an Armistice announcement.'

Nesbitt and his 14 staff writers researched and verified all the stories on the show, but he usually wrote the scripts an hour before broadcast.

8: The Passing Parade Shorts

Among the historical figures featured were Lord Clive of India, Abraham Lincoln, Dr Wilhelm Röntgen, Catherine de Medici and Nostradamus.

In 1938 MGM purchased the rights to the series, which Nesbitt produced as one-reelers to support whatever the main feature was.

The series ran from 1938 to 1949 and showcased upcoming young talent. Among the directors who went onto successful careers were Fred Zimmerman and Jacques Tournier, while a young Ava Gardner acted in a couple of the productions. The shorts contained no dialogue and were introduced by Tchaikovsky's 'Symphony No. 5'.

'The Hidden Master' consists of three stories, each lasting ten minutes, and focuses on how luck influenced the protagonists of each story. The second tale tells of how a stroke of luck brought about the invention of the X-Ray by Dr Wilhelm Röntgen (Emmett Vogan), while the third tale has a poor down-on-his-luck ordinary guy (Louis Jean Heydt) saving his family from a gas leak in his home after receiving a phone call from a drunk which turns out to be a wrong number.

Cushing stars in the first story. 'My part was the young Clive of India, who, in a state of black despair, tried to blow his brains out. He put a gun to his temple, and twice it refused to detonate. The third time, he aimed at a pitcher of water, which was shattered by the weapon suddenly responding. Clive regarded this as an omen, and history records the mark he made in an outstanding career.' Despite his many achievements, Lord Clive never escaped the black clouds. A lifelong opium addict, he took his life on 22 November 1774.

'The Hidden Master' was released on 20 April 1940. It was the 13th entry in the series, and the most memorable.

With limited screen time and no dialogue, Cushing gives his most effective Hollywood performance. As an actor who was insecure at best and self-destructive at worst, in the space of a few minutes he channelled his raw emotion to create a complex character plagued by despair and suicidal thoughts. By the end of the year, Cushing's Lord Clive attracted interest from the MGM bigwigs.

Cushing's next *Passing Parade* short, 'Dreams', explores the meaning of dreams in three tales, including one about President Abraham Lincoln dreaming of his assassination by John Wilkes Booth.

Cushing's story concerns a man who dreams about being chained to a railway line with a train heading in his direction. The narrator explains that the dream represents the man's desire to escape from the circumstances of his life but is held back by his devotion to a loved one.

Cushing invests his few minutes of silent screen time with an intense performance as a man wracked by the fear of his impending doom. Released in November 1940, 'Dreams' is not as memorable as 'The Hidden Master', but Cushing remains compelling throughout.

Cushing remained focused on getting home. 'I offered my services to everyone and everything, but I was too old for this and too old for that. I was getting desperate.'

'Having barely enough money to get me halfway to the East Coast, I had written to the Office of the High Commissioner for the United Kingdom in Ottawa, and the Department of National Defence in Regina, Saskatchewan, explaining my circumstances, both replies stating that "no provision exists to cover the cost of transportation from an individual's home to the point of enlistment".'

Once again, Cushing's career marked time, but at least his next film gave him a substantial role.

9: Laddie (1940)

Cushing with Virginia Gilmore and Spring Byington in *Laddie*.

Laddie, A True-Blue Story is a semi-autobiographical novel by Indiana born writer, photographer and conservationist Gene Stratton-Porter. Published in 1913, this was her fourth novel, and her most popular, with 2.5 million copies sold worldwide. It was inspired by the death of her brother Leander, who drowned in the Wasbash River, in 1872. The character of Laddie was closely based on Leander, with Little Sister being representative of Stratton-Porter as they shared similar personality traits. The novel was written while she was supervising the construction of her home in Sylvan Lake, Indiana.

Stratton-Porter was also an important pioneer of Hollywood's fledgling movie industry: her first novel, *Freckles*, was filmed by Paramount Pictures in 1917. Moving to Hollywood in 1923, she set up Gene Stratton-Porter Productions, one of the first female-owned movie studios. Subsequent film adaptations of her novels remained true to the original work, which included a 1926 version of *Laddie*.

Gene Stratton-Porter died in 1924, but her novels remained popular with filmmakers for many years. *Laddie* was filmed again in 1935 by RKO and directed by George Stevens. In 1940, the studio was ready to produce another version.

The situation in Europe became increasingly worrisome with many Americans pledging their support to the British war effort, and many more volunteering for military service overseas. To get audiences away from those harsh realities, RKO opted for simple, family orientated entertainment but emphasised their support for the war effort by making some of the main characters British.

Production began on 1 June 1940. Brought in as director was Jack Hively, who began as an editor at RKO and quickly emerged as one of Hollywood's finest filmmakers, successfully tackling a variety of subjects before moving into television.

Being a big budget film, no expense was spared when it came to recreating Indiana on the RKO lot. To achieve this, two large sound stages were converted by using 100 tons of soil, and plenty of trees and shrubberies to create an outdoor look. One assumes *Laddie* was too expensive to film on location.

RKO also cast their contract star in the title role. The son of silent cowboy star Jack Holt, Tim Holt had followed in his father's footsteps as a Western hero ever since he locked horns with John Wayne in *Stagecoach* (1939). Signing with RKO, Holt enlivened several B Westerns, but had a much wider range. In a surprising turn of events, he was cast against type as the obnoxious George Minafer in Orson Welles' masterpiece *The Magnificent Ambersons* (1942). Despite his critically acclaimed performance, the film wasn't a box office success, and he soon returned to horse operas.

Holt's second chance of cinema respectability was opposite Humphrey Bogart and Walter Brennan in *The Treasure Of Sierra Madre* (1948). *Laddie* was another rare opportunity to move away from Westerns.

The role of Pamela Pryor went to Anglo-American actress Virginia Gilmore, who was under contract with Sam Goldwyn Productions. Never achieving movie stardom, she is best known for being Yul Brynner's first wife.

Cushing was cast as Robert Pryor and his role consisted of two scenes and a couple of lines of dialogue. The character is pivotal to the plot and Cushing receives a screen credit. Turning up late on in the film, he shares a scene (and has his first onscreen kiss) with Virginia Gilmore as Joan Carroll's Little Sister. As the tortured and sickly Robert, Cushing evokes deep sadness and regret as he collapses in his sister's arms.

Cushing's second scene is briefer. He is in bed with Virginia Gilmore beside him. He does not speak, but his expression speaks volumes as he makes peace with his estranged father, a fine performance by Miles Mander.

Cushing also gives a good performance and looks debonair in period costume. He could have done more with the role, but the enthusiasm displayed in his earlier films is lacking. Had he been more committed, Jack Hively could have expanded the role and given Cushing more screen time.

Laddie is an honest, homespun drama. It is well made, and Joan Carroll is especially noteworthy as Little Sister. Like many child stars, she never made the transition to adult stardom but remained active on TV. Tim Holt acquits himself well, but like *The Magnificent Ambersons* and *The Treasure Of Sierra Madre*, *Laddie* failed to change the course of his career.

Laddie was released on 18 October 1940, and critical evaluation was unspectacular with Leslie Halliwell finding it a 'Rather dim, old fashioned rural romance.' The film was rated as average by most American newspapers, film magazines and journals, with one unidentified review stating that *Laddie* was, 'overall unremarkable and was best for the hinterlands.'

Peter Cushing's performance received no special mention from the critics. Not that he was bothered; his mind remained focused on going home.

RKO planned to produce a film version of Thomas Hughes' novel *Tom Brown's Schooldays*, and according to a press clipping of the time, 'Peter Cushing, the young English actor who recently completed a role in *Vigil In The Night* is being tested by Gene Towne and Graham Baker for *Tom Brown's Schooldays*.'

The film was released on 14 July 1940 but without Cushing (he would have made an excellent Flashman). Since his Hollywood career was progressing nicely, he may have been considered for other roles, and might have played bit parts in many more films. Perhaps one day, these obscure efforts may be rediscovered – much like his next movie.

10: The Howards Of Virginia (1940)

Cushing in *The Howards Of Virginia*.

Cushing never spoke about *Women In War* and *Laddie* in either of his autobiographies, but *The Howards Of Virginia* was completely omitted from his filmography, because he had no recollection of taking part. Considering his tiny appearance, it is understandable.

Columbia Pictures initiated the project early in 1940. With war raging in Europe, and public pressure mounting on America to get involved, the studio decided to produce more patriotic films.

The Howards Of Virginia is based on Elizabeth Merwin Page's *The Tree Of Liberty* (the film's original title). Published in 1939, the novel is 985 pages long so adapting it to a 116-minute movie was a challenge for screenwriter Sidney Buchman.

Production began in July 1940 with location shooting in Santa Cruz, California and the Pocahontas Trail in Williamsburg, Virginia. Another prominent location was the recently reconstructed Colonial Williamsburg. Restored by John D Rockefeller Jr, his intention was to use the town for education and tourism. He allowed Columbia to film the town exteriors,

10: The Howards Of Virginia (1940)

which saved the studio millions of dollars in sets and locations.

With Frank Lloyd directing, the pivotal role of Matt Howard went to an actor who epitomised Hollywood, Cary Grant. A star of several screwball comedies, *The Howards Of Virginia* was a change of pace for Grant as it would be shot in period costume. He was reluctant to play the role but was persuaded to by the head of Columbia, Harry Cohn. The decision also had a lot to do with Grant's wish to become an American citizen.

Although proud of his British roots, Grant's decision was looked upon unfavourably by his UK fans, and playing an American revolutionary fighting against the British was ill-timed under the circumstances, not helped by the fact the 36-year-old actor was too old to play Matt Howard, the character being 21.

Taking the female lead was Martha Scott, in her second film appearance (replacing Joan Fontaine). Best known as Charlton Heston's mother in *Ben-Hur* (1959), the Missouri born Scott was an inexperienced actress, but Grant helped her during filming. He demanded precise lighting and staging for Scott, who praised Grant's patience, assistance and professionalism throughout.

Now to Peter Cushing's five second appearance. The scene is set early on at a party where Richard Carlson's Thomas Jefferson introduces Matt Howard (and making him out to be a landed gentleman, instead of a backwoodsman) to several important guests, one of whom is Leslie Stevens, played by Cushing.

With his frock coat and flowing cravat, Cushing cuts a dashing figure. Carlson introduces him to Grant, referring to Stevens as, 'a great talent with music, practically none with the ladies.'

Sitting uncomfortably, Cushing rises to his feet stiffly and replies, 'Your servant, sir,' before bowing out of the film altogether. 'He does not even make most of the five seconds,' observed Deborah Del Vecchio. 'His inexperience is painfully obvious, and he exhibits none of the screen presence that would be his in the future.' One gets the impression that Cushing was chosen by a casting director, put into a costume, told to utter his line and then leave with his paycheque for what appears to be an hour's work.

'What is fascinating here,' said Del Vecchio, 'is whether Peter Cushing appeared in other films – perhaps in crowd scenes – that have not yet been noticed. It's more than likely (for the film) that a young man with an English accent was needed for a small part and Cushing was simply in the proverbial right place at the right time. At any rate, one can't help wondering.'

'Cushing's Hollywood career was, by any standards, going very well,' said David Miller, 'until the turn of the world events all but stopped it in its tracks.' With war raging in Europe, Cushing's desire to return home grew stronger.

Having this on his mind is reason enough for having no recollection of *The Howards Of Virginia*, although it is hard to believe he would forget a scene with Cary Grant.

The Howards Of Virginia was released on 19 September 1940, and while it is an excellent production (Richard Hageman was Oscar nominated for his music), the film isn't very good, the main fault being Cary Grant's miscasting.

The critics thought so too with the *New York Times* saying that the film was 'deficient in dramatic action. The only disappointment, and it is a major one, is Cary Grant.' Leslie Halliwell found it a 'Historical cavalcade in which the central miscasting seems to cast a shadow of artifice over the whole. Interesting, but seldom stimulating.' *Newsweek* is more forgiving. 'Obviously miscast, Cary Grant meets the exigencies of a difficult role with more gusto than persuasion. While ambitious, expensive and generally interesting, it comes to life all too infrequently.'

Grant knew he was miscast from the start. While adept at playing sophisticated, modern-day charmers, he struggles as a backwoodsman and his attempts to speak in the old English vernacular is unintentionally hilarious.

Grant hated the film, and audiences stayed away in droves. Receiving the worst critical reviews of his career, it caused a rift with Harry Cohn who he blamed for talking him into playing an unsuitable role.

Not surprisingly, Peter Cushing's 'performance' went unnoticed by the critics, but at least it was another film under his belt. 'Many of these were small roles,' said David Miller, 'although the money was useful.'

Towards the end of 1940, there was one more Hollywood film to make before his journey home.

11: They Dare Not Love (1941)

'I managed to get a few more engagements,' Cushing said of his final months in Hollywood, 'working once again with James Whale in *They Dare Not Love* (1941), which starred George Brent and Martha Scott.' This indifferent effort ended his Hollywood career on a low note.

Many things had changed since Cushing last worked with Whale on *The Man In The Iron Mask*. When Whale's temperament had reached breaking point at Universal, studio head Charles Rogers tried to buy out his contract. When Whale refused, he was assigned routine B movies.

Produced by Columbia Pictures, *They Dare Not Love* was a step up from Whale's recent output, but not by much, nor did it improve his standing in the film community.

Pre-production began towards the end of 1940, and Whale was hired for a small flat fee of $30,000, further emphasising the 'gun for hire' reputation he had acquired. Filming started on New Year's Day 1941.

Playing the lead was debonair Irish actor George Brent. After signing with Warner Brothers, he specialised in sophisticated English gentlemen, and became the perfect foil for Hollywood's most temperamental leading ladies, especially Greta Garbo, Hedy Lamarr, Barbara Stanwyck and Bette Davis. By the time he did *They Dare Not Love*, Brent was at the height of his popularity.

Unfortunately, the female lead was nowhere near as formidable as Brent's previous co-stars. Under contract with Columbia, Martha Scott was recruited from *The Howards Of Virginia* with Hungarian stage actor Paul Lukas playing the villain.

The route to Cushing's involvement in the film isn't entirely clear other than his being at the right place at the right time. He might have been hanging around the Columbia lot following *The Howards Of Virginia* and then got hired for his uncredited appearance as Sub-Lieutenant Blackler for the film's climax. James Whale might have used his influence when it came to casting the actor, but since Cushing never explained how he landed the job, it's really anybody's guess.

Nor does Cushing say anything about Whale's temperament on *They Dare Not Love*. Whale's bitter attitude and increasing insensitivity towards his actors made the film a difficult shoot for all concerned. He hated the script and quickly lost interest in the project, falling out with George Brent and Harry Cohn during shooting. Cohn replaced Whale with Charles 'King' Vidor three weeks into the shoot, with Victor Fleming filling in the gaps.

It was reported that Whale was replaced by Vidor after the former came down with flu. Further rumours indicated that the escalating personal problems were due to Whale's abusive behaviour towards the cast and crew. Writer Charles Bennett felt that the animosity between Cohn and Whale was personal and that Cohn's decision to fire Whale was, 'utterly ridiculous because James Whale was a magnificent director.'

The film marked a sad end to Whale's Hollywood career. According to critic John Brosnan, author of *The Horror People*, 'During the making of *They Dare Not Love* in 1941, which was about war refugees, he walked off the set after an argument and never returned. The film was completed by Charles Vidor. Whale never directed another feature though in 1949 he did direct a short, experimental film called *Hello Out There*, which was never released.'

Appearing at the end of the film, Cushing did his job unaware of any tensions on set; he probably had no idea that Whale had been fired since he finished his scene before it happened.

Cushing was already on his way home when *They Dare Not Love* was

11: They Dare Not Love (1941)

released on 16 May 1941, to a negative response from all concerned, with most of the backlash aimed at Whale. *The New York Times* felt that 'with all the proved talent Columbia put behind the manufacture of *They Dare Not Love* it is hard to understand why the new film should turn out to be the disappointment it is. Granting that James Whale's direction is pedestrian, that the performances of Martha Scott, George Brent and Paul Lukas are no better, we still feel that the root of all evil in this case sprouted back in the story department presided over by Charles Bennett, Ernest Vajda and James Edward Grant. Though the plot they whipped up probably is no more fantastic than some of the things happening in the world today it does not rouse either one's imagination or emotion. *They Dare Not Love* is vapid fare.'

The New York Herald Tribune thought, 'James Whale's direction is deliberate and fails to take fullest advantage of suspenseful opportunities in the script,' while the *Baltimore Herald* found the film 'scarcely inspired and, although it pains us to say so, the work of an ordinary able cast will do nothing to enhance its members' reputations.' Back in England Leslie Halliwell said the film was, 'curiously naïve romantic propaganda from this director; not at all memorable.'

They Dare Not Love is a poor film and Whale's lack of interest is evident. There is no chemistry between the leads and the supporting cast is weak. It is a lacklustre affair with few thrills.

Cushing provides a commanding presence in his few seconds of screen time as the British officer leading the rescue of the romantic leads. After his wooden turn in *The Howards Of Virginia*, it is refreshing to see him looking committed once more. Had circumstances been different and Whale showed more interest in the project, he might have expanded Cushing's role into something more substantial.

After *They Dare Not Love*, Whale never went beyond directing training films for the United States Army and turned down the occasional offer to direct a feature. He returned to the theatre but never achieved his earlier British success.

'After directing a few plays in both America and England,' said John Brosnan, 'Whale spent most of his retirement painting and set designing. He was financially well-off, having wisely invested his "fabulous salaries" in real estate. He was worth over $600,000 when he died in 1957.'

Whale's mysterious death prompted several conspiracy theories that included suicide and murder. 'Since he was a known homosexual,' said Brosnan, 'Whale's rather unusual death – he was found drowned in his swimming pool on the night of 29 May 1957 – provoked several rumours of a sinister nature, the most popular being that he was beaten up and pushed into the pool by one of his homosexual acquaintances. A much more likely explanation was that his death was entirely accidental. He had suffered a mild stroke earlier that year and it is possible that, having fallen in the pool, he was too weak to climb out. Nevertheless, the exact circumstances of his death remain a mystery.' The coroner recorded Whale's death as accidental.

The mystery was cleared up following the death of his former partner David Lewis in 1987. At the time in constant physical pain and deteriorating mental health, Whale took his own life and left a suicide note which Lewis withheld from the authorities. It wasn't made public until after Lewis' own death.

And what of Peter Cushing?

'By 1941 Cushing seemed to be on the verge of becoming a fully-fledged member of a film factory,' observed writer Mark Miller. 'MGM was pleased with two appearances he had made in their *Passing Parade* shorts, which had served, more or less, as screen tests for the young actor. He seemed poised to join the ranks of Hollywood's colony of distinguished British actors as an MGM contract player.'

David Miller agrees. 'Cushing's compelling portrayal of the young Clive, influenced no doubt by the actor's own self-destructive feelings before the start of his stage career, led to a talk at MGM of grooming him for stardom. However, as the war continued to rage in Europe and the horrifying news came through of the London Blitz, Cushing's thoughts turned more and more to returning home.'

'The powers that be were pleased with this "mini picture",' said Cushing, 'and there was talk of grooming me for stardom. But it was now 1941, and I had become desperately homesick. I wasn't all that keen to kill anyone in conflict, or to be killed for that matter, but I did want to get home, back to England. My heart and mind set upon this desire, I declined MGM's proposal, and with a longing to get a little nearer to the United Kingdom, I decided to go to New York, and work my way up to Canada, which was, at least, a British Dominion. I reckoned that "standing by" on the move would prove less frustrating. Even if I could have afforded the fare, it was not possible to book a boat or plane passage to England, all transport being commandeered for war requisitions.'

Salvation of sorts came from one of his understanding mentors. 'With extreme generosity, Louis Hayward kindly lent me the sum, so that I might have some cash in hand during my travels.'

Following her divorce from Hayward, Ida Lupino became an actor and director of some repute, tackling a variety of ambiguous and often controversial subjects such as rape, out-of-wedlock pregnancies and bigamy. 'People are tired of having the wool pulled over their eyes,' she said about the state of Hollywood during the fifties. 'They want realism. And you can't be realistic with the same mugs on the screen all the time.' Lupino's directing style influenced France's 'New Wave' cinema and

11: They Dare Not Love (1941)

inspired the careers of future American auteurs Nicholas Ray, Samuel Fuller and Robert Aldrich.

Lupino's prominence as a director, gives an indication as to how Cushing's career might have developed if he had stayed in Hollywood. As well as providing a strong influence, Lupino would have been 'his professional Helen,' an older, motherly figure, giving him the direction that he needed in his own personal development.

Shortly after completing *They Dare Not Love*, Cushing was ready to leave. 'By 1941,' said Mark Miller, 'he knew he had to abandon Hollywood and return to Britain, even if he could not serve in the armed forces. A long, arduous journey home began.'

Although he showed no regrets regarding his decision, Cushing remembered his time fondly. 'I have been treated with the utmost kindness and consideration during my two years in Hollywood and was deeply grateful for the experience it had taught me. And now, on 18 January 1941, I set forth on a pilgrimage, little knowing that another fifteen long months lay ahead of me, before I was to reach my journey's end.'

12: One-Way Ticket To Blighty

Playbill for *The Seventh Trumpet*.

'It took me eighteen months altogether to get home,' Cushing told John Brosnan in his book *The Horror People*. This arduous trip back turned out to be just as eventful.

Thanks to the financial support from Louis Hayward and Ida Lupino,

12: One-Way Ticket To Blighty

Cushing made it to New York where he put his plan into action. 'My immediate concern was to earn some money in whatever way I could, to pay my fare to Canada.'

'When I reached New York, the first thing I saw was a notice outside a hospital saying, "Give blood for Britain." As this was the only thing I had to give I went straight in, gave a pint, and walked out. And then I fell flat on my face, so they had to pull me back in and give me two pints of blood to revive me.

'They kept me there for a couple of weeks, apparently suffering from nervous exhaustion. I cannot recall my first war effort being an outstanding success.'

The next step was finding cheap accommodation. 'The YMCA was full, and upon their recommendation I booked a room at the Hotel St James, in West 34th Street, just off Times Square.' It was little more than a flophouse, but it served its purpose while Cushing looked for gainful employment.

'I scanned cards in shop windows, looking for any jobs that might be in the offing. One required a car park attendant on Coney Island, so I made a beeline for that popular summer resort in Brooklyn, Long Island, with its fine beaches and countless amusement arcades.'

Cushing turned up for his interview, and his new boss, who 'resembled Edward G Robinson – as a gangster – to a remarkable degree,' reluctantly put him to work. 'The customers drove to the entrance, leaving [their cars] there with the engines ticking over. Then I took charge, carefully parking them in whatever space was available.'

Cushing's consideration for the cars, and the time it took him, got him fired immediately.

Card spotting in the shop windows once more, his next job looked more intriguing. The card read 'Illusionist needs assistance'. 'Sounded more like my cup of tea, although I was wary about the last word, hoping it was merely mis-spelt, all he wanted was someone to assist in his act, and did not imply that he, too, was "skint" and in need of financial aid.'

'Cushing quickly learned the secrets of the trade,' said David Miller, 'such as various code signals and different ways to hold the cards, but the engagement only lasted three weeks and he was faced with the prospect of sleeping in a flophouse.'

'That added grist to my mill,' said Cushing, 'but I was still a long way from my target, and when the contract terminated, I went card spotting again.'

Cushing was also on the hunt for acting jobs. 'I could not find anything suitable until, while reading a copy of *Variety*, the American equivalent of *The Stage*, I saw that a radio network wanted actors to read commercials, and I did quite a few of these.'

Cushing's Hollywood success followed him to New York, and before long, he went beyond radio adverts. 'By this time *Vigil In The Night* had been shown, and greeted with a favourable press and public reaction, so my name meant a little more than it had when I arrived here in 1939.'

This led to better paid radio work, including the part of Tom Prior in an adaptation of *Outward Bound*, and a recurring role in the NBC radio serial *The Grandpa Family*.

It is surprising that *Vigil In The Night* did not lead to more lucrative radio, theatre and film work, which was preferable to the constant card spotting for less dignified jobs. He still had an agent and his various Hollywood contacts to help him. The only explanation would be Cushing's reluctance to commit himself to long-term acting assignments as it would hamper the journey home.

Vigil In The Night did lead to a chance meeting with another struggling actor in Greenwich Village.

'Standing in Times Square after yet another unsuccessful round of shop windows, I was contemplating what to do next, and wondering vaguely how the enormous smoke-rings were blown out of the open-mouthed effigy of a GI's head, advertising some brand of cigarettes, when I felt a tap on my shoulder, and heard a voice asking, "You are Peter Cushing, aren't you?"

'Delighted to be recognised, I shook hands with this stranger. "My name's John Ireland," he added, "I've seen some of your movies."'

Ireland and his wife Elaine Sheldon had just moved to New York and were looking for stage roles. Both men hit it off immediately.

According to Cushing, '(John) was trying to make a name for himself on Broadway, and with his wife Elaine, an actress, had just moved into the same hotel where I was staying. Like mine, their funds were low, so we pooled resources as far as meals were concerned. He made the most delicious porridge I had ever tasted, which he cooked on a gas-ring in their room.'

Ireland also helped Cushing out financially. 'John suddenly asked if I had collected my social security. I didn't know what he meant, and he explained that a certain amount of my earnings in Hollywood had been deducted at source, and therefore I was entitled to $18 a week unemployment benefit. We were able to supplement our oats for quite a few weeks following that most welcome information.'

In April 1941, Cushing was able to pay back Ireland's kindness after finding an opportunity in *Variety* and using *Vigil In The Night* as a bargaining tool. 'I read that a summer stock company was being formed, and pulling the slight rank I now held, applied for an interview, which was granted. Elaine and John went with me, resulting in all three of us being accepted.'

The company was situated at the Green Mansions Holiday Camp near Warrensburg, New York State. More importantly, it was situated near the Adirondack Mountains – the border between America and Canada.

According to David Miller, '(Cushing) had planned to make his way over the Adirondack Mountains to Canada, the better to secure a passage home, but fate briefly had other ideas.'

Cushing signed a four-month contract, and the tour began in May 1941. 'A diverse programme of entertainment had been planned for the fortnightly guests, including a selection of plays, to be directed by a gentleman who delighted in the name of Walter Sparrow. No salaries, but the company paid all expenses, plus $100 to each of us at the end of the four months' season.'

The plays on the programme were Robert E Sherwood's *The Petrified Forest* and Samuel Nathanial Behrman's character study *Biography*, Arnold Ridley's *The Ghost Train*, with Cushing as Richard Winthrop, and Emlyn Williams' psychological thriller *Night Must Fall* where Cushing played Inspector Belsize.

The programme also included a modern dress version of William Shakespeare's *Macbeth*, with Cushing as Banquo and the one-act comedy *Pound On Demand* featuring Cushing as an Irish policeman. This formed part of a double bill with Noel Coward's short comedy *Fumed Oak* with Cushing in the lead of Henry Gow.

The company moved into log cabins situated near a lake. 'Compared to the prison-like austerity in Palm Springs, the log cabins allocated to us here were spacious and beautifully appointed, situated among pine trees near a large lake, where canoes and rowing boats rocked gently at their moorings. Refreshed and invigorated by the clean mountain air, after the fetid atmosphere of summer in the metropolis, we could use these craft or swim if so inclined, to reach the theatre complex which lay on a farther bank.'

It turned out to be four invigorating months for Cushing. 'It was grand to be acting on the stage again, in such pleasant conditions, and I enjoyed the comradeship of my fellow actors.

'The pay was quite good, and not only was I able to build up my strength a bit but also to improve my finances.'

But Cushing still had his sights set on Canada. 'Under normal circumstances, it would have been an idyllic existence, but four months seemed an awfully long time, and the financial side of this deal would not improve matters to any great extent. Still, it was better than the alternative of hanging around the stifling city, and at the back of my mind lay the idea to cross the border when we finished. The company having paid my fare thus far, it seemed the logical thing to do.'

Or so he thought when his contract finally came to an end.

'Toilette items, cigarettes and the occasional round of milkshakes or coffee with the rest of the cast, were not regarded as legitimate expenses, and were quite rightly deducted from the $100 bonus, leaving me with only $25 when the time came to collect it.'

The situation was further complicated by talent scouts who came to the shows in Warrensburg. 'As a result of their intentions,' said David Miller, 'Cushing was invited back to New York to take part in a show on Broadway.'

It wasn't an easy situation for Cushing with Canada being just around the corner. 'Gazing wistfully at that mountain range, I resisted a wild temptation to climb over "them thar hills" and, instead, joined my good companions on the long coach ride back to New York City.

'I decided to accept this side track, reasoning that, with any luck, the play's run should consolidate my savings, and raise the sum I needed to make my next step towards home.

Playing Constable Percival, *The Seventh Trumpet* opened at the Mansfield Theatre on Broadway on 21 November 1941. Described as a mystical war play, it left everyone baffled. 'It mystified the audiences, the critics and the cast,' said David Miller. According to one review, '*The Seventh Trumpet* opened on Broadway last night and blew its last blast.'

'We were lucky to survive for as long as we did,' reflected Cushing, 'because it meant the curtain fell never to rise again.'

Cushing's only Broadway appearance was not a distinguished effort, but he worked with Ian MacLaren, who played Osbourne in the 1930 film version of Cushing's favourite play *Journey's End*.

The Seventh Trumpet ran for nine days, leaving Cushing to consider his options. The situation was further complicated by the attack on Pearl Harbour. American declared war on Japan and would soon join the Allies in Europe. It was now imperative for Cushing to cross into Canada.

Cushing's determination to get home cost him a lead role in a major Broadway play. 'The "concrete jungle-drums" had throbbed out a message regarding *Claudia*, Rose Franken's very successful play, which was enjoying full houses. That excellent actor John Williams was also in the cast as Jerry Seymour, but he was leaving soon to join the Royal Air Force. I fixed an appointment with Miss Franken, in the hope that I might replace him.'

The interview with Rose Franken was a success. 'We are set for a long run,' she told Cushing. 'And you are right for the part, but will you be leaving us soon?' Cushing said he wasn't, and she said she would get in touch soon.

Cushing made a bad judgement. When the letter arrived, Rose Franken expressed her disappointment that he wasn't going to return home and do his bit for Blighty and that she was unable to offer him the role. Being in the play would have meant that he would have been able to work through Christmas and most of the following year, making enough money to cross into Canada.

With America going into the war, he now could not wait. 'It now became imperative that Cushing return to England as soon as possible,' said David Miller. 'He redoubled his efforts to raise his fare home and was advised to go to Canada where a working passage would be more easily secured.'

It leaves an interesting question about what Cushing did between December 1941 and February 1942 when he finally left America. When *The Seventh Trumpet* closed, did he go looking for other Broadway roles? Was there radio work available? What other jobs were available while thousands of men were enlisting?

David Miller offered an insight regarding these final months. 'He eventually left New York in February, sent on his way by donations from friends and colleagues that included a significant sum from Rita Hayworth.'

On 8 February 1942, Cushing caught the Iron Horse north-bound for Canada, and on the final leg of his journey.

'Cushing arrived in Montreal and immediately made his way to the YMCA,' said David Miller. 'His varied jobs in Canada were no less varied than they had been in New York.' Once again, he put together a plan of action. 'My next objective was to reach Halifax, Nova Scotia, so I set about raising the fare for that penultimate journey.

'The YMCA needed a night porter, and in lieu of salary, I was given a small room and two meals a day.' With food and lodgings sorted out, Cushing began looking for paid work without having to worry about starving or freezing to death, Canada not being the warmest of places during the winter months.

That situation was quickly solved. 'One of the staff told me the Lowes State Cinema were short of an usher for the afternoon shift, and thought this would help to tide me over for a spell, leaving the evenings free for my duties at the Y.'

Cushing got the job and was kitted out with the regulation pill-box hat and an ill-fitting uniform. 'They only had one uniform, and it was obviously made for a dwarf. It was so tight under the armpits my shoulders raised up like one of your American football players. I walked around like a gorilla.'

The trousers weren't much better. 'I was unable to do up the fly-buttons, hoping this would pass unnoticed in the dark, but just to be on the safe side, I held the torch there. I think the effect was worse!'

Despite the uniform malfunction, Cushing began earning again. 'A nice perk which went with this assignment was the patrons' gesture of tipping those who showed them to their seats. These gratuities were gratefully accepted.

'I've always been a romantic. Loving couples used to come in and I knew they'd like to sit together, so I used to get my torch and say, "Would you mind pressing on one seat so these two could sit together." It probably annoyed a few patrons trying to watch the film, but at least the tips would have been more than generous.'

One of the films being screened was *Captains Of The Clouds* (1942), starring James Cagney, which was little more than a recruitment drive for the Canadian Air Force. 'Some years later, someone asked me if I'd seen this film, and I was able to say in complete Noel Coward fashion, "Yes, dear boy, 455 times".'

Cushing kept up with his artistic pursuits. 'To keep my mind occupied during the many idle hours forced upon me over the years, I often turned to painting or building small models. I was currently making a miniature Bernstein (piano) using odd bits and pieces of balsa wood and card. It was only in the early stages of construction, as yet unrecognisable to the untrained eye, and I had left the various sections on top of the chest of drawers in my room, so that the glue would be set by the time I got back from work.'

Cushing returned to his room one night to find his piano had gone missing. Thinking it might have been mistaken for rubbish by the Irish chambermaid working at the YMCA, he told her what had happened.

Rather than being helpful, the maid gave Cushing what his mother called 'an old-fashioned look', and scurried off to tell another maid about a madman living in room 42. 'There's hardly room enough to swing a cat,' she told her colleague, 'and he's after asking me what I've done to his grand piano!'

The grand piano incident came back to haunt Cushing when he got a job on another Canadian propaganda movie, *The 49th Parallel* (1942).

'There was one more incident that happened to me before I got a ship home. It seems amusing now, but it was quite frightening at the time. I was once again short of money and went to a small film studio which was doing some incidental work on *The 49th Parallel*. Although they had no work for an actor, the art department was looking for someone to make some war insignia.

'They required some flags depicting the Red Rising Sun of Japan and the Black Nazi Swastika - half a dozen of each. Short of draughtsmen, the Art Director kindly entrusted me with this task.' As well as earning extra money, Cushing carried out the job during his free time at the YMCA.

'I offered to make what they wanted, lots of miniature Japanese and Nazi flags to be pinned on a huge map. They had no space for me to work in the art department and gave me the materials I needed and told me to do it where I was staying.'

'In fact, I was in the local YMCA hostel where I was also doubling up as the night porter. My room was so tiny that I could barely turn round, there was just enough room for the bed, but I set up my equipment and began making the insignia. During the time when I was downstairs serving as a porter, a maid would go into my room and tidy up, and because she heard me talking about making things like a grand piano (in miniature of, course) thought I was a bit mad. And when I announced one morning that I actually lost this piano in my room, she was convinced of it.'

12: One-Way Ticket To Blighty

'I made a few before desk-duty, and after a catnap, finished the remainder next morning, pinning them to a board in a neat row. I left the board on the chest-of-drawers and, after taking an early lunch, went off to work.'

Leaving them on display in the room was Cushing's undoing.

'The Irish cleaner-up of unconsidered trifles had seen the flags where the piano used to be and with commendable, if somewhat overzealous patriotism, reported me as a suspect spy.

'When I returned to the hostel later that day, I found two huge Mounted Policemen waiting for me. They immediately grabbed me by the shoulders and said they were taking me to the police station where I was to be charged with being a spy!

'I immediately asked why, and they had said they received a report – obviously from the maid – that I was acting strangely and claimed to have lost a grand piano. And when they investigated my room, they had found the collection of swastikas I had been busy making. They seemed to confirm their suspicions about my nefarious activities, and they hurried me off to the station.

'Fortunately, I recovered my senses enough when we got there to have them call the film studio and get the producer to explain just why I was making the little flags!

'When I was released and walked out the police station, I was so thrilled to be free that I didn't look where I was going and tripped on a sheet of ice, cracked my head badly, and had to spend two days in hospital to recover.'

Cushing adds to the incident in his autobiography. 'The first thing I remember was standing in a snowdrift somewhere out in the "sticks", having wandered around in a semi-conscious state for several hours. On the opposite side of the street was a 'fleapit' showing Arthur Askey in *The Ghost Train* (1941). Something so English I just had to go and see. Buying the cheapest available seat, I went into the "Gods", sat down, and promptly fell asleep.'

One can assume from these tales, that Cushing had passed out in the cinema and was later discovered by a member of staff and was rushed to hospital for treatment.

Cushing's next acting job was playing Captain Roberts of the Royal Mounted Police for the Canadian Ministry Film *We All Help* (1942).

It was mid-March, and Cushing had made enough money to get him to Halifax. The next step was to find suitable transport. 'I covered the waterfront, mingling with Merchant Navy lads, trying to find out how I could get aboard any ship bound for the United Kingdom. On Sunday 15 March, I was rewarded with some information that the *SS Tilpala*, due to sail that night, was minus a deserter, and if he didn't show up, I could take his place.

'I remember that I was very lucky to get a place on this boat at all, for when I approached the captain, he said he had a full complement, and he could only take me on if any member of the crew failed to turn up.

'At midnight, after waiting for hours in the cold, I was finally told I could come on board as one man had not turned up. So, I got a passage home to England courtesy of a deserter.

'We steamed slowly up the River Mersey, making our way carefully between the hulks of sunken ships. Jutting from the graveyard of murky water, the silent sentinels of gaunt masts and criss-cross spars resembled uneven rows of broken crucifixes – fitting memorials to mark their final resting place.'

Despite seeing Liverpool ravaged by the severe bombings from German aircraft, Cushing was relieved to be back. 'It may not have been as imposing as the approach to Manhattan, but the sight of the grimy and bomb-scarred Royal Liverpool Building and Dock Board Offices held more magic for me than all the skyscrapers in the world, and I was filled with overwhelming joy as I walked down the gangplank and stood in England once again.'

And British to his core, Cushing made one final act that marked the end of his American dream. 'Like the Pope, I knelt and kissed the ground. I was so glad, and so thankful, to be home at last, and in one piece.'

Cushing's Hollywood career was over, but the globetrotting continued in one form or another.

13: Cushing Down Under

Cushing as Osric in *Hamlet*.

'It was March 1942 when I stepped onto English soil, and I hadn't the faintest idea what I was going to do.' First, he had to contact his family, who were staying at David's poultry farm in Norwood Hill, Reigate, and were unsure if he had returned home, the mail not being 100% reliable during wartime.

With his seaman's wages, Cushing took the train from Liverpool to Reigate, via London, celebrating his return with a cup of tea. Sitting in his third-class compartment, he reacquainted himself with England once more. 'Having seen so many vast, arid wastelands in the States, it was sheer bliss to sip my tea, and watch the panorama of our beautiful Shires unfold itself and pass peacefully by the window. It was a wonderfully soothing sight.'

Breaking up his journey by staying overnight in Ealing with the family of one his shipmates, Cushing saw the dark side of war. 'As I crossed London from Euston to Ealing, I saw signs of the appalling devastation the capital had endured during bombing raids.'

Unable to provide the specific date of his arrival, Cushing turned up at his brother's farm unannounced. With no one to meet him when he arrived in Reigate, he took in the woodlands and meadows of early spring as he walked to the farm.

'Arriving at the cottage,' he recalled, 'I knocked on the door. Mother opened it, took one look at me, and fainted!'

During his stay at the farm, Cushing considered his options. Since he was unable to get into the armed forces, he decided to resume his career. 'In fact, there was only one course open to someone in my profession – join the entertainment group for the forces, ENSA.' The troops called it 'Every Night Something Awful', but the actual title was the Entertainments National Service Association.

Returning to London, Cushing turned up at the ENSA offices in Drury Lane and met Henry Oscar, head of the drama department. Oscar was advertising for 'a presentable young man with talent' to replace an actor who had just been called up.

Cushing was assigned to a company touring with Noel Coward's *Private Lives*, a comedy about a divorced couple who meet on the French Riviera while honeymooning with their new partners. Oscar needed someone to play the lead of Elyot Chase opposite Sonia Dresdel as Amanda Prynne with Humphrey Morton and Yvonne Hills playing their respective partners.

Impressed by Cushing's determination, Oscar offered him the part despite having only a few days to learn it.

The role was significant for Cushing in that it allowed him to meet Helen Beck, the woman he later married.

'Sonia Dresdel, who had been playing the Gertrude Lawrence part for about a year and a half, was absolutely exhausted when I joined. The little leading lady who took over from her, Helen Beck, I married. I owe everything to her. She was a tremendous help to me in everything, not just my career. I always said that I was born in 1913, I started to live in 1942 when I met Helen, and I died in 1971 when she died.'

'It is difficult to imagine what would have become of Peter Cushing if Helen had never entered his life,' observed Mark Miller. 'In 1990 he stated that his insecurity and shyness all ended when he met Helen. Eventually she "knew me better than I knew myself".'

Violet Helen Beck was born in St Petersburg, Russia on 8 February 1908. Her father, Ernest Beck was a wealthy industrialist from Lancashire and proprietor of the James Beck Spinning Company, Russia's largest cotton spinners. Helen's mother was the daughter of Polish Baroness Bronikowska and the Swedish born General Carl Enckell.

The Becks lived a life of luxury under Tsarist Russia. All that changed in 1917 when the Revolution forced the family (comprising of three daughters and two sons) to flee, leaving behind a vast fortune that was never recovered.

Back in England, and almost penniless, the family lived a very different existence. 'Having been brought up in the lap of luxury,' said Cushing, 'with personal maids and servants in constant attention for all their needs, they were now compelled to fend for themselves, even having to learn how to cook. Helen adapted herself to this new way of life, with the result that she did everything superbly.'

'I spoke fluent French, German, and Russian and English,' Helen said. 'English was the worst of all. When I finished school in Switzerland my English was so bad something had to be done. So, my father sent me to Kate Rorke, the teacher of voice production who trained many of our actors and actresses, and there I learned to speak properly. That's how I went into the theatre.'

Helen had a varied theatrical career. She worked as a showgirl for revue artist C B Cochran and was selected from 500 girls to join Cochran in America. This led to her Hollywood film debut in Raoul Walsh's *What Price Glory?* (1926); her stage colleagues included Anna Neagle and Gertrude Lawrence.

Helen returned to England where she worked as an English tutor to Yvette Le Browse (who married the Aga Khan). Declining a permanent job in Egypt to remain with her family, she worked as a secretary for show business couple Jessie Matthews and Sonnie Hale.

With her parents' welfare to consider, Helen worked in a variety of jobs, which included acting in repertory theatre. She also endured a disastrous marriage to actor Kenton Redgrave, who walked out on her; she never spoke about him since.

Helen was working in Bath Repertory when war broke out. Returning to London, she moved back in with her parents and joined the Civil Defence. She finally joined ENSA where she met her future husband.

'From its beginning,' said Cushing, 'our relationship had been unique, as though we were continuing something that had begun in another age. It was a spiritual union, the physical element holding little importance. We just had a mutual desire to spend the rest of our lives together.'

The couple first met in May 1942 at the Theatre Royal prior to the company's coach trip to Colchester for their next performance. 'Can you think of a more romantic place to meet?' recalled Cushing. While travelling together, they went over their lines. 'Helen was word perfect, and soon we began to talk of other things.' They had many things in common and shared a love for literature and classical music.

'I wouldn't have said they fell in love straight away,' observed Joan Craft, who stage managed the tour, 'but they got on terribly well in the beginning. Peter wasn't tremendously mature; in fact, he never was. There was always a naiveté about him. Helen worshipped him. He was terribly fond of her, but she was just smitten.'

'It was a marvellous experience,' Cushing said of ENSA. 'I think the troops liked the play. It was a very good play. They had to be marched in at the point of a bayonet but once they realised it was a comedy they enjoyed it, especially the part where there was a fight, and I was hit over the head with the gramophone record. In the war the props men had to get what they could in the way of properties. They got bundles of what were supposed to be 75s – big old records that shattered easily – but amongst them were some that were unbreakable. So sometimes when Helen hit me over the head with these things they wouldn't break. It was a bit unfortunate, but the troops loved it.'

The company was billeted in Devizes, Wiltshire. 'One went to all sorts of the most beautiful country houses,' said Cushing. 'They were commandeered for the duration, so we were able to stay in these marvellous places. Mind you, they were stripped to the bare bones and all the wonderful bannisters had sacking over them. We slept in navvy beds which were always too short. We used to move these little camp beds into the vast bedrooms which had the posts of four-poster beds but no bed between them. We put our little beds in between them and tried to pretend we were sleeping in a four-poster. I adore England, and apart from doing a job I liked I was able to see a lot of the countryside. Of course, one had to guess where one was because there were no signposts. But I found it all absolutely wonderful and the general atmosphere was pretty marvellous.'

The couple continued touring with ENSA despite Helen's persistent cough, which led to a haemorrhage when they performed in Canterbury, Kent. 'Even then, Helen wasn't very well,' observed Joan Craft. 'She wasn't very strong. She was very ill towards the end of the run in Canterbury.'

'For almost two years,' Cushing added, 'we toured together with the play, but our happiness was marred by Helen's failing health, and we both had to leave the group and move to London.'

Cushing's health also took a nasty turn after being diagnosed with congestion of the lung. Helen devoted herself to nursing him back to health, and continued with the play until he was fit to resume work. 'I missed her dreadfully, and as soon as I could move, I joined her in Oswestry.'

'Helen never made any demands for herself,' recalled old friend Ann Redington, 'which was bad really because I think you have to make demands as a woman. But they were very happy together. Helen never spoke about her previous marriage because it was awful. She was very, very unhappy. She had a child which she lost, and the man deserted her. I think that coloured her whole idea of marriage. So, I think, in a way, Peter made up for the child as well as being her husband.'

Now fully recovered, Cushing returned to ENSA. 'In the New Year I was back at work, but the stress and strain of this arduous tour gradually took its toll on us both, and, in the end, we were invalided out of ENSA.'

The couple's courtship lasted from May 1942 to April 1943. After a brief holiday to recover, Cushing proposed to Helen. 'After nearly a year of fighting on the stage, we decided to try it at home.'

Peter Cushing and Helen Beck finally tied the knot. 'We did so quietly on 10 April 1943, at the Royal Borough of Kensington Registry Office. Her parents acted as witnesses – I had not told mine, in case there was any objection.

'Immediately Helen devoted her time to managing my career, a task she did so selflessly and successfully right up to the time of her death.'

Returning to London, the couple started house hunting. 'For a while we lived with Helen's parents in Kensington. We experienced little difficulty in finding somewhere to live, so many people having left to escape the incessant bombing.

'Then we found a flat nearby. Although it was a lovely flat, it had a lot of windows, hardly a place to be during an air raid.' Living in relative poverty, most of their furniture was provided by family members or converted by Helen from crates and boxes she picked up from bombsites. 'They looked very presentable,' said Cushing of his wife's handiwork, 'and were indeed serviceable.' Helen also sold her jewellery to make ends meet.

Cushing joined Al Parker's Agency. With theatres, cinemas and other entertainment venues slowly reopening, Parker contracted Cushing for two roles in a mammoth production of Tolstoy's *War And Peace* as the Emperor of Russia and the French officer Captain Ramballe. Directed by Julius Gellner, and boasting a 56 strong cast, the production opened at the Grand Theatre in Blackpool in June 1943, and then the Palace Theatre in Manchester the following month, prior to its London opening.

According to David Miller, '*War And Peace* was a mammoth 32-scene production that lasted nearly four hours. The scenery consisted of a series of raised levels and the backdrops were projected slides – a revolution in the theatre.'

The production was beset with problems. 'The slides frequently got muddled,' recalled Cushing, 'were placed upside down and sometimes didn't appear at all.' The advance publicity helped, and the reviews were positive, mainly praising the scale of the production.

The public weren't so forthcoming. 'We opened at the Phoenix Theatre, London in September 1943; the first night lasting nearly five hours, by which time most of our patrons had left, or were fast asleep in their seats. The spectacle did not survive.' The play was a resounding flop, lasting 20 performances.

Cushing's next play didn't even open. He could not recall the title but remembered Bernard Miles being in the cast, and the director being a Jewish refugee who escaped Europe. Cushing was to play a civil engineer. 'I had that sinking feeling we were doomed from the start, when he asked me quite seriously, "Doz this mean you are polite viz zere machines?".'

The rehearsals dragged on for a few days before it was abandoned to the relief of all concerned.

Cushing made his BBC radio debut on 8 September 1943 in *Memoirs Of Mendelssohn*, a one-hour biography of composer Felix Mendelssohn, played by Basil Langton. Other BBC radio work towards the end of the year included *Destination Unknown* and *The Lay Of Horatius*.

Cushing made his first appearance at the 'Q' Theatre on 16 November 1943 in Emlyn Williams' *The Morning Star*. This small independent theatre was run by Jack and Beatric De Leon, and was situated near Kew Bridge, Richmond. The De Leon's policy was to present weekly revivals of popular plays, along with new productions that might make it to the West End. It also provided a starting ground for Dirk Bogarde, Richard Attenborough, Flora Robson and Joan Collins. When acting roles were scarce, an odd week at the 'Q' allowed Cushing to maintain his stage career and consolidate his meagre finances.

Towards the end of 1943, Cushing was at the 'Q' for Joan Morgan's *The Dark Potential*. The play was popular enough to be transferred to the West End under the new title *This Was A Woman*, which ran for over a year. This should have been an amazing career advancement for Cushing, had it not been for Helen's poor health.

During the run of *The Dark Potential*, Helen was rushed to the Samaritan Free Hospital for Women with abdominal pain and had to undergo major surgery for a hysterectomy. A lifeless foetus was discovered in the womb. When Helen was discharged from hospital, Cushing decided to remain with her while *The Dark Potential* moved to the West End.

Following a quiet Christmas, Cushing returned to the 'Q' in March 1944 to appear in Ernest Hemingway's *The Fifth Column*. By mid-June, he played

Elyot in another production of *Private Lives*. With nothing forthcoming from the BBC, he returned to the West End in October to star in Paul Anthony's *Happy Few*.

Playing Free-Frenchman Private Charles, *Happy Few* met with good reviews and ran for two weeks. This coincided with a meeting Cushing had with Elsie Beyer, general manager of the theatrical management company H M Tennant Ltd. The company were producing Terence Rattigan's *While The Sun Shines* at the Globe Theatre. The play enjoyed an 18-month run when Eugene Deckers decided to take a break. When Cushing replaced him as Lieutenant Colbert, Elsie Beyer thought he was French!

'I have no languages, experiencing enough difficulties in learning my own, and it was ironic that my initial incursions into the West End should all be foreigners. Helen had taught me the accents by rote, and it was a tribute to her splendid tuition that Miss Beyer should have been so convinced by my portrayal in *Happy Few*.'

Directed by Anthony Asquith, *While The Sun Shines* enjoyed a long run at the Globe, making it Cushing's first stage success. He also became good friends with co-stars Michael Wilding and Ronald Squire. In March 1945, the play went on a provincial tour, and it was in Bolton on 8 May 1945, when the announcement came that the war in Europe had ended. 'The country as a whole had been living on its nerves for so long,' recalled a relieved Cushing, 'and now we were too exhausted to feel any real jubilation – just heartfelt thankfulness that it was over, but knowing we still had to face the hardship of the aftermath of war.'

The tour was in its last week when Ronald Squire met old friend Edith Evans, who had been asked to re-open the Criterion Theatre in London. She was assigned to direct a production of Sheridan's *The Rivals*. Squire recommended Cushing for the part of Faulkland.

The Rivals became Cushing's second stage success, enjoying an impressive run that enabled the actor to settle some outstanding debts. Following a brief tour in the North of England, the play opened in London to tremendous critical and audience acclaim, clocking up 166 performances and running through Christmas.

Working with Cushing was future horror icon Michael Gough. When *The Rivals* ended its run, Cushing was unable to secure stage roles: even radio work proved elusive. 'All too soon I was "resting" again, that discreet expression which always applied to out-of-work actors.

'The rent for the flat had risen, ten per cent of all earnings went to my agent and I was now just inside the income tax bracket. Soon I was heavily in debt.'

Despite the hardships, Cushing wasn't idle. There were several engagements at the 'Q' Theatre, many of which ran for two weeks. His credits at the 'Q' included Anton Chekhov's *The Seagull* and *The Curious Dr Robson*, and a Noel Coward triple-bill of *The Astonished Heart, We Were Dancing* and *Fumed Oak*. Cushing acted in all three.

Radio work was better paid. For Home Services Radio, he appeared in *A Fourth For Bridge* for *The Wednesday Matinee* and the BBC's 12-part adaptation of Anthony Trollope's novel *Orley's Farm*. By the end of 1946, he reprised his role as Faulkland in *The Rivals* for his old friend Peter Gray's repertory company, which opened at the Theatre Royal in Windsor.

The money for these engagements barely covered his general costs. 'For a time, I was able to get parts in several major plays, including Dame Edith Evans' successful production of *The Rivals*, but after the war things got much tougher and for a time Helen and I had a struggle to make ends meet. However, a stroke of good fortune kept the wolf from the door at this time thanks to my artistic leanings.

'One Christmas, not having enough money to buy Helen a present, I decided to hand-paint a piece of silk as a scarf for her. And it just so happened that a textile manufacturer saw this when we were out one night, and learning it was my handiwork gave me a nine-month contract to design more scarves. The money was an absolute godsend.'

It was still a financial struggle for Cushing. 'The remuneration only covered our weekly overheads, and the bank larder was beginning to look distinctly bare.' To keep things afloat, Helen found work. 'Apart from looking after me and her parents with tender loving care, Helen had taken up sewing to help make ends meet. I was still worried about her persistent cough, as there seemed to be no cure for it, and concerned that she was doing too much for everyone else, to her own detriment.'

This difficult period began to affect Cushing's mental health. 'I used to look through my cutting books, trying to reassure myself that I was destined to become an actor. I had been acting for 11 years. I had reached the goal of repertory actors, Harry Hanson's Court Players, at 24 and I had played second lead to Carole Lombard in Hollywood. I had a role on Broadway, then roles in London's West End. Even when the play was bad, the critics had singled me out for praise. So where had I gone wrong?'

Did this period of self-reflection make Cushing realise that leaving Hollywood was a mistake? After being on the verge of film stardom, he was unemployed for 18 months with limited finances and a career that was going nowhere.

'I went through a low period in my career when I almost gave up on acting, or rather it was giving me up. I hadn't worked for two years, and I was in such desperate straits. I had nothing, absolutely nothing. I've still got this terrible thing about being in anyone's debt and I think it all stems from that period when I was out of work. I eventually got a job designing ladies' head-scarves. I did that for nine months. I said to Helen that I think

I'll stick to this instead of acting, because at least we're sure of something coming in; and she nodded, but of course she knew I'd get back to acting.'

'Later I realised nothing was wrong. I believe those 18 months of disillusionment, depression and frustration were put into my life to widen my emotions.'

Cushing acted in two radio plays, *The Face Of Theresa* and *It Speaks For Itself*, and returned to the 'Q' to play Colbert again in *While The Sun Shines*. Although the assignment lasted a week, it was a beneficial move that led to his long overdue British film debut.

Laurence Olivier and his associate Anthony Bushell were producing *Born Yesterday* and were looking for an actor to play Paul Verall. 'Al Parker had put my name forward, and I had gone to keep my appointment at the Garrick Theatre with Laurence Olivier, who was directing.'

During the interview Olivier asked him, 'Can you speak with an American accent?'

'I had to be honest and say no, because I think there is nothing more phony than an English actor trying to be American.'

Olivier replied with, 'But you've been to America,' to which Cushing said something about going to Scotland but not being able to speak Gaelic.

'That's not quite the same thing, boy,' replied Olivier, but Cushing remained adamant about his ability to play an American. Olivier was impressed with Cushing's response, 'He looked at me and said, "That's awfully honest of you. You've saved us a lot of time – we shall be in touch again." I thought that was very kind of him, but believed it was just another polite brush off. I was soon proved wrong.'

Sometime later, Anthony Bushell watched *While The Sun Shines* at the Q, and was suitably taken by Cushing as Lieutenant Colbert.

He went back to Olivier and told him, and as a result, Olivier's party came down to a matinee. 'The great actor took one look at me and said, "Well, that's the chap who said he couldn't speak American. But he can certainly speak French!"'

This led to an interesting offer to star in Olivier's forthcoming film production of *Hamlet* (1948), playing the part of Osric.

'When production started, Larry was a kind, considerate, patient director. But as time went by, he became more and more autocratic. At first it was "Let's try it this way" or "What do you think?" but towards the end it was "do it this way, do it that way, and don't argue, goddamit!" We all started calling him Willie behind his back, after the stories we heard about William Wyler.

'I must say, the directorial methods he settled on got great results. Whoever said *Hamlet* couldn't be done on film was made to eat his words by Larry.' During filming, Olivier was knighted in the King's Birthday Honours.

Hamlet marked an important moment in Cushing's life. 'Although we never met at the time, this was also the first film in which Christopher Lee and I appeared together.'

Hamlet was Lee's second film. 'I smuggled myself onto the set as a soldier in order to watch Olivier directing. It was a totally unauthorised appearance.'

According to Mark Miller, 'In the film's sequence of the court play, a careful listener will hear Christopher Lee yell "Lights!" during all the racing around and confusion. Otherwise, he is not recognisable in his role as a spearman. If he actually appears in any of the shots used in the film, his face cannot be seen.'

Released in May 1948 (and July in the States), *Hamlet* met with a warm critical response with *The Times* calling it, 'nothing less than a masterpiece.'

Olivier made Cushing an interesting offer. 'Olivier was seemingly pleased with my portrayal of the courtier, for he offered me the same part in the Old Vic Australian tour, which he led with his wife, Vivien Leigh.'

Initially Cushing was reluctant to take up the offer. 'I said I'd obviously like to very much indeed, but that I wouldn't go anywhere without my wife as we'd had too many partings during the war. "I don't know what I can offer Helen," he said, "but she can certainly come along, even if it's just for the ride." But he did find her work, which was marvellous.'

Olivier's tour programme included Shakespeare's *Richard III*, Richard Brinsley Sheridan's *The School For Scandal* and Thornton Wilder's *The Skin Of Our Teeth*. Cushing's roles were, respectively, the Duke of Clarence and Cardinal Bouchier, Sir Joseph Surface and The Professor.

The tour would start in Perth, then move to Adelaide, before continuing throughout Australia and New Zealand. 'Our itinerary,' said Cushing, 'covered Melbourne, Sydney, Brisbane, and then went by flying-boat to Hobart, Tasmania, before proceeding to New Zealand, where we played the four principal cities in the North and South Islands – Auckland, Wellington, Christchurch and Dunedin.'

Rehearsals took place in Camden Town at a warehouse owned by Sir Donald Wolfit, and not far from Holloway Prison. '[It] had been used by a bankrupt theatrical management as a store for scenery, furnishings and the usual bric-a-brac associated with some long-forgotten offerings,' recalled Cushing. 'The damp hit us like a body blow as we trooped into this erstwhile "Aladdin's Cave".'

Everyone was affected by the unpleasant conditions; George Relph commented that the damp was caused by, 'the tears of all the actors who were never paid.' Ironically, the actors weren't paid for the rehearsals!

The company of 38 arrived in Liverpool, and boarded the cargo ship *SS Corinthic*, which set sail on 14 February 1948 for the 5-week voyage to Australia.

The ship docked in Western Australia on 14 March, to a late summer heatwave, and despite the humidity, the cast still had to rehearse *The School For Scandal*, for their first performance at Perth's Capital Theatre in a few days.

The Australian public wasn't used to watching live theatre, making *The School For Scandal* a surreal experience because the play was performed to complete silence from the audience, leaving the cast working twice as hard, with Cushing throwing himself into his role with comedic aplomb.

Richard III and *The Skin Of Our Teeth* were also met with a similar audience reaction. According to Cushing, 'All three plays were greeted with tumultuous applause at curtain fall, but we were mystified by the complete silence during the interpretations.'

The Oliviers were held in such high esteem by their Australian public, many felt it would be wrong to show their emotions during a performance. 'Laurence decided to educate and put them at ease,' said Cushing, 'by giving them a little lecture in front of the tabs before we began. He asked them to let us hear them enjoying themselves by laughing or crying, or whatever else they might feel like doing to express their reactions, rather than leaving it all until the end, because that would add to their pleasure and to ours, by letting us know as we proceeded that we were succeeding in our endeavour to please.'

The School for Scandal received excellent reviews, but the intimacy of Sheridan's play meant it never went beyond Perth, so the cast began rehearsing *Richard III*.

Richard III in Adelaide met with rave reviews and the performance coincided with the Cushings' fifth wedding anniversary, with Olivier providing champagne and oysters for the occasion. Olivier then busied himself with *The Skin Of Our Teeth*, an experimental piece he described as 'the Picasso of our repertoire.' According to David Miller, '*The Skin Of Our Teeth* was presented in a vaudeville style with the characters deliberately two-dimensional. Though the play baffled many Australians, it was generally well received.'

On 18 April, the company left for an eight-week engagement at the Princes Theatre in Melbourne. Away from the heatwave of the previous cities, Melbourne was a cold place, and the company quickly succumbed to tiredness and homesickness.

The next port of call was Hobart, Tasmania. 'Arctic conditions prevailed in Hobart when we appeared at the delightful Georgian Theatre, built by convicts years ago,' said Cushing, who observed Vivien Leigh, in full costume, drinking a large mug of hot chocolate and warming herself by an electric fire. 'I wished I could have joined her,' he added.

Following a short break, the company arrived in Sydney. *The School For Scandal* then opened at the Tivoli Theatre on 12 June and ran for eight weeks. Cushing returned to radio for NBC Australia to play the title role of *Beau Brummell* and later took part as guest panellist for the popular quiz show *Twenty Questions*. *The Skin Of Our Teeth* had a special performance on 19 July for Australian Prime Minister Ben Chilfrey.

The company travelled to Brisbane for a two-week run of *The School For Scandal*, by which time Olivier, who had been removed as director of the Old Vic, prepared a season at the New Theatre that included *The School For Scandal* and *Richard III* with Jean Anouilth's short play *Antigone* replacing *The Skin Of Our Teeth* and Anton Chekhov's *The Proposal* added to make up the running time.

And then it was the final leg of the tour when the company flew to Auckland, New Zealand.

'New Zealand made a refreshing change from Australia,' said David Miller, 'it resembled England somewhat and alleviated the company's homesickness a little.' Their arrival was greeted equally well by the population with 33,000 attending the 17 performances at the St James Theatre in Auckland. Similar crowds also attended the St James Theatre in Christchurch and at Her Majesty's Theatre in Dunedin.

The tour ended in Wellington where Olivier suffered a knee injury. On 9 October, the exhausted company boarded the *SS Corinthic*, but there was little time to rest on the journey home as they were rehearsing for a proposed season at the West End.

The second phase of Cushing's overseas career ended in great style. 'The triumphant tour had been a worthwhile experience, and we had been showered with hospitality and enthusiasm. But we were not sorry when it finished for there is no place like home, and we were wanting to get back to where our hearts belonged.'

Cushing had one last word about the tour, which he mentions in his autobiography. 'In all those past months I never caught sight of wandering Uncle Bertie.' Whatever became of the elusive Albert Cushing will forever remain a mystery.

With everything set up for the New Theatre, Cushing played the lead role of the hypochondriac Lomov in *The Proposal*, a one-act comedy included as a forerunner for *Antigone*, which was too short to provide an evening's entertainment. 'The normal running time was about half-an-hour,' said Cushing, 'but Sir Laurence suggested we performed it in the fashion of a speeded-up Keystone Kops car chase. Once we got into our stride it was all over and done in 19 minutes flat. It took me another 19 minutes to recover.'

The Proposal was a three-hander with the actors made up as marionettes and performing in front of a painted background with no furniture or props. Cushing, who was well known for his use of props, had to sit in mid-air against a painted chair.

Cushing's performance was singled out for praise, but it was achieved with some difficulty. The lengthy Australian tour had left him exhausted.

The financial situation didn't improve. 'We had been working consistently for some time now, but subsidised theatre salaries were notoriously low and after we closed in February 1949, apart from the odd week at the Q (Theatre), I had no engagements worthy of note until early 1950, by which time Helen and I were close to insolvency once more.'

Emotionally and physically exhausted, but concerned about his financial welfare, Cushing received an offer from Olivier, who had just been appointed manager of the St James Theatre in London. He was mounting an ambitious production of Bridget Boland's *The Damascus Blade* and offered Cushing the familiar role of the Free Frenchman.

Cushing's first rehearsal proved disastrous when his failure to understand a simple cue brought about a nervous breakdown.

'In 1941, the "V for Victory" campaign had been launched, using the letter V in Morse code as a recognisable signal, which resembled the opening thematic statement of "Beethoven's Fifth Symphony No'5 in C Minor".' All Cushing had to do was knock on the door with the composer's famous opening piece.

During rehearsals, Cushing started his scene with a knock on the door. For that he used a conventional rap, only to be challenged by Olivier who asked him to use the *V for Victory* sign instead. 'My mind not functioning properly, I withdrew, and entered again repeating the same knock as before.'

Olivier tried to correct him, but it was too much for Cushing, who broke down in tears, the stress of everything finally came out in the open.

'He was at my side immediately, consoling and compassionate. He told me to go home to Helen, and to get some nice, healthy fat around my tired and jagged nerves.'

Thanks to his breakdown, Cushing didn't work for the next six months. In recognition for his loyalty and hard work, Olivier kept him on the payroll until he was fit enough to return to work, which Cushing considered, 'an act of kindness not to be forgotten.'

Thanks to Helen's care and devotion, Cushing returned to the stage. Still in a fragile state, he made his comeback in September 1950 in *The Gay Invalid*, a musical adaption of Moliere's *le malade imaginaire*, where he played the young soldier Valentine.

The production marked the return to the London stage for celebrated Polish actress Elizabeth Bergner as Toinette with the cast rounded by A E Matthews as Crank and the barnstorming Tod Slaughter, a star of many stage melodramas and of several British horror films made in the thirties. *The Gay Invalid* would be one of his last stage roles.

The play opened at the Manchester Opera House and following an extensive tour, ended up at the Garrick Theatre, London for two months until it closed in March 1951.

1951's *The Festival of Britain* was a government sponsored event designed to show the country as a major force in the world and to lift the morale of the population after the gloomy years of war. With entertainment that included an exhibition and a funfair, Olivier had plans for an ambitious stage production.

Continuing his managerial role at the St James Theatre, Olivier presented a festival season in May, with Vivien Leigh playing Cleopatra in Shakespeare's *Anthony And Cleopatra* and George Bernard Shaw's *Caesar And Cleopatra*. Aware of Cushing's fragile health, Olivier gave him small roles as Alexas Diomedes in the first play and Ben Affris for the prologue of the latter.

When Wilfred Hyde-White left *Caesar And Cleopatra* to honour another commitment, Cushing replaced him as ancient Briton Brittanus, a comic character which Helen thought was perfect casting, 'because she claimed I was so British anyway, that if I cut myself, I bled woad.'

The Festival of Britain was a huge success and when the St James season came to an end in October 1951, Olivier took the plays for an extensive Broadway run, a golden opportunity for Cushing to re-establish himself on the American stage. Sadly, it never happened. 'Wilfred Hyde-White was returning as Brittanus,' said David Miller, 'and the other parts would be recast. Perhaps Olivier, in his wisdom, realised that Cushing could do better than these minor roles, and that staying in London would advance his career further. Helen suspected that Larry had been nobbled.'

'You have been unaware of the jealousy in high places,' she told her dejected husband, 'but I've heard and seen things going on behind your back. You received a standing ovation every time you played Lomov, and practically stopped the show as Brittanus. That is why you weren't asked to repeat your performance on Broadway. Larry was not the instigator of this injustice; we have good reason to be grateful to him, but there are others at court whose influence is very strong. Wilfred is excellent of course, but he's older than you and well established. You are a "new boy" and represent a threat. They cannot stand that sort of competition. You must become independent. You have the qualities of true leadership and are loved and admired by those that count – your audience.'

Even with the pep talk, Cushing still needed to establish himself, and Helen dismissed the backward step of returning to repertory theatre. She had other ideas.

'Around about 1951, I said to Helen, "Now what?" And she said, "The thing of the future is going to be television and we shall get into that." So, she got a copy of the *Radio Times* and got all the names of the producers from the programme credit lists and wrote a sort of round-robin letter saying that Mr Peter Cushing finds himself unexpectedly available and is free anytime you would like to offer him work. And I said, "Darling that is awful!" And she said, "Perhaps you're not very well known with the public, but you've done enough work with enough well-known people for your name to be known in professional circles."

'And she was absolutely right. She had an incredible instinct about these things. I got wonderful letters back, one in particular from Harry Clayton who said that he knew my work and would be delighted if I would play the leading part recently done at the National Theatre. It was *Eden's End* by J B Priestley. And it was in December 1951 that I did my first television play.'

14: Homegrown Television

Cushing (left) with José Ferrer and Suzanne Flon in *Moulin Rouge*.

It was on 12 November 1951 when Cushing received the offer to appear in *Eden's End*, and after three weeks rehearsing, his first venture into television felt like, 'a criminal about to be executed.'

'When a mistake is made in filming, the director shouts "cut" and the scene is shot again until you get it right, and in the theatre, you can usually cover up anything that goes wrong. But not on television. In that confinement there is no escape, those cameras with lenses like probing microscopes picked up everything that happened, as it happened, as if you were a goldfish in a glass bowl. Added to this terror was the fact that the audience was the largest you could ever play to, and at the same time, the smallest, consisting mainly of family groups in their sitting rooms.' Fearful of something going wrong, Cushing learnt the whole script.

Playing the lead of alcoholic actor Charles Appleby, Cushing experienced the true horror of live television as a large sign in the studio flashed VISION ON. 'My head went numb, as if it had suddenly come into sharp contact with a plank of wood, and my voice seemed to be coming from somewhere else, far, far away – like the view seen through the wrong end of a pair of binoculars. I proceeded with my performance like an automation, paralysed with nerves.'

Cushing felt the whole enterprise was a doomed failure. 'When it was all over, I said to myself, "Right, that's it. I'll never be wanted again, so I might as well pack the game up altogether." I couldn't face anyone, so I disappeared unseen from the building.' He did so, still in his makeup and, 'with my clothes sticking to me.'

Helen watched the show at a friend's house and was more than impressed, reassuring her husband that everything went well. Harry Clayton also phoned Cushing to convey his congratulations, and as soon as he hung up, producer Fred O'Donovan called with an offer of a juvenile role in another Priestley comedy, *When We Are Married*.

'Thereafter I had three solid years of what was laughingly called "live television", and this undoubtedly established me in the profession.'

Cushing still had to overcome his nerves. 'It was called "live". My heavens! You rehearsed three weeks, which is as much as you would do in the theatre, and then gave this "live" performance, then three days passed, and you repeated the "live" performance on the following Thursday. That was a pure form of torture, because your nerves carried you through the first night and afterwards you had people ringing up and saying that was marvellous and so on, so that you had to be as good as they thought you were, or try to be better, on the second performance.'

Cushing's next role sealed his TV stardom. Many actors have played this role on film and television, but Peter Cushing was TV's first Mr Darcy in a six-part dramatization of Jane Austin's *Pride And Prejudice*.

'It was terribly hard work. It really was. The strange thing was that people would congratulate you for playing hysterical scenes and bursting into tears but oh, it was so easy, compared to playing someone who is cool and calm. Usually in the television plays I was always playing people who were in control of the situation and that was difficult. But it was certainly a wonderful thing that had happened to me because overnight I was well known in England. It was a big audience, even in those days, at least a million (TV) sets, and at that time there was only one channel so there was no competition. I did that for several years and it was through all this TV work that I got back into films.'

Cushing's TV profile was high enough to get him cast in a new film. Directed by John Huston, *Moulin Rouge* (1952) was a fictionalised account of Parisian artist and bohemian Henri de Toulouse-Lautrec (an Oscar winning Jose Ferrer) and his strong association with the city's most infamous burlesque nightclubs.

This prestigious production was shot in Paris with Cushing making a brief appearance as the wealthy Marcel De La Voisier, who battles with Lautrec over the love of a former mistress (and Lautrec's lover), played by French actress Suzanne Flon.

The French accented Cushing has one scene, which is a day at the races. He doesn't have much to do but makes the most of his screen time as a conniving manipulator who takes Flon's Myriamme back as his mistress.

Christopher Lee turns up earlier in the film as artist Georges Seurat. He has the same amount of screen time but isn't credited. Lee's scene was shot in Paris while Cushing's was filmed at Kempton Park Racecourse.

Despite the high-profile work, The Cushings were still struggling financially, and when Helen suffered a serious injury, she was told by their doctor that she needed to relax and take in the sea air. A friend offered them a weekend place on the Cornish Riviera, but such was the financial situation, Cushing reluctantly asked his father for assistance.

George Cushing on handing his son a cheque said, not unkindly but in no uncertain terms that he was 'nearly forty, and a failure,' his idea for success was how much money was in the bank. 'On that basis, he was dead right, but it hurt deeply.' It seems George Cushing was unaware of his son's extensive TV credits.

While holidaying in Cornwall, Cushing was ready to pack in acting and devote his time to painting. Such was his state of mind and concern for Helen's health, he told nobody of his departure, not even his agent, which probably robbed him of lucrative film and television work. As an established TV star, the possibility of further film offers following *Moulin Rouge* may have taken his career into another direction.

Cushing would never give up acting. 'You see, to become an actor you've got to be raving mad to start with. It really is a vocation, dear boy. We're all born with gifts and it's up to us to use those gifts to the utmost that we can because we're lucky to be born with them. It's only the love of the thing that keeps you going because there are so many times that the actor is, politely called "resting", which is really being out of work. If it was something you absolutely loved, then you'd be forced to give it up.'

Returning to London, Cushing heard that Robert Helpmann had tried to contact him. A former ballet dancer who choreographed *The Red Shoes* (1948) and *Tales Of Hoffmann* (1951), Helpmann previously worked with Cushing in *Anthony And Cleopatra* for the *Festival of Britain* season. He later achieved cinema immortality as the Child Catcher in *Chitty Chitty Bang Bang* (1968).

Helpmann offered Cushing a role in a new play produced by his long term partner Michael Benthall. *The Wedding Ring*, written by Simon Wardell and Kieran Tunney, was Helpmann's directorial debut. Set in a marriage bureau, Cushing was joined by Adrienne Allen, Irene Brown, Shelagh Fraser, Irene Handl and newcomer Patrick MacNee.

14: Homegrown Television

The Wedding Ring started out in Manchester and was planned to open in London prior to a lengthy tour. According to Patrick MacNee, 'The play, however, was hugely unfunny, opened in Manchester, and finished three weeks later at the Cornwall Theatre, Worthing, in disgrace. Noel Coward said when he came to Manchester that it was the worst play he had ever seen.' Helpmann's advice to the cast was 'speed, speed, speed' which didn't help alleviate the gloom felt by the cast. The play never reached London, not that Cushing was bothered. 'Unhappy and fretful when away from Helen, I wasn't upset when the notice appeared on the callboard, even though it meant I'd be "resting" once more.'

Cushing didn't need to 'rest' for long. Now firmly entrenched in television, Cushing appeared in 12 BBC productions in as many months. His output included *If This Be Error*, *Asmodee*, *A Social Success* and *Number Three*, the latter coinciding with his departure from Al Parker's Agency. 'I received a congratulatory letter from John Redway. In my "thank you" acknowledgment, I asked if he would take me under his wing.'

Cushing's TV fame continued through 1953 with adaptations of *Tovarich*, *The Face Of Love* and *Beau Brummell*, interspersed with a theatre production of *The Soldier And The Lady*, directed by Sam Wanamaker, who introduced Cushing to the art of Method acting.

In September 1954, Cushing returned to movies, playing a role that marked his future screen image. It also took him out of the country.

15: The Black Knight (1954)

Cushing in *The Black Knight*.

'As an itinerant actor, donning the guise of an arch-villain Sir Palamedes, I jousted with Alan Ladd in *The Black Knight*, within the massive castle walls of Manzanares el Real, Castilla la Nueva, Central Spain, and plotted against him in the foreboding granite Palace of El Escorial.'

The Black Knight is a fun medieval romp set during the reign of King Arthur. Not a trustworthy history lesson, and the casting of Alan Ladd in the title role has to be taken with a large pinch of salt – his armour is actually white.

The Black Knight is the first of four films Cushing made in Spain. Most of the interiors were shot at Pinewood Studios with other UK location work taking place in Castell Coch, Wales.

Produced by Irwin Allen and Albert R Broccoli for Warwick Productions, shooting began in early September 1953 on a £297,728 budget, plus an additional $450,000 to cover the cost of Ladd, Allen, Broccoli, and director Tay Garnet, who previously tackled the Arthurian legend with *A Connecticut Yankee In King Arthur's Court* (1949), starring Bing Crosby.

The Black Knight was Alan Ladd's fourth and final British movie and he was contracted to do them for tax exemption purposes. Receiving a $200,000 flat fee, he was Britain's most popular Hollywood star of 1954, but was never happy about working in England. 'Despite the heart-warming

15: The Black Knight (1954)

jaunt to locations in Spain,' said David Miller, 'Ladd was weary of the British drizzle and anxious to return to America.'

Ladd's arrival in England was typically Hollywood. Donald Sinden, who was under contract with Rank and had his own dressing room at Pinewood, observed the fanfare first hand. 'He brought in his entourage, a double-cum-stunt man who bore an uncanny resemblance to him. The double did all the long shots, most of the medium shots and even appeared in two-shots when the hero had his back to the camera. The "star" only did eleven days work on the entire film. He was extremely short in stature and unless he was alone, the camera could never show his feet, because if he was stationary, he was standing on a box; if walking, the other actors were in specially dug troughs or ditches and for anything between, all other actors were required to stand with their legs apart and their knees bent.'

Cushing became friends with Ladd, and found him a quiet, sensitive individual far removed from his tough guy Hollywood image. In his second autobiography, Cushing recalled a wonderful act of kindness from the star.

'Having no car, I took the tube from Kensington (where Helen and I lived) to Uxbridge, and then walked some three or four miles across fields and along county lanes to the studios. Returning home one evening, a sleek limousine pulled up beside me. Alan leaned out of the window and asked if he could give me a lift. I accepted gratefully, and asked to be dropped off at the station, but he insisted on driving me all the way to my doorstep before going home to the Savoy Hotel where he was staying. "Any time Peter," he said, "otherwise you'll be worn out before we finish the movie."

'He was a shy reserved person, and this gesture was typical of his kind thoughts for others. At the end of the shooting, I presented him with a tiny replica of the Black Knight as a souvenir, which I had made by a modeller who specialised in miniatures. Some months later, Alan wrote from Hollywood saying how grateful he was: "I've never had any hobbies until now, thanks to you, I've started collecting figurines and have already filled a large cabinet, representing uniforms throughout the ages. Thanks a million."'

Spanish locations were shot in Castilla le Nueva. Irwin Allen thought Spain was, 'a wonderful country to make pictures in.' There were over 2,000 old castles in the country and 12 were used for the film. 'While it provided some substantial granite castles for the backdrops,' observed David Miller, 'it meant that the Stonehenge sequences featuring a kind of druidic orgy were shot rather unconvincingly on the Spanish plains.' There is one scene where the Druids are about to sacrifice Patricia Medina's Lady Linet, who had to wear a blonde wig at the last minute because the stunt girl was blonde, and her brunette wig kept slipping.

Filming wasn't without incident as Deborah Del Vecchio explains, 'Patricia Medina sustained a couple of cracked ribs during one of the scenes when she is attacked by Cushing's servant. In typical Hollywood style, Medina's chest was bandaged, and she went on with the scene, no doubt in considerable pain. Another incident took place during the druid ceremonies at Stonehenge. A stuntman who was hired to play one of the sacrificial monks was nearly roasted alive when the basket he was suspended on caught fire and his costume began to smoulder.'

Cushing had his own issues during one scene. 'I was cast as the villainous Sir Palamides, and I wore a large, jewelled ring on my finger. Whilst haranguing my servant, I had to deliver a vicious backhander across the poor fellow's face. It worried me that he might be scarred for life, so as a precaution I asked the first assistant director if he would kneel beside me, out of shot, remove the ring before the blow was struck and replace it when I let my hand fall back to my side. This succeeded, but it was strange to play such a scene with someone fiddling about with my digit, as if we were becoming engaged on the sly.'

The Black Knight was released through Columbia Pictures on 28 October 1954. Reviews were positive although every critic thought Ladd was hilariously miscast with Jeffrey Richards saying he was, 'playing the part like a tired American businessman prevailed upon to take the lead in a revival of *Merrie England*.'

The Monthly Film Bulletin was equally unimpressed. 'Alan Ladd galahads with wild west gentilesse in this Technicolor rampage through British history,' while Leslie Halliwell found it a 'Hilarious travesty of English historical legend, meant seriously for Anglo-American consumption. Shades of *Zorro*, *Babes In The Wood* and *1066, And All That*.'

Time Out had a similar view. 'Low budget Arthurian antics featuring vengeful armorer Ladd's specially scaled down sword and very little cinematic sorcery. Erratic veteran Garnett coasts through the second-hand motions of a hastily concocted patchwork script.'

At least Cushing's performance was praised by *Variety*. 'Peter Cushing does a sterling job as Sir Palamides, the principal villain. Other principal roles are enthusiastically played by a competent team of British performers.'

About as realistic as *Monty Python And The Holy Grail* (1975), *The Black Knight* is entertaining *Boy's Own* nonsense, and while Alan Ladd doesn't cut it, the solid supporting cast of Patricia Medina, Harry Andrews, Andre Morell, Laurence Naismith, Patrick Troughton and John Laurie are in fine form. For all its faults, the film is undemanding fun, with plenty of action to keep everyone happy.

Peter Cushing steals the show as the sadistic Saracen villain out to usurp King Arthur (Anthony Bushell), only to be thwarted by Ladd's

15: The Black Knight (1954)

gallant hero. With the dark make-up, goatee beard, a succession of weird hats, ostentatious mannerisms, sardonic insults and exaggerated hand gestures, Cushing's performance is full of camp menace, and cool one-liners, that includes this absolute classic, 'There is a saying in my country. When a puppy yelps at his master, it is time to cut off his tail.'

Cushing's appearance hardly looks acceptable today, as David Miller observed, 'We have Cushing (from Kenley), playing a Saracen, disguised as a Viking. Not politically correct, certainly, but surely no more unlikely than Alan Ladd in King Arthur's Court.'

Despite the air of pantomime, the well staged climax between the Black Knight and Sir Palamides, who is, 'battered to pulp by Alan Ladd, who used a jumbo-sized mace for the purpose,' rounds things off in great style. The film did well at the box office, boosting Cushing's profile considerably.

Returning to the UK, Cushing was offered the lead role of *Peer Gynt* for the BBC but couldn't accept it because he was contracted to a new film starring Deborah Kerr and Van Johnson. This allowed him to stretch his acting reputation further; the TV star was emerging as a solid supporting actor in films.

Directed by Edward Dmytryk, *The End Of The Affair* (1955) was based on Graham Greene's complex novel concerning the writer's feelings of guilt and the examination of his Catholic faith following his affair with Lady Catherine Walston. Regarded as one of his finest works, it is a difficult book to adapt to film, and this version was a misfire despite the hard work from all concerned.

Told in flashback, Sarah Miles (Kerr) is the unsatisfied wife of senior civil servant Henry (Cushing), who is described as a man with a 'mind as neatly creased as his trousers.' Although a dull person, Henry loves Sarah, but doesn't know how to express it.

Things become complex after Henry introduces Sarah to Maurice Bendrix (Johnson) an American writer working on a book about the British civil service. They quickly start an affair, but following a crisis of conscience, Sarah abruptly ends it. The film focuses on her reasons for doing so and examines her crisis of faith.

Henry cannot fathom out her erratic behaviour, especially when he cannot answer Sarah's questions about religion. Eventually Henry hires a shady private detective, Parks (John Mills, providing some much-needed humour), but decides not to pursue the case despite the evidence incriminating Sarah and Bendrix.

Before long a desperate Henry realises how dull he is for Sarah, and when she dies from a fever, his world falls apart, but he is unable to comprehend why.

The End Of The Affair is as dull as Henry, who remains the most sympathetic character. Neither Sarah or Bendrix evoke any kind of likeability. The original choice for Bendrix was Gregory Peck, who Greene wasn't keen on and vetoed the casting. When Johnson came on board instead, the author was really unimpressed. 'I stymied Gregory Peck. But then to find that Van Johnson took his place was a disaster.'

A miscast Johnson bulldozes his way through the film without any conviction. Kerr fairs slightly better, but there is no chemistry between them. Working opposite a different actor might have improved her performance, but sadly she comes across as a pathetic woman who doesn't deserve the kind hearted Henry.

Deborah Kerr enjoyed working with Cushing. 'I only wished we had worked more together, but Peter gave a lovely, understated performance as my shy and retiring husband. The last time we met was some years ago in the coffee shop at the Castlanna Hilton in Madrid. We sat over tea and reminisced over the years. Such a sweet man.'

The End Of The Affair belongs to Cushing, and it's difficult to watch the film without becoming emotionally involved with Henry. When he first appears, Henry discusses his job processing widows' pensions, and then breaks down slightly when he speaks about the number of young war widows he must deal with, but quickly returns to his stiff upper English persona. It's enough to tell the audience how deeply caring Henry is. So much so, it is impossible to feel any warmth towards Sarah for her unforgivable actions.

Although the film received mixed reviews, the critics singled out Cushing's performance. Deborah Del Vecchio felt that this was his best film to date. 'As Henry Miles, Peter Cushing delivers what is one of his finest screen performances. Here we see his career as it might have been if not for his association (for better or worse) with horror films. He creates an unforgettable picture of a man losing everything – including his self-respect – but is unable to understand why. Had Peter Cushing been a bigger name, an Academy Award nomination surely would have been his.'

Cushing's growing reputation as a TV star meant salary increases, and the new independent stations were equally keen to use him. Film roles were also coming in, and his next assignment took him overseas.

16: Magic Fire (1955)

Cushing (left) with Valentina Cortese and Alan Badel in *Magic Fire*.

Playing another wronged husband, Cushing took a paid vacation abroad, this time 'to the heavy Gothic and Baroque architecture of Munich, capital of Bavaria as Otto Wesondonk in *Magic Fire* (1955), to be cuckolded by Alan Badel's Wagner.'

Magic Fire was a big budget international venture that should have boosted Cushing's profile further, and the Hollywood connection continued with the casting of Yvonne De Carlo as Wagner's wife Minnie.

Produced by Republic Pictures, *Magic Fire* began shooting on 11 September 1954. With the studio expanding their production facilities to make bigger pictures, this became one of Republic's most ambitious films, with location work in Zurich, Paris, Venice, Dresden and Munich.

The Hollywood link continued with William Dieterle directing. A veteran of the silent era, German born Dieterle previously directed *The Life Of Emile Zola* (1937), *The Hunchback Of Notre Dame* (1939) and *The Devil And Daniel Webster* (1941).

Dieterle always wanted to bring the life of Germany's greatest composer to the big screen, although the film was actually an adaptation of Bernita Harding's novel of the same name, which was described as 'not strictly a biography, but not quite fiction.' Dieterle had previously directed *Juarez* (1939), which was based on another Harding novel, *The Phantom Crown*.

Dieterle bought the film rights to *Magic Fire* in 1953 and co-wrote the script with David T Chandler with Bernita Harding providing additional re-writes. He then approached Herbert Yates at Republic Pictures to bankroll the project. Yates wanted to move from low budget westerns and serials to big 'event' pictures and felt *Magic Fire* was a perfect subject to film. Shooting took place between September and December.

Yates took the project seriously, making use of the overseas locations, massive, opulent sets, period costumes and a cast of thousands. The opera scenes were staged by Professor Rudolph Hartmann of Munich and the ballet sequences were choreographed by Latjana Gsousty. Brought in to supervise and arrange Wagner's music was the distinguished composer Eric Korngold, whose Oscar winning work included *Captain Blood* (1935), *The Adventures Of Robin Hood* (1938) and *King's Row* (1941). He had previously worked with Dieterle on *Juarez*.

Magic Fire was Korngold's final film, although he continued writing music until his death in 1957. He also makes an uncredited appearance as conductor Hans Richter. When the original actor failed to show, Dieterle persuaded Korngold to play the non-speaking role for a scene featuring over 1000 extras in full costume on set.

For the coveted role of Richard Wagner, Charlton Heston and Howard Duff were seriously considered before settling on British actor Alan Badel, in his second Hollywood film. Badel previously worked with Dieterle in *Salome* (1953).

Although Badel was a fine actor, he proved difficult to cast in films and never achieved the stardom he deserved. He maintained a successful career in character roles until his early death in 1982. Badel has fifth billing in the film.

Cushing's former mentor Ida Lupino was considered for the role of Wagner's wife Minnie, which eventually went to Yvonne de Carlo, best known as Lily Munster in the popular TV sitcom *The Munsters*.

The international cast included Austrian Gerhard Reidman as King Kudwig II and Argentinian Carlos Thompson as Franz Liszt. Thompson specialised in suave, continental womanisers, and briefly had an affair with De Carlo during the making of *Fort Algiers* (1953), which had ended by the time they made *Magic Fire*.

Cushing's scenes were shot in Germany. He appears halfway through the film in the thankless role of Wagner's friend and sponsor. 'His time

16: Magic Fire (1955)

onscreen totals only minutes,' said Deborah Del Vecchio, 'and he is photographed in only medium shots – no close-ups.' Exiled from Germany, Wagner takes up residence at his friend's Swiss estate and then has an affair with his wife Mathilde (Valentina Cortese).

A step down from *The Black Knight* and *The End Of The Affair*, the film allowed Cushing and Helen to take an extended holiday in Munich. His time on *Magic Fire* was a foretaste of things to come as David Miller observed. 'Cushing's brief appearance is notable at least for showing him in an outfit like the one he will famously wear as Frankenstein, with frock coat, waved hair and side-whiskers.'

Miller also noted Cushing's growing stature as a film actor. 'With *Magic Fire*, Cushing consolidated his position as an attractive and reliable supporting player.'

Magic Fire doesn't light any fires. It suffers from a feeble story, uninspired handling and a miscast Badel and de Carlo sporting ropey German accents. Failing to give any light to this complex man, the film falls between two stools.

Magic Fire received a Royal Film Performance on 15 July 1955. The original cut, which ran for 150 minutes, was trimmed to 120 minutes for the special screening before being cut to 90 minutes for its general release in America on 29 March 1956. Critical evaluation was largely negative with Robert Cass, writing for *Catholic World*, calling it 'romanticized slush overloaded with pretentiousness and bad acting.' Leslie Halliwell found it a 'Remarkably boring biopic with much music and little characterisation. Ugly colour minimizes German locations.'

Magic Fire bombed at the American box office and faded into obscurity. Dieterle wanted to shoot a biopic of Wolfgang Amadeus Mozart, but plans were scrapped following the film's failure.

By 1954, Cushing's TV career had peaked. 'During this time, I was lucky to win the Best Actor Award three times, and appear in two quite outstanding television productions, *The Creature* and the controversial version of George Orwell's *1984*.

The Creature was written by Nigel Kneale, creator of the classic BBC science fiction series *Quatermass*. The production also took Cushing on location, 'as Dr Rollason in search of the abominable snowman, I climbed up to the frozen, snowy height of 13,000-odd feet on the Jungfraujoch in the Bernese Oberland, Switzerland, where the equipment had been tested for Sir Edmund Hilary's successful assault upon Mount Everest in 1953.'

Cushing was now more comfortable about travelling abroad. 'I couldn't be more willing or eager to go on location for *The Creature*. I'm never keen on the idea of a double being used as I like to know what I'm doing in a play all the time.' When Hammer remade *The Creature* as *The Abominable Snowman* (1957), Cushing filmed his scenes in England.

Cushing's desire to travel had a lot to do with his wife. 'Helen always went on "safari" with me, and I looked forward so very much to her greeting when I returned in the evenings from those various hinterlands, and to a refreshing bath and cosy chats over our meal.'

In *The Creature*, Cushing plays Dr John Rollason, a botanist more interested in seeking the truth about the mysterious Yeti rather than capture it for commercial gain, which is the intention of his associate Tom Friend (Stanley Baker). Being a Nigel Kneale science fiction drama, the expedition is subjected to extra-terrestrial mind control from the creatures. Only Rollason survives, but he keeps the secret of the Yeti to himself.

'I became known as "The Horror man of the BBC" long before my connection with the type of film which carried that certificate. Poetic justice gone a little awry, perhaps?' If *The Creature* began Cushing's horror career, Nigel Kneale's TV adaptation of *1984* sealed it for good.

'I played Winston Smith and to me it is the only true *horror* film I've ever done, for the sort of horror pictures I normally appear in are pure fantasy and impossible to a degree. But in *1984* is not only possible – it's practically happening. You only have to look around you, and nearly everything Orwell predicted has come true – and unless we are very careful it will *all* come true.'

'In my opinion, Winston Smith is one of the greatest heroes in the world of fiction, for he stood alone against everything. He knew the odds and was certainly frightened, but he stood by his principles. And although he was defeated, he stands as an example to us all.'

Cushing was correct with his feelings about the modern world, and this compelling play, which was broadcast in December 1954, struck a chord with the public, clearly demonstrating the BBC's attempts to push boundaries and face the hostilities from the press and the critics. *1984* did exactly that, sparking off a heated TV debate between critic Malcom Muggeridge and the director Rudolph Cartier. There was even talk in the House of Commons about whether the play's scheduled repeat should go ahead.

While there is little to shock a modern audience, *1984* is an outstanding drama with Cushing giving the performance of his TV career.

'One good thing that came out of the controversy,' he recalled, 'was that it helped to get me better known still. However, I wanted desperately to get into films in England.' Keeping busy with starring roles in the TV adaptations of *The Browning Version*, *Moment Of Truth* and *Richard Of Bordeaux*, Cushing's next film was a big budget affair that again took him outside the UK.

17: Alexander The Great (1956)

Cushing (centre) with Claire Bloom in *Alexander The Great*.

Returning to Spain once more, Cushing 'went to my death in battle as the Athenian General Memnon, against Richard Burton's Alexander the Great on the parched plains of Andalucia.'

With a stellar cast of Fredric March, Claire Bloom, Harry Andrews, Stanley Baker, Niall McGinnis and Michael Hordern, *Alexander The Great* (1956) was shot in Cinemascope and Technicolour by United Artists with Robert Rossen directing, this big budget epic gave Cushing his highest profile film role to date.

Rossen had long been fascinated by the life of Greece's greatest historical figures and spent years researching into Alexander's brief rise to power. He began working on a proposed film version in 1952.

Rossen's company, Rossen Films along with C B Films entered a co-production deal with United Artists, and with a $4 million budget, the film was shot in Spain over 110 days from February to July 1955. Interiors were filmed at Madrid's Sevilla Studio.

Location work was extensive with El Molar being used to depict Pella, El Vellon passing for Persepolis and Athens, and Alexander's battles shot in Spanish Morocco. The Battles of Chaeronea and Guagamela were filmed near the Sierra de Guadarra and the Battle of the Granicus took place near the river Jarama. Acting as historical advisor was Prince Peter of Denmark and Greece.

The impressive sets were designed by Andre Andrejew and the costumes by David Ffolkes, a total of 11,000 outfits were made; Burton's wardrobe alone cost $87,000. For one battle sequence there were 6,500 spears, 4,000 shields, 430 horses, and 42 chariots. 5,000 extras were used, and 1,000 cavalry horses were loaned from the Spanish military.

'In a film of this size and scope,' observed Deborah Del Vecchio, 'simply moving the cast and crew provided Robert Rossen with problems similar to those encountered by Alexander in moving his troops. Transporting everyone across Spain involved the use of 14 cars, 9 buses, 2 trailers, 20 trucks, 5 vans, 2 ambulances, 1 jeep, 9 portable dressing rooms and 1 water tank.'

For the pivotal role of Alexander, Rossen wanted Charlton Heston, who turned it down saying, '*Alexander* is the easiest kind of picture to make badly.' The part went to Richard Burton, who had appeared in the epic *The Robe* (1953).

At 29, Burton looks too old for Alexander (who was 32 when he died), especially when he had to play him as a teenager during the first half. Danielle Darrieux, who played Alexander's mother Olympias, was eight years older than Burton.

Cushing arrived in Madrid with his wife around mid-March to play Memnon, the Athenian general who is exiled for not pledging allegiance to Alexander. Another cuckolded husband, Memnon loses his wife Barsine (Claire Bloom) to Alexander before meeting his death at the Battle of Granicus.

Cushing gives the best performance in the film. He looks so convincing in costume, and Burton suffers in comparison. As David Miller correctly points out, 'In his long black wig and saturnine beard, Cushing cuts a more heroic figure than poor Richard Burton, who with his peroxide blond curls looks like nothing so much as an elderly blond cherub.'

'Cushing's athletic background again served him well,' said Del Vecchio, 'as the role acquired a great deal of physical ability and stamina. Although he often discusses his horseback riding as "at my peril", he is really quite an accomplished rider and appears natural in the saddle, or in this case, riding bareback.'

Cushing had come a long way from his early horse disaster on *The Man In The Iron Mask*. 'Helen was a first-class equestrian, and it was she who taught me the fundamental principles, enabling me to at least to look as if I knew what I was doing.'

Cushing has several excellent scenes with Burton, but his finest moment is opposite Claire Bloom. Their final meeting is the most bittersweet of farewells when she decides to leave him for Alexander. It's a well-acted

17: Alexander The Great (1956)

scene that provides the only grit in a gritless epic.

'As the Athenian General Memnon, having taken a fond farewell of my wife, played by Claire Bloom, I rode a horse, bareback, to be slaughtered in the Battle of Granicus by Richard Buron's legions.' Sadly, Memnon's death is anti-climactic. What makes epics impressive are the amazing battle scenes utilising a cast of thousands fighting to the death.

Memnon is killed before the battle starts and we don't see anything else other than Cushing getting cut down by advancing Greek soldiers, a poor exit to put it mildly, and one that infuriated critic Alexander Walker. 'Cushing's performance has a perfectly pitched theatricality, but the emotions are brilliantly controlled. Among some very powerful actors, his is quite possibly the finest performance in the film.'

Because filming took longer than planned, the cast became restless, and Burton had already lost interest. Cushing's Greek excursion prevented him from playing the lead in a BBC production of *The Sun And I*.

When the production wrapped in June 1955, United Artists spent $1 million on advertising with $251,000 spent on magazine and newspaper advertising, which included a 13-page feature in *Life* magazine. Additional advertising came from UA after hiring 6ft 7inch David Ballard to dress up as Alexander.

Alexander The Great received a Royal World Premier in London on 22 March 1956. Critical evaluation was mixed with *Time Out* seeing it as 'A sprawling, misbegotten epic that undercuts its serious intent by constantly declaiming it and fails to strike a balance between spectacle and speechifying. Burton's Alexander, with his hatred and fear of father figures, comes in for some heavy-handed, cod-Freud analysis as he sweeps across Europe and Asia in his search for glory.'

The New York Times was more positive. 'Its moments of boredom are rare, and the battle scenes make a colourful and thunderous show. As Alexander, Richard Burton contributes a serious and impassioned portrayal of a man inspired by but still repelled by his father.' In his write-up of the Los Angeles premiere, Edwin Schallert stated: 'The initial audience had a chance to view some very powerful individual portrayals by Burton, March and others and to witness some overwhelmingly big and spectacular battle and crowd scenes. However, as a piece of storytelling, historical or otherwise, mainly revolving around the title character as a great conqueror for Greece, the film seemed to run off in a dozen and one different directions at practically every stage.'

The Monthly Film Bulletin felt that 'Conviction is considerably dissipated here by Rossen's refusal, in spite of obviously serious intentions, to present characters in terms much more convincing than those of comic strip history. The battle sequences are well composed, but the generally pedestrian style and approach of the production ultimately reduce *Alexander The Great* to a well-intentioned historical jamboree, protracted and intermittently quite enjoyable.'

The Guardian was less impressed describing the film as 'a great, unwieldy blunderbuss of a film.' *The Times* singled out Cushing's performance, 'Memnon is played with saturnine inscrutability by Mr Peter Cushing.'

Alexander The Great is more talk than action, despite Rossen's admiration for the subject. 'Robert Rossen was clearly fascinated with the character of Alexander and his world,' said Del Vecchio. 'He devoted years to researching the man and the legends that grew around him and was determined to bring the epic story down to a human level. He succeeded to some degree.'

The human level that Rossen projects on screen backfired on him, resulting in a dull epic, not helped by Burton's flat performance. The film is well staged, the cast is reliable, but overall, it is a plodding bore.

The film did well at the box office. United Artists needed to make $7 million in order to break even. *Alexander The Great* replaced *Carousel* (1956) as the highest-grossing movie for the first week in April 1956, before being knocked into second place by *Carousel* the following week. The film finally earned $2.5 million by the end of 1956, making it the 32nd highest-grossing film of that year.

Helmut Dantine, who played Nectanabus the Soothsayer was dubbed by Christopher Lee, making *Alexander The Great* the third unofficial collaboration between Lee and Cushing.

Cushing returned to England to take part in another movie, and once again there was a strong Hollywood link in the shape of director Joseph Losey.

Moving to England in the fifties, Losey directed several interesting films, mainly in association with Dirk Bogarde, and this included two for Hammer: the short film *Man On A Beach* (1955) and the science fiction feature *The Damned* (1963).

Based on Emlyn Williams' play *Someone Waiting*, *Time Without Pity* (1956) is a downbeat thriller starring Michael Redgrave as David Graham, an author whose estranged son (Alec McCowen) has been sentenced to death for murder. Convinced of his son's innocence, the recovering alcoholic carries out his own investigations, only to find the situation far more complicated.

Joining a solid cast of Leo McKern, Ann Todd, Lois Maxwell and Joan Plowright, Cushing plays Jeremy Clayton, Graham's by-the-book lawyer who breaks the news of his son's imprisonment. The first meeting between Cushing and Redgrave establishes a solid relationship between the characters. After that Cushing is reduced to a couple of brief scenes but he makes the most of them with a good performance.

18: Homegrown Star

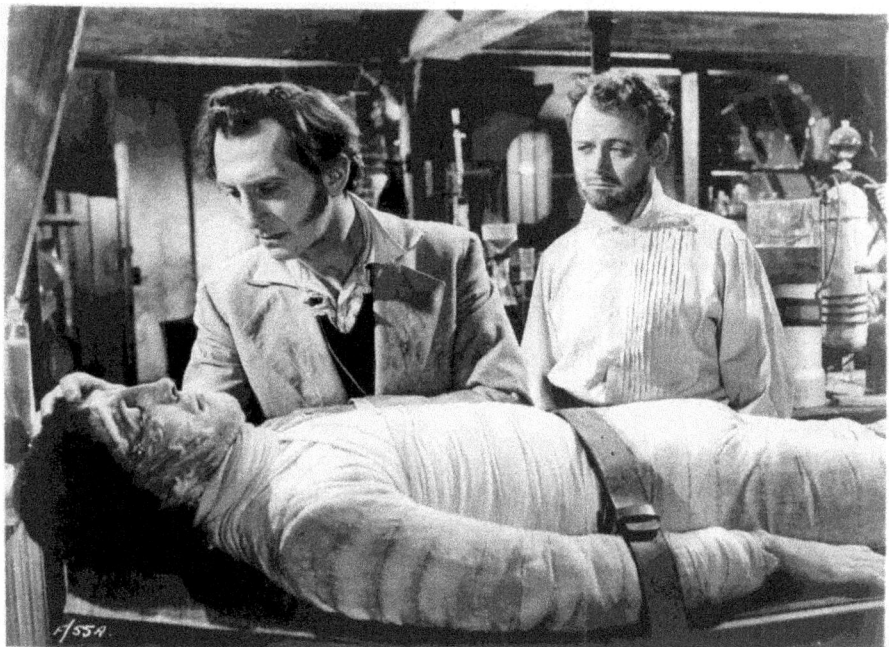

Cushing with Robert Urquhart and Christopher Lee in *The Curse Of Frankenstein*.

The timing couldn't have been better. There was a slight lull in Cushing's TV commitments due to a couple of projects that didn't materialise. There were also major changes to the British theatre scene in the late fifties which saw the sort of play that Cushing preferred start to fade from view. The catalyst seemed to be the arrival of John Osbourne's anti-establishment tirade *Look Back In Anger*, first staged in London's Royal Court Theatre in May 1956.

Into the breach stepped James Carreras and Hammer Films.

'It started after I did the television play of Orwell's *1984* which caused a bit of a furore at the time. Soon afterwards, Jimmy Carreras started to call my agent once a week almost regularly saying, "When's the boy going to be free? We must have him." So, I read in the (trade) papers that they were going to remake the *Frankenstein* pictures, which I remembered being very thrilled by as a boy, so I rang my agent and said if they're still interested, I'm free now as this is the one I'd like to do.'

Carreras wanted Cushing to play Baron Victor Frankenstein. 'I had seen the original James Whale version with Colin Clive and Boris Karloff and enjoyed it immensely. Nevertheless, I still wanted to be sure that I was getting into the right thing and asked to see Hammer's latest film.

'They very kindly showed me *The Quatermass Experiment* (1955) with Brian Donlevy, and I thought it was a splendid film. No one at all connected with the *Frankenstein* films realised where it was going to lead.'

The Curse of Frankenstein (1956) began a lifelong friendship between Cushing and Christopher Lee, who played the monster. According to Cushing. 'The very first time we met he was wearing his grotesque make-up conceived by Phil Leakey, and a story was put about by the publicity department that when it was removed at the end of the day's work, he came face to face with me in the corridor, and then I screamed! He is a man of so many attributes, among them a most marvellous sense of humour plus the ability to laugh at himself, and an uncanny skill as an impersonator, which helped to lighten the darkness hanging over Count Dracula's entombed habitat when we were shooting.'

Christopher Lee had his own version of their meeting. 'From the first time we met on the set of *The Curse of Frankenstein* at Bray (Studios), Peter Cushing and I were friends. Our first encounter began with me storming into his dressing room and announcing in petulant tones. "I haven't got any lines!" He looked up, his mouth twitched, and said dryly. "You're lucky. I've read the script." It was a typical wry comment. I soon found Peter to be a great perfectionist, who learned not only his own lines but everybody else's as well, but he had a gentle sense of humour which made it quite impossible for anybody to be pompous in his company.'

Lee added that it 'was the start of a very deep friendship between myself and Peter Cushing, whom I found to be a person of exceptional character and deep understanding. I would certainly liked to have played some of Peter Cushing's parts, notably Baron Frankenstein – but only once.'

Shooting began at Bray Studios on 19 November 1956 and ran for 14 days. To avoid copyright infringement with Universal, Hammer wisely avoided comparisons with the Boris Karloff classic, to the amusement of Jimmy Sangster, who took up the screenwriting duties after a previous script by Milton Subotsky was rejected. 'It didn't take a Clarence Darrow [an American lawyer who became famous in the 19th Century for high profile representations of trade union causes] to point out that Mary Shelley, who wrote the novel, had been dead for over 100 years and therefore [the story] was in the public domain. "Point taken," said Universal, "but make sure your monster in no way resembles the old Boris Karloff version. That is our copyright.".'

Sangster made the shrewd decision of avoiding any reference to *Frankenstein* (1931) by returning to the novel. Unlike the Universal series, Hammer's subsequent sequels focused on the creator and not the creation.

And who better to fill that role than Peter Cushing? Unlike the pathetic wet blanket of the novel, and Colin Clive's neurotic, guilt-ridden interpretation, Cushing's Frankenstein is cold and ruthless, a man who would stop at nothing to achieve his goal to create life.

'The first major change I made was to make the Baron the villain, as opposed to the monster' said Sangster, 'Let's face it, the monster couldn't help doing monstrous things. Having great body parts isn't going to be much good if his brain is full of broken glass before it's even planted in his reconstructed skull. The Baron, on the other hand, was well-educated, brilliant, a seemingly charming man. He didn't set out to create a monster, he just wanted to create life. Unfortunately, everything got screwed up and that's where his true character came out. He became an evil, cold-blooded murderer. And when confronted with the fact, he was unable to understand what all the fuss was about.'

The Baron's narcissism is an important factor in the novel, but in the film, Cushing takes it further. 'I have a tremendous amount of affection for Baron Frankenstein for all the obvious reasons. I based the original character on Mary Shelley's novel, which I never read until I knew I was doing the film. You couldn't put all of the novel into an hour and a half's screening, but it was adapted very well, I thought, by Jimmy Sangster, and there was a certain charm I could bring into it. In the subsequent films he became more ruthless.'

'It is interesting how the Baron's motives were honourable for a good chunk of the movie,' added Sangster. 'He sets out to build a perfect human being. Nothing wrong in that. We're already having ethical discussions and arguments about it. First a cloned sheep! Then a monkey! What next? Victor actually says to Paul [Krempe – Robert Urquhart] in one scene that he's doing no real wrong – just robbing a few graves. The first evil thing he does is murder the professor by pushing him off the first-floor gallery.'

Frankenstein isn't that altruistic when he gets his pretty maid Justine (Valerie Gaunt) pregnant, yet he shows no interest in his beautiful wife Elizabeth (Hazel Court). In essence, Frankenstein creates life on two occasions, one of which is through impregnating a poor girl. The Baron's treatment of both the maid and the monster shows his lack of empathy.

These characteristics are brilliantly conveyed by Cushing, who gives an outstanding performance, vindicating Carreras' trust in bringing a TV name to a film. Cutting an immaculate figure in period costume, many books and critics have commented on his Byronic screen persona. The handsome, charming dandy gives way to a cold figure too immersed in his own self-importance and following misguided goals that succeed in destroying more lives than those he creates. As the series progresses, the Baron becomes older, twisted and more murderous.

Cushing is well supported by Christopher Lee as the monster, Valerie

Gaunt as the tragic Justine, and Melvyn Hayes as young Frankenstein. Hazel Court does her best in a poorly written role while Robert Urquhart as Victor's disillusioned mentor walks through the proceedings with no conviction; he had scant regard for the film as he felt it hampered his career.

Brilliantly directed by Terence Fisher, who makes excellent use of the low budget and Sangster's economical script, *The Curse of Frankenstein* was a massive box office success, despite critics' unanimous disapproval about the level of gruesomeness that had never been seen on the big screen before. It's all there in glorious colour, blood, guts, eyeballs, brains, the lot. That said, *The Curse of Frankenstein* has its own grizzly sense of style.

Following the film, Cushing returned to the stage in *The Silver Whistle* and made further TV appearances in *Gaslight*, *The Winslow Boy* and *Uncle Harry*. Now on the road to stardom, his BBC contract had come to an end and with the financial security that came with his newfound status, he focused entirely on film work.

Returning to Hammer, Cushing reunited with Terence Fisher in the sequel *Revenge of Frankenstein* (1958). Thanks to Jimmy Sangster's intelligent script, he plays Frankenstein as a more multi-faceted individual, still focusing on his misguided goals, but not without a great deal of black humour.

Cushing's next Hammer film sealed his horror status when he reunited with Christopher Lee and Terence Fisher for a new version of *Dracula* (1958).

After the cruelty of Baron Frankenstein, Cushing finally plays the heroic role he enjoyed reading about as a child. 'To me, Van Helsing is the essence of good, pitted against the essence of evil, and I think the *Dracula* films have the same appeal as the old morality plays with the struggle of good over evil and good always triumphing in the end.'

Dracula opened to massive box office success on London on 21 May 1958. A few days later the actors attended the New York premiere.

Joined by James Carreras and Anthony Hinds, the screening coincided with the actors' birthdays. 'As his birthday was the day before mine,' said Lee, 'we celebrated it together on the peak of the Empire State Building, which gave me vertigo, and again at a party given by Universal Studios when I launched myself on the cake with its 36 candles and stabbed it in the heart. There was a picture of me several storeys high – some fifty feet of bloodthirsty Count holding a girl in his/my arms – on a building beside the cinema in Times Square.'

Then came the premiere of *Dracula*, at the Mayfair Theatre in New York. 'The midnight screening for the profession and the media had me worried,' Lee recalled. 'Not a few of that exuberant audience were well tanked up and greeted each new character with a Bronx cheer and a fusillade of cracks and laughs.

'Peter and I sat right under the projection booth at the back and the crowd came in; they were shouting, they all knew each other, they were really in high spirits. Somebody fired a gun – a blank cartridge – and got a few people's attention. Finally, the lights went down. Along came the credits and there's the tomb with the name *Dracula* – blood spattering on it – and they roared! At that point, I said to Peter, "I'm leaving; I can't take any more of this. This is awful." And Peter said, "No, just stay," and this kept going until the famous scene in which Jonathan Harker meets me for the first time. He feels the presence and he turns around and there, at the top of the stairs, is the silhouette. I tell you, the place erupted. The roof nearly came off.'

Expecting another Bela Lugosi take-off, the audience reaction quickly changed upon hearing a well-spoken Englishman with a booming voice taking centre stage, as Lee continued, 'The ordinary conversational tone of the Count switched them off like a knob being turned off on a radio. From then on there was only direct reaction. The Count tamed them.'

The premiere was followed by an autograph party where Cushing and Lee met the fans who caused the uproar. 'At two in the morning,' said Lee. 'Peter and I sat in the foyer and signed our wrists stiff. At last, I knew what it was like to taste blood.'

Little is said about Cushing's stay in America other than making several TV appearances across the country promoting *Dracula*. Lee remained in the States for a further fortnight where he visited old friend Richard Burton. After trying to conquer Hollywood all those years ago, Cushing became a film star in his own country.

The youth culture in England ran parallel with America, and although the UK films weren't as high profile as *On The Waterfront* (1954), *Blackboard Jungle* (1955) and *Rebel Without A Cause* (1955), they had their moments with the screen adaptation of *Look Back In Anger* (1959) and Jack Clayton's gritty Northern drama *Room At The Top* (1959) spearheading a new wave of realism in British cinema which extended to location work outside London.

The Liverpool based *Violent Playground* (1957) focused on juvenile delinquency. 'England was having its own problems,' said Deborah Del Vecchio. 'A post-war depression, decaying urban areas, and a dissatisfaction with class distinctions caused a similar situation. For the first time, British teenagers were viewed as potential menaces.'

Starring Stanley Baker as police community liaison officer, Inspector Truman, the film's James Dean is played by David McCallum, a gang leader responsible for several arson attacks in Liverpool.

Now completely off the rails, the young man buys a machine gun and holds the children in his old school hostage. With recent school shootings in America, *Violent Playground* makes disturbing viewing, despite many dated moments – women in headscarves and plain clothed cops in trilbies and trench coats, and not a single Scouse accent, other than the one provided by an uncredited 12-year-old called Freddie Fowl, who later became comedian Freddie Starr.

Playing Father Laidlaw, a streetwise inner-city priest who tries to help McCallum's disenfranchised Johnny, the classically trained Cushing looks surprisingly at home with this new style of gritty realism. As the film's moral tone, he gets to show his trademark steely resolve during the siege when the priest climbs up a ladder to enter the besieged classroom to try to talk Johnny down, only to injure himself when the boy pushes him off the ladder.

Violent Playground is an interesting forerunner to the kitchen sink dramas that engulfed British films in the early sixties. It would also have a negative effect on Cushing's film career when he tried to break away from the horror genre in the early sixties.

19: John Paul Jones (1959)

Cushing in *John Paul Jones*.

Cushing took a welcome break from Hammer to star in another Hollywood production, and this could have been a turning point in his career and a chance to break away from the horror genre. As it turned out, *John Paul Jones* would be his final blockbuster for quite some time.

Set during the War of Independence, with Robert Stack playing the eponymous Scottish merchant turned navel captain for the colonial forces, this historical drama gave Cushing the decent supporting role of Captain Pearson, the British naval commander of the *Serapis*, who engages in a sea battle off Flamborough Head against Captain Jones' ship the *Bonhomie Richard*

There were several attempts to bring the life of John Paul Jones to the big screen. Warner Brothers purchased the rights to Clement Ripley's biographical novel *Clear For Action*. James Cagney and director Michael Curtiz were both attached to the project before it was abandoned due to the heavy costs involved.

In 1946, independent producer Samuel Bronston obtained permission from the US Navy to make his own version. Forming Admiralty Pictures Corporation in 1955 with a group of New York investors, Bronston made a deal with Warner Bros to resurrect the project with Jesse Lasky providing the script.

John Paul Jones was the first of several films Bronston shot in Spain. Various American companies and leading entrepreneurs invested in the project in order to retrieve funds frozen by Spanish dictator General Francisco Franco. Bronston persuaded Franco's government to release the money to finance future filmmaking in Spain.

Pre-production went underway in January 1956 with Admiral Chester Nimitz as technical advisor. Shooting was due to start in May 1956 with Glen Ford playing Jones and William Dieterle assigned as director.

Dieterle preferred Richard Todd or Richard Basehart over Ford and Ben Hecht was hired to re-write the script when Basehart secured the role. *John Paul Jones* was intended to be shot at Warner's Italian studio, but the studio pulled out when production was pushed back to October 1956.

By October 1957, Warners returned as distributor following lengthy negotiations with the US Navy. John Farrow replaced Dieterle and production moved to Spain. In February 1958, Robert Stack replaced Basehart.

With a $5 million budget, shooting took place between January and August 1958, with location work in France, Scotland and Italy. Most of the production unit was based in Denia, Spain, and the government allowed filming to take place at the Royal Palace in Madrid.

Farrow was determined to keep things as realistic as possible. According to Deborah Del Vecchio, 'This sense of authenticity was further enhanced by adviser Alan Villiers, who, in 1957, sailed a replica of the *Mayflower* from England to Plymouth, Massachusetts. A search by Villiers uncovered two ancient hulls of sailing ships used to haul fruit between Spain and France. With different riggings and cosmetic changes, they represented the *Bonhomie Richard* and the *Serapis*.'

Cushing arrived in Denia in July 1958 to film his scenes. 'Given Cushing's love of swashbuckling,' said David Miller, 'he must have been happy to make a film like *John Paul Jones*.' This was reflected in Cushing's committed performance.

Cushing described the battle scene between the *Serapis* and the *Bonhomie Richard* as being close to the real thing. 'To give the impression of

19: John Paul Jones (1959)

gunshots hitting planks and bulwarks, small charges of gunpowder were placed in strategic positions all over the decks. At given moments they were detonated electrically by the special effects department, but in the fury of the mock battle with so much noise and action, plus things to think about, it was extremely difficult to remember where these explosions occurred, so we had to leave our safety solely in the hands of those splendid experts, and to their credit, we all emerged from those dangerous skirmishes unscathed.'

The cast and crew were stationed in Benidorm, long before it became the infamous party town, and, as always, Helen accompanied her husband. 'It was the only spot with decent accommodation,' recalled Cushing.

'Filming also presented problems,' he added, 'especially when canvas sails needed the wind to blow in the right direction. That element has a will of its own, paying no attention to the whims of impatient filmmakers.'

Robert Stack also found filming difficult. 'Shooting in the deep Spanish summer heat was very hard to bear for the crew, because of heavy suits and uniforms to wear. And also, the final battleship sequence took place near the coastline, very close to an area that served as one of the main outlets of the sewage system; the stuntmen who jumped into the water had to hold their noses.'

John Paul Jones was released on 16 June 1959 and critical reaction was mixed. Leslie Halliwell found it a 'Fragmented biopic with a succession of guest stars, which turns it into a charade almost as silly as *The Story Of Mankind* (1957). On that level, it is not unentertaining.' *Time* magazine described the film as 'A full colour saga of the sea on which movie makers have lavished $4,000,000 and infinite care.'

The New York Times found it 'an unexciting picture, so far as dramatic action is concerned, and utterly unexpressive of the recorded nature and character of John Paul Jones. Stack looks as though he were a slightly dull but talkative member of a conservative gentleman's club.' *Variety* felt it 'could be shortened drastically and tightened to give it better pace and emphasis. The strong portions would then show to better advantage and eliminate the drag of unnecessary plotting.'

John Paul Jones turned out to be a box office failure. It has its moments, but like *Alexander The Great*, it's dull and talkative, not helped by Robert Stack's stolid performance and Bette Davis' silly guest appearance as Catherine the Great. The sets and costumes are outstanding, and the battle scenes are well-staged.

Cushing makes the most of his limited screen time. Looking magnificent in the King's uniform, his Pearson maintains a solid presence. The scene where Pearson surrenders to Jones is memorable. Impressed by Pearson's courage in battle, Jones refuses to accept his sword as was customary in defeat.

John Paul Jones was an enjoyable experience for Cushing, and with Helen alongside him, he was happy to travel abroad. He returned to Bray Studios to play Sherlock Holmes in Hammer's adaptation of *The Hound Of The Baskervilles* (1959). Cushing was a natural choice to play The Great Detective.

'I think Sherlock Holmes is the most complex character I ever had to play – having appeared in the film, *The Hound Of The Baskervilles* in 1959 and made a television series based on the short adventures in 1967. I have always been a great admirer of Conan Doyle's work and possess a collection of material relating to Holmes, including copies of the *Strand Magazine* in which his stories were first published.'

Cushing felt his portrayals of Frankenstein and Van Helsing were, 'more or less as myself', but this time he was playing an established character that had been prominent in the cinema. 'When I was offered the part, I was thrilled. It's a marvellous opportunity when you've got so much detail to base your character on.' Cushing's dedication extended to buying his own costumes.

Some of his preparation was unintentional. When he arrived at Bray for the start of filming, Hammer's second-in-command, Anthony Hinds, was impressed by the amount of weight he had lost. 'I'm afraid I hadn't been as conscientious as that,' Cushing replied, 'It was Spain what done it! I'd been out there filming *John Paul Jones* and a mild bout of dysentery had fined me down.'

Cushing's stardom gave him a degree of financial security and better health care for Helen, which included a stay at a health farm at Le Mont-Dore in France to help get rid of her persistent cough. The couple still lived in Kensington but had since bought a cottage in the seaside town of Whitstable in Kent, where the sea air was helpful to Helen's breathing. Initially used as a weekend getaway, the couple permanently moved to Whitstable a few years later.

Cushing consolidated his horror stardom with *The Mummy* (1959), again for Hammer Films. His first independent chiller saw him play Dr Robert Knox in *The Flesh And The Fiends* (1959), which was then followed by *The Suspect* (1959), a low-key espionage drama for Roy and John Boulting. 'It was one of the quickest pictures I appeared in,' Cushing said of the three-week shoot, 'but it stands to this day as a lesson that such budgets and tight shooting schedules can sometimes work.'

The tight schedule on *The Suspect* and his appearance as Charles Norbury in the West End stage production of William Fairchild's *The Sound Of Murder* became so stressful, that the actor started to fluff his lines on the fifth day of filming. 'I do not recommend making a film and at the same time appearing in a play. I did it once and lived and learned never to do it again.'

19: John Paul Jones (1959)

Working on the film and arriving at the Aldwych Theatre after work to play Charles Norbury in the play finally took its toll on Cushing's mental health. Suffering from nervous exhaustion, he took advantage of a 'get-out clause', and was replaced by Michael Goodliffe. *The Sound Of Murder* was his last stage appearance for some time.

Cushing's horror career reached an artistic and commercial peak when he returned to the role of Professor Van Helsing in *The Brides Of Dracula* (1960), but not without some reluctance.

Jimmy Sangster's script, originally called *Disciple Of Dracula*, received a second re-write from Peter Bryan that omitted Dracula altogether, however, Cushing turned down the role; he wasn't happy about Van Helsing using magic to destroy Baron Meinster (David Peel) as it was out of character, and that the Professor's only means to defeat a vampire were stakes and crucifixes.

After many years of struggle, Cushing could pull some weight regarding his assignments. 'Peter Cushing just wouldn't tolerate anything that he thought was second best,' said Anthony Hinds, 'and he used to nag me if he thought I was taking the easy way out of a difficulty, and quite rightly too.' To add polish to the script, Hinds hired playwright Edward Percy on Cushing's suggestion in addition to carrying out further uncredited re-writes himself.

The Brides Of Dracula has been long regarded as one of the best of Hammer's *Dracula* series with Cushing giving his finest performance as Van Helsing. He has stiff competition from David Peel, who holds his own as the youthful but decadently evil Meinster, although they are both upstaged by Marita Hunt's creepy Baroness and Freda Jackson's cackling maid.

Cushing's lack of compromise on a project may have succeeded in limiting his film offers, although it had little to do with personal ego and more with the good of a movie. There was also an indication that he had grown disillusioned with horror and was itching to play other roles.

Cushing was set to star in Hammer's *The Man Who Could Cheat Death* (1959), an adaption of Barrie Lyndon's play *The Man In Half Moon Street*, but he decided to turn it down. He wasn't happy with the level of violence.

Cushing also wanted to take a break from film work to devote his energies to an exhibition of his paintings in London's West End. *Here and There – An Exhibition of Watercolours by Peter Cushing* opened at the Fine Art Society in December 1958 and ran for several months.

Cushing retained star billing when he played alongside Michael Craig, George Sanders, Bernard Lee, Andre Morell, Noel Willman and Marne Maitland for the aeronautical drama *Cone Of Silence* (1960). This efficiently made film is a decent addition to his movie portfolio, but it never had the same impact as his horror work.

20: Sword Of Sherwood Forest (1960)

Cushing with Sarah Branch in *Sword Of Sherwood Forest*.

Sword Of Sherwood Forest (1960) was the first of four Hammer films Cushing made outside the UK. Instead of shooting at Bray Studios, the producers opted for another Bray, the town in County Wicklow in the Republic of Ireland.

Intended to be a sequel to Hammer's previous Robin Hood adventure *The Men Of Sherwood Forest* (1954), the project was on the schedules back in 1957, only to be put on hold following the success of *The Curse Of Frankenstein*.

Getting the green light in May 1960, the film capitalised on the successful TV series starring Richard Greene. Greene previously enjoyed Hollywood success as a 20th Century Fox contract player, and was best known as playing Sir Henry Baskerville opposite Basil Rathbone in *The Hound Of The Baskervilles* (1939).

Movie stardom didn't last long, and after military service during World

20: Sword Of Sherwood Forest (1960)

War 2, Greene had returned to England looking for work when he was offered the role of Robin Hood on television.

The Adventures Of Robin Hood ran from 1954 to 1958 and 143 episodes were made. It proved an immediate success on both sides of the Atlantic. Greene had good reason to be grateful for the show when marketing products and comic books using his likeness sorted out his financial problems.

Wanting to play Robin on the big screen after the show ended, Greene formed Yeoman Films with series producer Sidney Cole and approached Hammer with the idea. Terence Fisher, who directed eleven episodes of the series, was also brought in.

Production began on 23 May 1960 at Ardmore Studios in Bray. Cushing replaced Alan Wheatley from the series as the dastardly Sheriff of Nottingham with the supporting roles taken by Nigel Green (Little John), Niall MacGinnis (Friar Tuck), Richard Pascoe, Oliver Reed, Dennis Lotis and Desmond Llewellyn. Greene was the only actor from the series to star in the film.

Cushing found Ireland more to his liking and the beautiful countryside piqued his artistic interests. According to Terence Fisher's wife Morag, 'Peter Cushing and his wife were staying at the same hotel and Peter was out painting when he wasn't shooting. He does lovely watercolours.'

Filming caused one problem for cameraman Len Harris. As part of the second unit team, he nearly lost an eye in an incident on the set. 'We constructed a Saxon village, all thatched roofs you know. The Normans were to ride through and set fire to the village. It would have been no problem in England, but [in Ireland] they had no horses trained for film work. We would just go around farms and ask to borrow regular horses! When we waved the torches, the horses panicked. I was working a huge Cinemascope camera, and a horse knocked it on top of me – blood everywhere! It was practically the last shot, so no one was overly concerned. It was lucky it was just me that was damaged – we hadn't got another camera!'

Working on the film for the first time as continuity supervisor was Pauline Wise, who filled in for Hammer's resident supervisor Tilly Day. 'Tilly was at Bray, and they needed someone for *Sword Of Sherwood Forest*. They did have somebody to start on it, but Richard Greene had her replaced. They sent me over there, very nervous, reading the script going out on the plane. I was picked up in Dublin and they never told Richard Greene that I'd not done it before. They told me one of the big problems he'd had was with the arrows in his quiver. He'd either be sent into battle without any, or he'd had spent them in fighting and would then ride into a clearing where he'd have a quiver full of arrows and that's what mostly annoyed him. So, I made sure he always had arrows!

'I do remember one of the very first scenes, where I was scared stiff. It was a sort of rape and pillage scene in a monastery, where Oliver Reed and Richard Pascoe were attacking the nuns and fighting. In comes Richard Greene as Robin Hood and there was this free-for-all and, really, I hadn't got anything written down in my pad. I didn't know who was who, I didn't know who to watch. It was scary, but that was just an early experience. Anyway, I seem to have got through that film all right and they told Richard Greene on the last day that I was a new girl – well trained, but new all the same. Terry Fisher was the director, and he was lovely.'

Playing the villainous Edward, Earl of Newark was Cushing's lifelong friend Richard Pascoe. 'I first knew Peter at the start of my career in 1943 when I was 16 years old at a little theatre in a suburb of London. The war was on. This little theatre was what you would call stock, I suppose. It was the "Q" Theatre at Kew Bridge, which is near Kew Gardens in London – demolished years ago. It no longer exists, sadly. A different play was produced every week, very often with totally different actors each week too. I was a student-apprentice assistant stage manager, which is the lowest of the low. I swept the stage, and I washed the teacups and did all that kind of stuff. Peter would come down and be the leading juvenile, the leading man. For instance, we did a stage adaptation I always remember of *Anna Karenina* in the tiny little theatre on this minute stage. I can't remember the names of the other plays in which he appeared, but he was around in my life at that time.'

The actors kept in touch for many years prior to reuniting on *Sword Of Sherwood Forest*. 'We resumed talking where we'd left off years previously. He was so welcoming. "My dear old chap! How are you, my dear boy! How are you Dickie!" He's one of the world's saints, you know, Peter. He would help anybody in trouble and is so patient. Peter is one of the kindest, gentlest men I've ever known in my life, the antithesis to how he often appears on screen. He's a darling man.'

Filming wrapped on 8 July 1960 after a seven week shoot and the cast and crew returned to London for post-production. *Sword Of Sherwood Forest* was released through Columbia Pictures on 26 December 1960 on a double bill with Hammer's *Visa To Canton* (1960).

Critical evaluation was decent but unspectacular. Leslie Halliwell found it, 'a rather feeble addition to the legend, but the actors try hard.' *Kinematograph* thought the same, 'Jolly, disarmingly naïve adventure comedy melodrama.' *The New York Times* said, 'It's business as usual, but hold on. Alan Hackney's script and Terence Fisher's direction keep the incidents jouncing, a nicely tinted Sherwood Forest is as pretty as could be, and Sarah Branch is certainly the curviest Lady Marian we've ever seen. Mr Greene is aptly limber, and Peter Cushing, Richard Pascoe and an unidentified Archbishop of Canterbury (Jack Gwillim) are excellent.'

Despite solid work all round, *Sword Of Sherwood Forest* isn't great. Away from the horror genre, Terence Fisher is unable to inject the same excitement he brought to *The Brides Of Dracula*. The fight scenes lack spark, and the script is dialogue heavy.

The film's strongest point is the acting, although Richard Greene looks a tad too old and heavy to make a convincing Robin, and Oliver Reed's camp, nasally voiced villain is annoying. Other performances are solid enough.

Cushing gives a menacing performance, and even though he was older than Greene, he looked far more athletic when it came to wielding a sword. Sadly, he gets an anticlimactic death scene when Oliver Reed stabs him in the back, disappointing fans who wanted to see the obligatory duel to the death between Robin and the Sheriff.

Sword Of Sherwood Forest made little impact at the box office, but that did not affect Hammer's production line approach to filmmaking, which was successful enough to withstand the occasional flop.

The swashbuckling continued in England with *The Hellfire Club* (1960) starring Keith Michell, making his film debut and proving himself a versatile and acrobatic action hero, although his career remained rooted in the theatre.

With a strong supporting cast of Peter Arne, Adrienne Corri, David Lodge and Francis Matthews, Cushing has an amusing guest appearance as the bumbling but sly lawyer Mr Merryweather. He makes the most of his comic performance, and while the film is an improvement on *Sword Of Sherwood Forest* it's easy to watch and easy to forget.

Cushing's next film should have reunited him with Christopher Lee. *Im Namen des Teufels*, or *The Devil's Agent* (1961) is a bizarre, haphazard Irish/German espionage drama described by Mark Miller as 'an odd sidelight to the Cushing/Lee films.'

According to Lee, 'The Irish venture had German money behind it, was made in English, included Peter Cushing in the cast (though I never once met him), was called *The Devil's Agent*, used me as a Krupp-like industrialist, put the cast up in a delightful hotel whose suites were all named after Irish writers, and staggered from crisis to crisis as it was never certain whether the money would be coming in for the next reel.'

Perhaps there wasn't enough money to pay Peter Cushing because his role was deleted from the final print. 'Due to the episodic structure of *The Devil's Agent*,' said Deborah Del Vecchio, 'it would not have been difficult to cut out Peter Cushing's (or anyone else's) scenes to keep the running time down. However, since Peter Cushing was the best-known name in the cast, why him?'

Cushing had a cameo appearance as solicitor Evan Wrack in *The Naked Edge* (1961) which reunited him with Deborah Kerr and gave him the chance to work with Gary Cooper, in his last film role: he died before *The Naked Edge* was released. Appearing as the prosecuting council at Cooper's trial, Cushing rises above the convoluted thriller with some credit. He also enjoyed working with one of his western heroes. 'Gary Cooper was an especial favourite of mine, and it was a great pleasure to work with him.'

Returning to Hammer, Cushing gave a great performance as the tyrannical bank manager Harry Fordyce in *Cash On Demand* (1961), an excellent crime thriller that reworks Charles Dickens' *A Christmas Carol* with Fordyce as a modern-day Scrooge. 'I don't mean he's evil, he is simply a man who lacks charity and warmth. In his office, as manager of the bank, he is stern and forbidding. He derives smug satisfaction from holding the threat of dismissal over his staff. This, then, is the man who suddenly finds himself the centre of a drama that rocks him to the core and alters his life.'

The events that undermine Fordyce's world occur following the arrival of André Morrell's Colonel Gore-Hepburn, who claims to be a representative of the bank's insurance department, but in reality, is a classy thief who has kidnapped Fordyce's family, forcing him to assist in robbing his own bank.

What makes *Cash On Demand* interesting is Gore-Hepburn's fascination with Fordyce's miserable persona. The film is an intriguing two-hander between Cushing and Morrell, as the Colonel pricks Fordyce's impregnable suit of armour to the point of an emotional breakdown. Fordyce now must rely on his staff, especially downtrodden senior bank clerk Pearson (Richard Vernon) to help him when Gore-Hepburn is caught by the police and is briefly incriminated as Fordyce's accomplice.

Directed by Quentin Lawrence, *Cash On Demand* is an atmospheric and menacing thriller. 'I remember thinking,' recalled Len Harris, 'as we were doing it that the picture would have worked just as well if Peter and André had switched roles. How many actors are that versatile? Both men were kind, considerate and professional, always a delight to work with.'

Cushing returned to swashbuckling with *Fury At Smuggler's Bay* (1961), which was the closest Cushing ever came to starring in a western. 'The scenario contained all the traditional ingredients,' he recalled, 'lots of shootin', the inevitable brawl in the saloon, a *High Noon* confrontation between the duellists, using swords instead of six-shooters and the cavalry charging to the rescue in the nick of time.'

In Cushing's eyes the main characters were typical western stereotypes. 'Bernard Lee was the "baddie", George Coulouris the alien homesteader-in-trouble and Miles Malleson the comic hick-town governor, Liz Fraser "set-em' up" behind the bar in the tavern, quenching the thirst of the roysting pirates. John Fraser and William Franklyn played the James Stewart and Richard Widmark parts, Michele Mercer the heroine, I had the grumpy-old-dad-who-turns-up-trumps-in-the-end Lee J Cobb part, with a beautiful daughter, thrown in for good measure, in the shapely form of June Thorburn. It was written and directed by John Gilling.'

With a change of setting, scenery and costume, *Fury At Smuggler's Bay* would work as a western. Cushing gives an excellent performance, dominating the film with every scene, but much like his previous swashbucklers, it is forgettable fluff.

The swashbuckling concluded with *Captain Clegg* (1962), and being a Hammer film, horror elements were added to the proceedings. Once again, Cushing was involved with smugglers, only this time, he is in charge of the illegal operation taking place in the coastal village of Dymchurch not far from the infamous Romney Marshes.

Based on Russell Thorndike's novel *Dr Syn*, *Captain Clegg* is a remake of the 1937 Gainsborough film of the same name starring George Arliss as the infamous pirate posing as village parson Dr Syn, and organising a lucrative smuggling ring, using the legendary marsh phantoms to scare off intruders. When Walt Disney Productions secured the rights to the title *Dr Syn* for their own 1963 film version starring Patrick McGoohan, Hammer changed the character's name to Dr Blyss, but retained his real identity of Captain Nathanial Clegg. Thorndike's story remained unchanged.

Cushing threw himself into the role with total conviction; his persona changing the minute he removed his spectacles, from twittering, whimsical Dr Blyss to the forceful Clegg, running the smuggling ring with ruthless efficiency aided by the former pirates under his command and some of the village locals.

The smugglers included one of Hammer's most enduring actors, Michael Ripper as Mr Mipps, the sardonic undertaker, and Clegg's former first mate. Ripper steals the acting honours from under Cushing's nose, not an easy task with the star on top form.

'I had a good part in that opposite Peter,' recalled Ripper. 'It was the only time we worked together at Hammer. I didn't get to know him that well, he was a very quiet man, but like Christopher Lee, a brilliant actor, perfectionist and a very important part of Hammer films. I am sure without them both, the company would not have become as successful as it did.'

The story begins with Captain Collier (Patrick Allen) and his revenue men arriving to expose the smuggling ring. This leads to a series of mind games between Clegg and Collier, complicated by Collier's mulatto (Milton Reid) a former pirate left to die on an island, his tongue cut out, after assaulting Clegg's wife.

Captain Clegg is an excellent movie, directed with verve by Peter Graham Scott and filled with first-rate performances. Cushing was so enthused by the project, he wrote a script for an unnamed sequel. It is not known as to whether Hammer optioned the script as a future production.

The British film industry suffered a brief slump that left Cushing unemployed for 18 months, not helped by the many changes within the industry.

Kitchen sink dramas were all the rage with a new generation of aggressive, testosterone-fuelled young men making their cinematic mark.

Albert Finney, Richard Harris, Alan Bates and Tom Courtney represented this new, charismatic leading man of British film, leaving classical actors like Cushing almost redundant.

Cushing was approaching 50 and his youthful looks had given way to a more gaunt appearance, not helped by his thinning hair. Hardly the right image for the all-important youth market the cinema relied on. Nor did the recent films he made do any favour to his box office standing.

It remains a mystery why Cushing never went further afield. International co-productions were commonplace and British actors such as David Niven, Jack Hawkins, Trevor Howard and Alec Guinness were being used to great effect in several big budget epics. Cushing could have easily lent his presence to these large-scale efforts.

Cushing's one film of 1962 reunited him with Stanley Baker and Quentin Lawrence. Shot at Shepperton Studios, *The Man Who Finally Died* (1962) is a convoluted thriller set in Bavaria with Baker playing Joe Newman. After receiving a mysterious phone call from someone claiming to be his late father, Newman arrives in Konigsbaden, where he learns that his father had been a Russian prisoner-of-war who escaped to Germany and married a young woman (Mai Zetterling).

Cushing turns up as Dr Peter Von Brecht. 'I played quite a good chap really. Although I still went around with a gun in my hand. I have no doubt people will remember me in this picture as the villain.'

This uninspired film now has a cult following thanks to a series of TV commercials for Holsten Pils Lager where Griff Rhys Jones acts opposite old movie footage featuring several famous actors, including Cushing.

There was still a demand for classically trained actors and in January 1963, the BBC offered Cushing a role in an ambitious production. *The Spread Of The Eagle* featured an excellent cast of Barry Jones (Caesar), Paul Eddington (Brutus) and Keith Michell (Mark Anthony) with Cushing well cast as Cassius.

Further TV work followed with an appearance as Albert Fawkes, descendant of Guy Fawkes. 'The Plan' was a one-off episode of the *Comedy Playhouse* series where Albert follows in his ancestor's footsteps with the help of a former IRA member played by Irish actor P G Stephens. It is a rare treat to see Cushing playing a comic role.

The TV work continued with 'The Caves of Steel', Terry Nation's adaptation of Isaac Asimov's 1954 novel with Cushing playing Elijah Bailey. Directed by Peter Sasdy, 'The Caves of Steel' was adapted for the anthology series *Story Parade*. The episode was so well received, further adaptations of Asimov's novels followed including the sequel 'The Naked Sun', which Cushing did not appear in.

Around November 1963 Cushing returned to Hammer to reprise his most famous role.

The Evil Of Frankenstein (1963) was not a sequel to *The Revenge Of Frankenstein*. Rather than follow continuity, Anthony Hinds' script went back to the beginning with a new story. A deal with Universal meant Hammer could use Boris Karloff's famous monster makeup (although Australian wrestler Kiwi Kingston added no subtlety to his mimed performance), but the result was a misstep.

Directed by Freddie Francis, who had previously helmed a couple of Hammer's low budget thrillers, this was his first horror film for the studio, but he had no sense of gothic melodrama. Cushing gave a lacklustre performance, further undermined by a weak supporting cast, laboured script and a threadbare production.

More satisfactory was *The Gorgon* (1964). Production began in December 1963 and was notable for reuniting Cushing, Christopher Lee and Terence Fisher. It was a partial return to form for all three, even if it wasn't their best effort. It was also a rare opportunity for the actors to swap roles, with Cushing making a superb villain and a miscast Lee, fitted with a grey wig and walrus moustache, playing the good guy. '*The Gorgon* was one of the very few films in which I played an evil man, although to be fair even this character, Dr Namaroff, had a secret reason for behaving as he did. Namaroff was not a neurotic raving villain, but a reserved, thinking man, shy, retiring, rather sad and without too much to say. Yet he had the power to collect and sustain around him an undiluted aura of menace.'

The Gorgon was the first of four films Cushing and Lee made together in rapid succession. Their next effort was their first for Amicus Productions. Founded by Milton Subotsky and Max J Rosenberg, Amicus became Hammer's main rival in British horror, specialising in the portmanteau movies, the first of which was *Dr Terror's House Of Horrors* (1964).

'*Dr Terror's House Of Horrors* actually gratified a long-standing ambition,' said Cushing. 'I had always loved trains, and in that picture my entire section took place in a railway carriage as I played the link man Dr Shreck, who dealt out the tarot cards of fate to his fellow travellers.' The unfortunate travellers were Christopher Lee, Roy Castle, Alan Freeman, Neil McCallum and a pre-stardom Donald Sutherland.

With his grey beard, heavy eyebrows and Germanic accent, the trilby-hatted Cushing gives a casually menacing performance that also brings out his sense of fun.

The third Cushing/Lee collaboration would be filmed abroad.

21: She (1965)

Cushing with John Richardson and Rosenda Monteros in *She*.

An adaptation of H Rider Haggard's famous novel *She: A History of Adventure*, called simply *She* (1965) was Hammer's most expensive production to date. 'It will be the biggest picture we've ever made,' said James Carreras, who had high hopes for the new film's success, 'it will have spectacle, colour, scope, and one of the most horrifically exciting climaxes since the disintegration of Dracula became a talking point five years ago.'

She marked Hammer's commercial peak, an event picture in the Hollywood tradition which Michael Carreras had always envisaged.

Carreras saw *She* as a golden opportunity to move away from low budget horror and into bigger features and he was convinced that it could be achieved. 'There's no doubt the future lies with big budget productions.'

Carreras' vision of mainstream acceptance proved a false one. According to Jonathan Rigby, '*She* was in line with Hammer's short-lived

21: She (1965)

belief that they should "think big" in future, a belief fostered by the ever-quixotic Michael Carreras. Despite being Hammer's most expensive film to date, *She* is the first instance of the company's reach visibly exceeding its grasp.'

She had been filmed many times, the most recent being in 1935 starring Helen Gahagan, Randolph Scott, Nigel Bruce and Helen Mack. '*She* was a natural choice for Hammer,' said Mark Miller, 'a studio that specialised in transplanting the terror and exotic sensuality of famous novels to the big screen. Although Hammer's scriptwriter David Chandler preserved most of the novel's plot points, he updated the period of *She* to 1918 and changed the location to Palestine after the war.'

She is notable for being the first Hammer film to be built around a female star. Following her legendary bikini turn in *Dr No* (1962), Andress landed the title role, her first with top billing, through her association with Kenneth Hyman of Seven Arts Productions and her husband John Derek. 'I did *She* because John wanted me to make some films. Seven Arts financed them. I had the guarantee that I would work in case those films did not make back the money. So, I guaranteed two films. The first one they put me in was *She*.' Andress wasn't keen on her character aging rapidly. 'It's something I'm not looking forward to. Growing old slowly is bad enough.'

It was Kenneth Hyman's idea to bring *She* to the big screen, and Michael Carreras was happy to be involved. Hyman's father Elliott was a close friend of James Carreras and being vice-president of the Seven Arts European production base, he had previously financed several Hammer projects for Stateside distribution. *She* would be Hyman's first official film collaboration with Hammer and securing Andress' services was a major step towards mainstream acceptance.

'I had been a house guest in the New Forest and found an old paperback which I read one evening,' Hyman said about his introduction to *She*. 'I walked into Tony Hinds' office with it and said, "I think I've found another Hammer movie," which he agreed with and acquired the rights, and it came into being.' With finance provided by Seven Arts and ABPC, Tony Hinds commissioned John Temple-Smith to write the screenplay.

Additional finance was required, but despite Andress' involvement, Universal, Joseph P Levin and American International Pictures turned the project down. Hinds passed the production chores to Michael Carreras, who obtained a generous £350,000 budget from MGM that included location work in Israel.

With Andress on board, the rest of the casting fell into place. For the pivotal role of Leo, Kenneth Hyman hired John Richardson. A former 20th Century Fox contract player. Richardson had made uncredited appearances in several British films, mainly for Rank Studios.

Richardson's first credited role was the lightweight comedy *Bachelor Of Arts* (1958), which featured Barbara Steele. They both travelled to Italy to star in Mario Bava's horror classic *Black Sunday* (1960). Steele was the first of several formidable leading ladies that Richardson worked with over the next decade.

After a leading role in *Pirates Of Tortuga* (1961), Richardson's career marked time until producer Ray Stark spotted him hanging around the Seven Arts office. Richardson's Greek adonis good looks made him perfect casting for Leo.

For the role of Ustane, the producers opted for Mexican actress Rosenda Monteros, who was best known as Petra in *The Magnificent Seven* (1960) and had filmed extensively in Mexico and Hollywood. Bernard Cribbins, a familiar face in British film and TV was cast as Job, and being a Hammer film, Peter Cushing, Christopher Lee and André Morell (as Ustane's father Haumeid) added familiarity to the proceedings.

Brought in as director was Robert Day. After a varied career as camera operator and cinematographer, Day made his directorial debut in *The Green Man* (1956). He dabbled in comedy with *Two-Way Stretch* (1960) and *The Rebel* (1961), directed several Tarzan films on location, the best being *Tarzan The Magnificent* (1961), and was no stranger to British horror after helming the Boris Karloff chillers *Grip Of The Strangler* (1958) and *Corridors Of Blood* (1958). Relocating to America in 1960, he became prolific on TV.

'My *Tarzan The Magnificent* may have something to do with being given *She*,' Day recalled. 'Producers see your shows and you get offers – they don't always tell you why you were hired. I personally cast many of the roles, including André and Bernard, but not Peter and Christopher. They were part of the Hammer package, and the film was planned around them. Michael Carreras and Tony Hinds were a great team. They knew what the people wanted to see. Sir James was the one who kept it all together. *She* was financed by MGM, and we spent six weeks in Israel.'

Day brought in David T Chandler to rewrite the script, and remove the story's more sadistic elements, making *She* a standard adventure film. '*She* was made on a bigger budget than the Hammer films produced at Bray,' said Mark Miller, 'but it is still a modestly budgeted movie.'

With Hammer's regular team working on *The Secret Of Blood Island* (1964), Michael Carreras reluctantly took on the producer's chores. Brought in as associate producer from his company Capricorn Productions was Ada Young, who had worked in various capacities for Hammer. 'Michael was highly amused by *She*, having a woman there,' she recalled, 'but we got on terribly well and we were friends socially as well. So, I learnt a lot from him, but he really didn't want to be a producer, you know. He really only wanted to be a director and writer. He hated being a producer, so he left me a lot to do. As associate producer I would mainly stand in for

21: She (1965)

Michael, who sometimes wasn't there, and make sure everything ran smoothly, and act as liaison between the director and he. I tried to stop things from happening before they happened. In a way I was a superior production manager but had more responsibility. You had the responsibility of the cast, and you were in the script meetings and so on.'

The scaled down version tells the story of three recently demobbed British soldiers, Major Horace L Holly (Peter Cushing), a former professor of archaeology at Cambridge, his handsome ward Leo Vincey (John Richardson) and their faithful, wisecracking manservant Job (Bernard Cribbins).

Spending a rowdy evening at a cheesy looking nightclub enjoying the delights of the dancing girls (one of whom was the former Queen of Iran), Our heroes are reluctant to return home after experiencing adventure and excitement in the Middle East during their war service.

As the evening progresses, Leo leaves the club with the beautiful Ustane (Rosenda Monteros) while his friends are flirting with the dancing girls, and only minutes before a brawl breaks out between Holly, Job and a group of British soldiers led by stuntman Nosher Powell. We never find out who wins the punch-up, but we get to see Cushing strutting his stuff on the dance floor; that alone makes *She* worth watching!

Leo is brought to a house where he meets the impossibly statuesque Ayesha (played by the impossibly statuesque Ursula Andress) who gives him a map that leads to the lost city of Kuma. Tempted by the prospect of fame and fortune, the trio embark on a perilous journey across the desert, unaware of the real dangers that lie within the city walls, which is ruled with a manicured iron fist by Ayesha, who, after discovering the secret of immortality, believes Leo to be the reincarnation of her lost love Kallikrates, the high priest of Isis who was murdered by Ayesha in a jealous rage centuries ago. Also on hand is Ayesha's faithful high priest Billali (Christopher Lee), who has his own not-so-faithful agenda.

Production began on 24 August 1964 in Southern Israel's Negev Desert. Because Bray was too small, interiors were shot at Elstree Studios where the sound stages were used for both Kuma's main hall and the nightclub. Except for Lee and Morell, who filmed their scenes at Elstree, the cast and crew arrived in the small coastal town of Eilat. Prior to their departure, Cushing and Cribbins went to Chessington Zoo to learn how to ride a camel in preparation for what was to come.

According to writer Wayne Kinsey, 'By six am the unit would be on their rugged 90-minute journey into the desert in an armada of army trucks loaded with equipment. By eight, everything was ready and director Robert Day could begin rehearsals. It was an arduous shoot for all in the baking heat of the Negev Desert. It was so hot the artists didn't visibly perspire so make-up had to apply a fine spray of moisture to their faces to simulate it. Miss Andress was merely on hand to keep the press and photographers happy.'

Author John Doran who accompanied the crew to the Negev Desert, shared his own travelling experiences during filming. 'We arrived at the first location after a drive of 90 hair-raising minutes. The one road out of Eilat – little more than a narrow strip of tar over the undulating sand – provided the Israeli drivers with great sport. Whenever they met a truck coming in the opposite direction, the drive developed into a "chicken" run, with the first one off the road a "sissy".'

Doran also experienced a frightening incident during a shooting break. 'It occurred when one of the technicians put up a huge umbrella and a large black scorpion fell to the ground. Immediately it froze – its venomous tail raised to strike. A heavy Israeli boot was raised and fell, and the threat was removed. "No need to worry about the black scorpions," said the local. "Their sting only makes you very bad. It's the yellow one you watch out for. If they sting – you dead!" It was a typical day's outing and all for the sake of about three minutes of film.'

Cushing remembered how tense the atmosphere was while shooting. 'We were in Israel during a very heavy political climate. We had to start very early in the morning, starting at four am, and work was impossible in the afternoon as the heat was unbearable. While we were in the Danago Desert, the Arab sector was quite near, and they just sat there with their machine guns in their laps. In the meantime, we were popping off our prop guns hoping we would not be attacked. We were lucky they seemed to be enjoying us; it was quite an exciting period.'

'We did have problems with explosives and camels,' said Robert Day, 'Peter had more problems with his camel than I can count!'

'I had to ride a camel,' recalled Cushing. 'Now that is a mode of transport I do not recommend to the uninitiated, especially when that capricious quadruped takes into its mulish head to sit down and/or get up. If you are ever in contact with one, be warned – get nowhere near its breath!'

In addition to the intense heat, John Richardson contracted dysentery. 'Unfortunately, the water was contaminated,' said Cushing, 'and John was laid up for several days with a bout of gyppy tummy. Production had to be held up until he was fit again, and Ursula, a kind lady with deep maternal instincts nursed him back to health.'

Bernard Cribbins suffered an awful injury during filming. According to Robert Day, 'We had a scene where they were being ambushed by these guys on the camels. The special effects man was an Israeli explosives expert. He'd wired some of the bullet-shots-in-the-sand explosives wrong, and Bernard was over this bunch of them when they were detonated. It peppered his behind. We had to rush him to the hospital. This Israeli guy was so distraught and upset with it all that he tried to pull all his wires out and rewire them. The damned thing went off again and blew one of his fingers off. I rushed over to him, and he screamed, "Just stay away from me!" and picked up his finger and stuck it back on! Then we rushed him off to hospital. When I went to see him that evening, he couldn't apologise enough. Anyway, they saved his finger – stitched it back on. It was a gory deal.'

Without a word of complaint, Cribbins was soon back to work. 'He was sent to hospital for treatment,' said Cushing, 'but the next day he insisted on returning to work, not wishing to delay filming again, manfully struggling on in considerable pain, yet managing to keep us all amused with his irrepressible sense of fun. "It could have been worse," he philosophised, "if I'd been the other way down, I might have been blinded." He smiled ironically when he read a critique after the film was shown, which commented, "What a pity Mr Cribbins tried to get laughs by adopting a funny walk."'

Throughout filming, the cast and crew were aware of the crossfire that could occur at any time between Israeli and Jordanian forces. 'It was nerve wracking, but fun,' said Robert Day.

John Doran enjoyed his time with Cushing. 'Standing behind the camera, Bob Day acted each of the parts being played before him; grunting and groaning when things didn't go according to plan, enthusing when it went as planned. Peter Cushing sat in the shade and talked. It is a measure of his ability, that so gentle a man can chill the blood with performances in the horror films with which his name is synonymous. A highly intelligent man, Peter talked about the autobiography he had thoughts of writing, a work for which Bernard Cribbins had suggested the title *I'm All Right Drac!*'

'Peter Cushing is a wonderful man,' said Day, 'and a pleasure to work with. I was struck by his sincerity. He puts himself completely into a role and gets away with the most melodramatic lines because he probably believes them himself.'

Back in England, Hammer's editor Eric Boyd-Perkins was kept informed of events in Israel. 'We stayed back at Elstree. As far as I remember they sent over the film each day and we would run the dailies and they would see it when they got back. We would look at it and send out reports of how it was and if anything extra was needed. These days its different; they have bigger budgets and people order double prints and you keep one print back and send one print away, whereas with Hammer, that wouldn't be in their budget to do that. We would start cutting it while they were away.'

After the real-life action and adventure of the Negev Desert, the crew returned to Elstree Studios to complete the interior shooting.

After living for some time in Switzerland, Christopher Lee returned home. '*She* was Lee's first film since he, Gitte and Christina had moved back to England from Switzerland after a bout of homesickness,' said Mark Miller. 'They purchased the London flat that is still their home today, and a neighbour, until his death in 1969, was Lee's friend Boris Karloff.'

Despite her Bond success, Ursula Andress was still an inexperienced actress. 'Ursula Andress had to do more acting in *She* than was required in *Dr No*,' said Day. 'She's a great presence but had little experience. I really had to work with her. It wasn't easy!' Andress' strong Swiss-German accent was dubbed by Nikki van der Zyl, who had previously re-voiced her in *Dr No*.

'I was forced to do *She*,' Andress admits with some embarrassment. 'It was a very cheap Hammer film and the only thing I adored was the costumes. I was lucky to look good in it because they photographed me so beautifully.'

Andress' death scene provided a challenge for makeup artist Roy Ashton. 'You see, the problem with most sequences of this sort is that during the process of aging the face wastes away. The skin becomes very fine, the bones become pronounced, and the hair thins extensively. Instead of diminishing the features, the makeup artist has to build up what was already there, fattening and rounding of the face to such a degree that the result is often, I think, implausible. If you ever have the misfortune to actually see a real corpse in an advanced state of decomposition, you'll see that it is just putrescent skin and bone.'

Ashton planned Ayesha's demise by using several women instead of Andress. 'I suggested four or five women of successive ages, ending up with an old woman without any teeth. Unfortunately, when the time came, they only provided me with one old dear, upon whom I had to apply the pieces needed to make her look far in excess of her advanced years, but she had a prominent nose and features totally dissimilar to Ursula's.'

'She couldn't bear the sight of herself,' Ada Young said of the aging process Andress had to endure. 'She burst into tears and all her makeup was ruined. I was called in because she wouldn't have it done, but finally she did.'

She wrapped on 17 October, with post-production work completed by editors James Needs and Eric Boyd-Perkins, and sound editor James Groom. 'Robert Day used to view the scenes as I completed them,' said Boyd-Perkins, 'but didn't get involved an awful lot. On those sort of schedules, the directors, apart from Seth Holt, wouldn't be able to have too much influence, because there wasn't time on the schedule. If you produced something good that was acceptable, you didn't have time to play around with it.'

Hammer then launched a huge publicity campaign with posters

21: She (1965)

promoting Andress as 'The World's Most Beautiful Woman', which flattered and embarrassed the actress. 'I don't say myself that I'm the most beautiful girl in the world. I never have, but I know I'm not ugly.'

She went into the cinemas on 18 April 1965, and for added publicity, the film's release coincided with Andress posing nude for *Playboy Magazine*. The photos were taken by John Derek, who by that time had separated from the actress, divorcing her the following year. Free from her husband's obligations, Andress gave Hammer's proposed sequel *The Vengeance Of She* (1968) a wide berth.

The Stateside release on 1 September 1965 was marked by a triple-page advertisement in the American trade press with MGM boasting that '*She* is the biggest box office news in England since *Goldfinger* (1964)!'

She is not the epic movie that Michael Carreras envisaged. Despite the box office success, it never achieved mainstream respectability.

Lacking the Cecil B DeMille style budget, the skimpy studio interiors gives *She* a claustrophobic look that fails to live up to the location work. The film cries out for a cast of thousands and massive outdoor sets, not unlike the epic *Cleopatra* (1963): Elizabeth Taylor's famous entrance into Rome shows the awesome sense of power that *She* desperately lacks.

The main hall of Ayesha's palace looks like a function room, and Kuma's population consists of a small detachment of troops, an equal number of Amahagger slaves, three guys blowing trumpets on top of what looks like a large fireplace, a couple of well-oiled musclemen bodyguards and two handmaidens who follow Ayesha. Not exactly a cast of thousands!

She also lacks action. The final punch-up between Ayesha's soldiers and her rebellious slaves isn't the Battle of the Alamo, although the swordplay between Leo and Billali is effective. The tedious native dancing could have been removed.

Looking every inch the Queen of Kuma, Ursula Andress is genuinely scary, especially when her beautiful face hardens with sadistic glee while dishing out brutal punishments to her slaves and reeling with jealousy when she catches Leo and Ustane together. Sadly, her acting abilities cannot match her screen presence.

Richardson on the other hand gives a wooden performance. 'John Richardson was a great looking guy,' said Day, 'and a nice one, but wasn't much of an actor. Anyway, most of his scenes were with Peter, and he didn't stand a chance!'

Despite their stiff performances, Andress and Richardson are a stunning couple who work well together and do not embarrass the picture.

What gives *She* its true centre are the excellent performances from Peter Cushing and Bernard Cribbins.

Unlike the ugly, Jewish misogynist in Haggard's novel, Cushing's Holly is a handsome, bearded charmer, a bit of a rogue with an eye for the young ladies and a sense of adventure in his veins, a forerunner to Indiana Jones. Unlike Harrison Ford's iconic archaeologist, Holly is motivated by the glory and wealth he would get for discovering the lost city of Kuma.

'*She* gives Cushing the chance for some traditional derring-do in the sort of entertainment he adored,' said David Miller, 'In this unashamed family film, he proves once more that he could enliven any genre, and that he was particularly suited to action and adventure.'

Holly also has a serious side. As Leo's protective mentor, he reluctantly supports his ward's decision to become immortal, but after losing Leo to Ayesha, the desire for glory, wealth and a possible knighthood evaporates. 'All my life I've dreamed of finding a city such as this,' he laments. 'And now that I have, I'd like to see it destroyed and all it stands for.' With his friend beyond his reach, fame and fortune is not important. It is a moving journey of self-discovery for Holly who would rather have Leo back.

Holly is equally insightful of Billali's intentions, which are not obvious on screen. This is represented by an excellent scene between Cushing and Lee. Suspicious of Billali's motives in bringing Leo to Kuma, Holly questions the high priest's devotion to Ayesha. 'No one was born to be a vassal of another,' he remarks. 'You know and feel this too. I've seen it in your eyes. Your body does her bidding, but your spirit cries out to be free. Is that not true?'

'Each man has his own destiny to fulfil,' replies Billali, but Holly is unconvinced. 'And yours I suppose is to fill the next alcove. I can't believe you're such a fool, Billali,' to which the high priest responds with, 'No Mr Holly. I am not such a fool.' The scene doesn't advance the story, but it is brilliantly played by Cushing and Lee; their onscreen chemistry remains as magnetic as ever.

Lee's Billali is far from the white bearded, benevolent figure of Haggard's novel. The dark goateed figure of the film demonstrates his stomach crawling loyalty to Ayesha but has no intention of joining the other high priests in their respective mummified alcoves upon his death. Craving immortality for himself, he engineers his own destiny, regardless of what Ayesha wants.

Holly sees immortality in the form of fame and fortune, and Leo desires it out of love for Ayesha, but Billali wants it for his own ends. It was probably his idea to bring Leo to Ayesha and keep him alive while remaining in Ayesha's good books until the time is right. He also allows Ustane to remain in the city. 'He is a man of soul and conscience,' he tells Ayesha, knowing Leo's 20th Century logic may prevent him entering the flame. Lee invests Billali with a scheming, deep-rooted determination that culminates in the climactic sword fight. The part isn't a great stretch for Lee, but it is another colourful villain to add to his impressive portfolio of screen heavies. His eventual death (a spear in the back from Ayesha) and his final crawl towards the flame before expiring is melodramatic stuff, but nonetheless brilliantly conveyed by Lee.

Providing a humorous presence throughout, Bernard Cribbins' Job is closer to the novel, fiercely loyal to Holly and Leo, but always speaking his mind when necessary. He's not so much an employee but an equal partner in their adventures, and reliable when needed. Cushing and Cribbins form a nice double-act and the chemistry between the actors is so humorously heartwarming, one wishes for further adventures starring Holly and Job.

It is Rosenda Monteros who gives *She* real heart and soul, with a deeply moving performance. Monteros invests Ustane with an emotional fragility, making her off-screen demise more heart-breaking. She is the antithesis of Ayesha, not interested in power, unselfishly devoted to Leo and even accepting his desire for Ayesha. Monteros bestows a warmth that captures her deep sadness.

'André Morell was another marvellous actor,' said Robert Day, 'he was able to go back and forth between big and small films. Like Peter Cushing, he came from a school of acting with too few students today. When an actor of Morell's quality has seventh billing, it speaks well of any film.' Morell has presence, but it's difficult to evaluate his performance because he was revoiced by Egyptian actor George Pastell.

She received mixed reviews with *Variety* staying, 'Production values save the day, with crowd scenes and palace pomp worthy of far more expensive films,' further stating that the film, 'adds colour and widescreen to special effect, all of which help overcome a basic plot no film scripter has licked. Director Robert Day's overall excellent work brings out heretofore unknown depths in Miss Andress' acting.'

Kinematograph Weekly felt that a 'little too long, perhaps, is spent on the early trek across the desert, but once that has been perilously accomplished, events keep excitingly on the boil and the romantic interludes between Leo and Ustane and Ayesha fit naturally without slowing the pace. Ursula Andress certainly has the physical attributes for the title role, and those tried and trusty veterans, Peter Cushing and Christopher Lee, do their stuff as Holly and Billali respectively. Rosenda Monteros is a charming Ustane.'

The New York Daily News wasn't overly impressed, calling the film, 'Ridiculously old fashioned,' but adds, 'Cushing is by far the best for his cynical attitude towards this nonsense.' *Time Magazine* felt, '*She* is for children, television addicts and those who relish cinema clichés.' *The Monthly Film Bulletin* found it, 'a flat and uninspired affair,' while Alan Frank thought the film was, 'banal and slow, only the special effects keep the whole movie from sliding into tedium.'

Paul Taylor's *Time Out* review was equally unimpressed. 'Rider

Haggard's *She* emerges predictably in this low rent exotica from Hammer as She-Who-Must-Be-Ogled, and the olde fashioned hunt-for-lost-city formula doesn't even cut it as camp. At least the setting returned to warmer climes from the Arctic setting of the 1935 version, no doubt to explain Andress' undress.'

The New York Times was also unforgiving. 'It lacks style, sophistication, humour, sense and, above all, a reason for being, since it isn't even as good (excepting that it is in colour) as the last remake with Helen Gahagan in 1935. John Richardson gives a very weak imitation of Peter O'Toole in a famous desert film, and Peter Cushing and Bernard Cribbins are foolish as his veddy English friends. David Chantler's screenplay and the direction of Robert Day are as fustian as such can be.'

Films and Filming's Raymond Durgant gives the most negative of reviews. 'Robert Day's rather flat direction never sparks off the exotic feeling the film needs. He gets some lively movements from camels in the early scenes, but Cushing hardly gets into his part. Bernard Cribbins looks very out of place in the dated comic, ever faithful valet, and we couldn't care less whether the anonymous black slaves get their freedom or not. Little Ustane is played with a nice, tender vitality, and Ursula Andress queens it nicely with her eerie, bony, sumptuous face and sad voice. All in all, *She* is too gawdy and odd a film to be depressing, but it falls sadly below the level of (Terence) Fisher's *Dracula* or (Don) Chaffey's *Jason And The Argonauts*.'

While *She* could have been a better film, there's plenty to enjoy thanks to some spirited scenes, good performances and competent direction. It may not be a Hammer classic, but it is an entertaining one.

She also marked the commercial peak in Peter Cushing's film career. With Helen's health restricting oversea excursions, he remained busy making homegrown British horror. The output at this time had gone down market, and meeting the demands of his wife's medical bills, he took on work that was beneath his talents.

22: Marking Time In Blighty

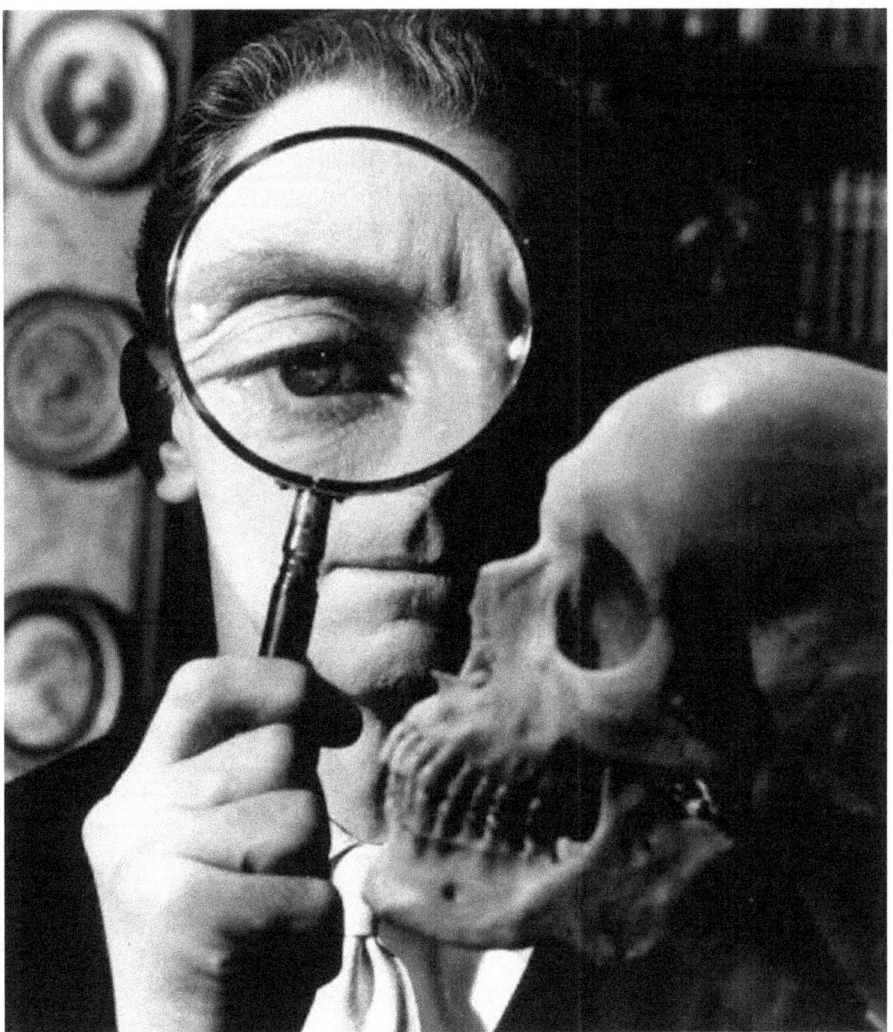

Cushing with friend in *The Skull*.

Based on Robert Bloch's short story, *The Skull* is regarded as a horror classic thanks to Freddie Francis' stylish directorial touches that overcome Milton Subotsky's plodding script. Cushing plays Christopher Maitland, a wealthy collector of occult literature and relics, who falls under the spell of the skull of the Marquis de Sade.

The Skull boasts an exceptional cast playing small roles – Patrick Wymark, Jill Bennett, Nigel Green, Michael Gough, Patrick Magee, Peter Woodthorpe – and Christopher Lee receives guest star billing, but despite its reputation, the film is style over content, saved by Cushing's excellent performance.

Far more satisfactory is *Dr Who And The Daleks* (1965). Produced by Milton Subotsky at Amicus (called AARU on release), it was a big screen adaptation of the popular BBC science fiction series starring William Hartnell as the Doctor.

Subotsky's script demystified the lead character, making him an elderly human scientist called Doctor Who, living with his two granddaughters, played by Jennie Linden (Barbara) and Roberta Tovey (Susan).

'The difficulty with playing Doctor Who,' said Cushing, 'was that one couldn't expect everyone in the world to know about him and his TARDIS and the television series. So, we decided to play him simply as a professor who invented this machine that travels through time and space and I created my own character out of that idea, realizing that a lot of people in Britain might be disappointed. Actually, most people weren't.'

Shot at Shepperton Studios, *Dr Who And The Daleks* did well at the box office. Gordon Flemyng's direction is solid, the performances transcend the production, and the Daleks remain the stuff of nightmares. Cushing makes an amusing Doctor Who, with his *Dr Terror* co-star Roy Castle providing the comic relief as Barbara's boyfriend, Ian.

Daleks' Invasion Earth 2150 A.D. (1966) is the better film, benefitting from a bigger budget and location shooting in London. Due to a bout of bronchitis, Cushing is a lot less eccentric. He agreed to reprise the role on the condition that Roberta Tovey returned as his granddaughter Susan. Jill Curzon (as the Doctor's niece Louise) replaced Jennie Linden.

Daleks' Invasion Earth 2150 A.D. boasts superior special effects, an excellent Dalek spaceship, a solid plot and convincing interiors. The locations add realism and there's a stronger supporting cast of Andrew Keir, Ray Brooks, Godfrey Quigley, Philip Madoc and Sheila Steafel. Playing the comic relief this time is Bernard Cribbins. Around the time of their collaboration making the film, Cushing appeared on a one-off BBC Variety Show fronted by Cribbins and called *Cribbins* (1965).

Daleks' Invasion Earth 2150 A.D. didn't repeat the success of the first film and plans for further films were scrapped. The movies still maintain a cult following.

In between the *Doctor Who* films, Cushing returned to the stage with a revival of Ben Travers' haunted house farce *Thark*. Directed by Ray Cooney, *Thark* had a short run at the recently opened Yvonne Arnaud Theatre in Guildford with Cushing playing Benbow and Alec McCowan as Gamble. Kathleen Harrison and Cushing's *Doctor Who* co-star Jennie

Linden made up the supporting cast. The play then transferred to the Garrick Theatre in London.

Cushing's performance was greeted with enthusiasm from Harold Hobson of *The Sunday Times* who wrote, 'It was a considerable pleasure to see Peter Cushing as the middle-aged gentleman with roving eyes.' Hobson rounded his review off with a reference to Christopher Lee. 'If only Mr Lee had emerged from the grandfather clock on that ominous staircase, my pleasure would have been perfect. What am I saying? It was perfect!'

Following a TV role in 'Monica', for the anthology series *30 Minute Theatre*, Cushing returned to films with *Island Of Terror* (1966), a horror/science fiction hybrid with monsters that wouldn't have looked out of place in *Doctor Who*. It also reunited him with Terence Fisher, who admitted, 'I detest most science fiction films. The future holds no interest to me.'

The action takes place on a remote island off the coast of Ireland as the inhabitants protect themselves from an invading force of blob-like thingys accidentally created by an ill-fated scientific research team based on the island. It might have worked better if the creatures had been humanoid, but the creatures on screen were unconvincing, even for 1966.

Fisher effectively builds up the claustrophobic tension and the first-rate cast of Cushing, Edward Judd, Carole Gray, Eddie Byrnes, Niall McGinnis and Sam Kydd add gravitas. One of the strengths about many low budget British chillers was the ability to bring together a group of solid actors who couldn't give a bad performance if they tried.

It's refreshing to see Cushing playing a modern scientist. He gives a good, humoured performance filled with several amusing lines, the most memorable coming when his Dr Stanley, after having his arm hacked off with an axe by Edward Judd's Dr West, sardonically tells his colleague, 'Watch it boy, or I'll sue you for malpractice!'

Island Of Terror was shot at Pinewood Studios, and from then on, Cushing's output remained entrenched in British made chillers. 'The horror boom was already on the wane in terms of quality,' said writer Bruce Lanier Wright, 'and the seeds of its economic failure were present as well, although continuing strength at the box office helped disguise that fact for a while.'

This was the time that Cushing should have stepped away from British horror and worked more in international ventures which many of his colleagues were doing in the late sixties. Helen's declining health was another major factor in his reluctance to work abroad. Being unable to travel, it was a case of taking on whatever homegrown work was available to pay the medical bills.

Returning to Hammer, Cushing reunited with Terence Fisher for

Frankenstein Created Woman (1967), which is a vast improvement on *The Evil Of Frankenstein*. The Baron is lodging at the home of muddle-headed local physician Dr Hertz (Thorley Walters) in what looks like Mittel-Europe's most underpopulated village. Unlike the previous efforts, Frankenstein is not on the run from the authorities. Residing under his own name, the locals tolerate his presence even if he is still viewed with suspicion.

Assisting Frankenstein and Dr Hertz in their experiments in metaphysics is young Hans (Robert Morris), the son of a convicted murderer. He is in love with Christina (Susan Denburg), the local innkeeper's disfigured daughter. Christina is also taunted by three arrogant upper-class goons (played with relish by Peter Blythe, Barry Warren and Derek Fowlds) who push their luck too far and end up getting clobbered by Hans.

Shortly after closing time, the aristocratic thugs break into the inn to resume their binge drinking and beat Christina's father to death. When Hans is framed and executed, the devastated Christina takes her own life. Frankenstein then transfers Hans' soul into Christina's body. After intense surgery, Christina returns to life. Now very beautiful, she has no memory of her past life.

Hans' spirit takes hold of Christina, turning her into a sexually alluring predator who stalks and kills the toffs. Her work completed and despite pleas from Frankenstein, the confused girl takes her life a second time.

Frankenstein Created Woman explores social class represented by the moronic toffs at the top, Dr Hertz being the middle order, and Hans and Christina as the lowly misfits, with Frankenstein being the glue that holds it together. Every character is flawed, including the romantic leads, which makes a nice change from the bland juveniles in previous Hammer films. Hans doesn't do himself any favours with his short temper and lack of respect towards authority.

Delivering an impeccable performance, Cushing moves away from the cold, flamboyant figure of the first two films. Older and mellower, he doesn't murder anyone but still has a negative impact on those around him. The narcissism and arrogance remain intact. Frankenstein's lack of humanity is reflected by his unsympathetic attitude towards Christina. Now that she's been created, he doesn't know what to do with her other than have her cook his breakfast.

Frankenstein becomes a more peripheral figure during the film's second half as Christina takes centre stage with her murderous antics, all this brilliantly conveyed by a tragic performance from Susan Denburg.

Frankenstein Created Woman is an uneven affair. Anthony Hinds' script is full of plot holes and the low budget shows. These quibbles aside, it is an enjoyable effort. Terence Fisher brings back the fairy-tale element, which would soon disappear when Hammer moved from Bray to Elstree.

Cushing returned to Amicus for his second anthology chiller *Torture Garden* (1967), adapted by Robert Bloch from four of his quirky short stories.

Torture Garden takes place in a creepy fairground attraction, where unsuspecting customers are told their fortunes by a bizarre mannequin that represents Atropus, the Goddess of Destiny. Overseeing it all is Dr Diablo, played with creepy relish by Burgess Meredith.

With Bloch completing the script, Max Rosenberg approached Columbia to bankroll the project. Shooting began at Shepperton Studios in November 1966 with Freddie Francis returning as director.

Torture Garden was intended as a vehicle for Peter Cushing and Christopher Lee, but Columbia was doubtful that it would work. 'Away from Hammer,' said writer and critic Alan Bryce, 'neither were punching their box office weight, and Columbia decreed that two American names were needed and that the film should be as Anglicized as Amicus' previous effort had been.'

Dr Diablo was written with Cushing in mind, but rather than repeat his Dr Schreck character from *Dr Terror's House Of Horrors* in a different setting, he was replaced by Meredith. Wishing to retain Cushing's services, Subotsky cast him in the fourth story, 'The Man Who Collected Poe'. Lee was due to play opposite Cushing but pressure from Columbia prompted the actor to be replaced by Jack Palance.

Robert Bloch had great admiration for Cushing. 'I've had the pleasure of watching a live performance by Peter Cushing in a West End theatre where he played the lead in a revival of *Thark*, but never had the privilege of meeting him. What little I have known about Mr Cushing as a private person was related to me by Christopher Lee, who regarded him as a veritable candidate for a sainthood. From what he's told me, I've no doubt that Mr Cushing deserves such a posthumous nomination.'

Despite good reviews and an admirer in Martin Scorsese, *Torture Garden* is a weak effort that did not repeat the success of *Dr Terror's House of Horrors*. The first story, 'Enoch', works reasonably well, but the middle tales, 'Terror Over Hollywood' and 'Mr Steinway', are complete duds.

'The Man Who Collected Poe' is the most effective final tale, and one that makes the most of the film's modest budget. Palance plays Ronald Wyatt, a collector of Edgar Allan Poe memorabilia who meets another obsessive bibliophile in the shape of Cushing's Lancelot Canning. Canning invites Wyatt to his Maryland home which is completely dedicated to the author.

The collectors get drunk, and Canning takes Wyatt to a locked room where he shows him unpublished work written on modern paper. As it turns out, Canning is an occultist who made a pact with Satan to bring Poe (Hedger Wallace) back to life so he can write further stories and poems.

Things turn nasty when Cushing gets killed in a no-holds-barred fight with Jack Palance. Wyatt then agrees to swap places with Poe as Canning's house goes up in flames.

'The Man Who Collected Poe' is an excellent short film, Bill Constable's production design creates the right Poe atmosphere and Cushing and Palance give topflight performances.

Cushing enjoyed working with Palance. 'I was the title character, Lancelot Canning, and Jack was the man who came to see my extraordinary collection, which included Poe himself in a back room. We were involved in a fight and after one scene, Jack, who is one of the strongest men I have ever met, asked if he had hurt me. I said no, and he replied that he certainly thought he had by my expression! I was quite pleased at the compliment because I could only add, "Oh, I was just acting."'

Cushing's next film cast him alongside Joseph Cotton and Martha Hyer in the espionage thriller *Some May Live* (1966). Set in Saigon during the early days of the Vietnam War, location work was confined to Twickenham Studios. This turgid, low budget effort has uninspired direction from Vernon Sewell and a boring central performance by Joseph Cotton.

Cushing and Martha Hyer rise about the muddled premise, cheap sets and stereotypical oriental characters to give decent performances, but *Some May Live* didn't advance the careers of anyone involved.

Cushing joined Christopher Lee and Terence Fisher in an adaptation of John Lymington's 1959 science fiction novel, *Night Of The Big Heat* (1967). A small island off the English coast is experiencing a record heatwave during the winter months. The heat is causing problems among the locals who spend their time propping up the bar at the local hotel run by Patrick Allen and his real-life wife Sarah Lawson. Things are further complicated by the arrival of Allen's former mistress (Jane Merrow) and a bad-tempered scientist (Christopher Lee), who suspects there's something far more sinister about the heatwave.

Receiving special guest billing as local GP Dr Stone, Cushing also props up the bar and looks concerned as he constantly dabs his forehead with a damp cloth. 'One can't help wondering why he doesn't remove his sweat-stained jacket in the stifling heat,' observed Deborah Del Vecchio.

The real weather didn't live up to the movie's sweltering heat when it was shot at Pinewood during a freezing February 1967, 'We wanted the illusion of 115 degrees Fahrenheit,' recalled Christopher Lee, 'so Peter, Patrick Allen and I worked in shirtsleeves, and the girls had bikinis. That was fine, except that it was in the middle of the night in winter. To foster the impression of sweat we were drenched in glycerine.'

The aliens were as silly as the ones in *Island Of Terror*. 'It dealt with the invasion of Earth by alien protoplasm,' Lee added. 'Looking like fried eggs, they ruined the climax.'

The claustrophobic atmosphere works well, and there are a few suspenseful moments, but otherwise, the film lights no fires. The cast go through the motions and the aliens raise a few laughs, which goes to show that when it comes to low budget British science fiction, extra-terrestrials work better off camera.

Jane Merrow had fond feelings of working with Cushing on the film. 'Peter just took a very modest position, got on with it, and was a total gentleman from top to bottom.'

Following completion of *Night Of The Big Heat*, Cushing didn't work for four months. His next assignment was for television in an episode of *The Avengers*.

'The Return of the Cybernauts' was a sequel to an episode featuring Michael Gough as a mad scientist who created an army of robots for evil purposes, only to be thwarted by John Steed (Patrick MacNee) and Emma Peel (Diana Rigg).

Peter Cushing plays Gough's vengeful brother Paul Beresford. Beresford is an art expert, a likeable villain who happily flirts with Mrs Peel, to Steed's jealous reaction. But behind the bonhomie, Beresford has a sadistic streak when he uses a mind controlling device to turn Mrs Peel into a human cybernaut to exact revenge – he fails of course!

'The Return of the Cybernauts' is a fun episode, and Cushing is back on form after his previous, lacklustre movies. 'Peter was a delight to direct,' said the show's creator Brian Clemens, 'totally trusting our expertise.'

MacNee and Cushing had become lifelong friends when they first worked together on Robert Helpmann's production of *The Wedding Ring*. 'Peter Cushing was the first glamorous actor I had ever met. He was extremely nice, had this wonderful John Barrymore profile. He'd been in Hollywood, he'd been Carole Lombard's leading man, he'd come back to England, he'd met Olivier, he'd been with him on his wonderful tours, he'd played Osric in the film of *Hamlet*. And he was the most quiet, reserved man I ever met. From Manchester he would walk up the hills outside Cheshire and paint. He was a dear sweet, giving and humorous man.'

Cushing's next film, shot at Isleworth Studios for Titan Films, marked a depressing direction British horror took during the sixties. According to Jonathan Rigby, '*Corruption* (1968) is the film many Peter Cushing fans would prefer to ignore. In it, Cushing plays a reluctant Jack the Ripper whose blood-spattered career points forward to the more disreputable strain of British horror which would emerge in the 1970s. It could even be seen as a distant ancestor of the slasher film which became depressingly popular in the early 1980s. And yet Cushing is excellent in it.'

Director, Robert Hartford-Davis wanted to push the boundaries of British horror, but the result here is nasty exploitation, not helped by Columbia using the ad line that '*Corruption* is not a woman's picture', when the film got its American release. Alan Frank found it, 'A clinically nasty exploitation movie, derivative and gory, and made with a complete absence of style,' further adding that, 'the film is totally unworthy of Cushing's talents.'

Despite giving a thoroughly gripping performance, Cushing wasn't happy with the film. 'It was gratuitously violent, fearfully sick. But it was a good script which just goes to show how important presentation is.' He plays eminent surgeon Sir John Rowan who goes to a wild psychedelic party with his young model fiancée (Sue Lloyd, whose eye rolling nuttiness acts Cushing off the screen). When an accident leaves her permanently scarred, he stops at nothing to restore her beauty, murdering young women for their pituitary glands. The results being short-lived, it's only a matter of time before the couple go completely bonkers.

Cushing felt that *Corruption*, 'could have been made a little more subtle.' But subtlety is not one of Robert Hartford-Davis's strong points as he directs like a bull in a china shop. Seeing Cushing groping his female victims before slicing them up makes uncomfortable viewing. That said, *Corruption* was a commercial success

Cushing's next picture was his first for Tony Tenser's Tigon Productions. *The Blood Beast Terror* (1968) was originally entitled *The Horrors Of Frankenstein*, until a quiet word from James Carreras changed all that despite Mary Shelley's novel being in the public domain

Assigned to direct was Vernon Sewell, who liked the script. 'It was by a good friend of mine, Peter Bryan, and I thought it was very clever. I thought it would be good fun. I said to Tony, if Peter Cushing was in it, I'd do it.'

A less enthusiastic Cushing often regarded *The Blood Beast Terror* as the worst film he ever made, which is a little unfair when compared to the ghastliness of *Corruption*, it actually marks a quaint return to Hammer-style heroics and period costume.

As Scotland Yard detective Inspector Quennell, Cushing plays a policeman for the only time in his career, although the character has a distinctly Holmesian bent. The Holmes association was strengthened further by another link to his Hollywood days. Cast as Professor Mallinger was the screen's greatest Sherlock, Basil Rathbone.

Rathbone received an offer from the BBC to play Sherlock Holmes in a radio series. His return to London also coincided with Tenser offering him *The Blood Beast Terror*. Being a British-made period chiller, the film suited his Shakespearian stage presence. Conscious of script changes when he signed up in July 1967, and ever the perfectionist, Rathbone said of his preparations, 'I like to get the part under my belt, as I find it difficult to unlearn.' His enthusiasm for the project may have had a lot to do with the prospect of working alongside Cushing.

Sadly, this historic teaming never happened. After being given the all-clear by his doctor to travel, Rathbone suffered a fatal heart attack two weeks before production began. Robert Flemyng stepped in at the last minute.

Now increasingly tired of the genre, Cushing became surprisingly difficult on the set. If he wasn't happy about something, he made his feelings known. Aware of how versatile Cushing was in developing a character, Sewell left him to his own devices, until one day early in the shoot.

According to Sewell, 'Peter and I hadn't discussed the film or the script at all, which I had thought unusual: he was a very professional actor. Then after a day Peter came up to me and he obviously wasn't happy. He said, "I think this is perhaps the worst film I've ever made." I was quite flattered really.' Tenser was also aware of Cushing's frustration with the script and allowed him to rewrite his dialogue.

Cushing's script rewrites added depth to Roy Hudd's memorable cameo as a sardonic morgue attendant. 'I was called for makeup,' recalled Hudd, 'and there, in the next chair, was the great man himself. "Good morning," he said, "I'm Peter Cushing," as if I didn't know. "Have you seen the script?" he asked. "Not very good, is it?" "Well," I blustered. "No, we can do better than that." "Can we? How can we make it funnier?" asked the great man. That was the start. Together we rejigged the whole two scenes.' Their collaboration was enough for Hudd to steal the acting honours.

The Blood Beast Terror did well at the box office especially in America, and despite Cushing's protestations, it's certainly not his worst movie.

During the 1968 British Film Academy Awards, master of ceremonies Kenneth More asked Cushing what he was up to. 'I'm going to play Sherlock Holmes,' he replied. 'A series for television. Will you come and be Watson.' More was happy to oblige.

The series in question was actually the second Holmes series from the BBC. They had already made a pilot (under the series title *Detective*, 'The Speckled Band') and a first series (called *Sherlock Holmes*) both starring Douglas Wilmer as Holmes and with Nigel Stock as Watson.

For the second series, *Sir Arthur Conan Doyle's Sherlock Holmes*, Nigel Stock repeated his role, it was to be shot in colour, and also included location work. There was talk of Peter Ustinov, Orson Welles, George Sanders and even Sean Connery being guest stars. For Cushing, who desperately wanted to return to television, the series became a baptism of fire that drove him back to the horror genre.

Douglas Wilmer declined the second series because of the restricted rehearsal period. 'Poor Peter Cushing unwisely accepted,' he lamented. 'He was, of course unaware of the consequences into which he was to find himself, and when he did, coupled with the insecurity of a beggarly ten-day rehearsal, the results were not good.' With hindsight, Cushing should have got in touch with Wilmer beforehand.

'I think Peter wanted to raise his profile a bit,' recalled the show's script editor Donald Tosh. 'He had done some films which he thought were not tremendously wise choices. This was a prestige project, back at the BBC, back on his old ground. But it had changed beyond recognition. And I don't think he knew he was second choice to Douglas Wilmer, which would have upset him if he had known.'

Cushing quickly got into shape exercising on Whitstable Beach and making sure costumes and pipes perfectly matched the Conan Doyle character and the Sidney Paget drawings. His commitment was astounding with all the scripts memorised before the rehearsals were completed.

The series was fraught with budgetary and technical difficulties. The limited rehearsal and chaotic production schedule was further undermined by Helen's absence, which affected Cushing's performance. 'I missed her presence in the control box, which gave me the self-confidence I lacked. She was my sternest critic, and I felt lost without her guidance.' Cushing also had to go through the ordeal of smoking Holmes' trademark pipe, which often made him violently sick.

Roger Jenkins, who directed one of the episodes, recalled the introverted Cushing's lack of connection with Nigel Stock. 'Peter Cushing was very spare always. They didn't provide, I thought, the best possible foils to each other although I was always very fond of Nigel Stock as an actor. Peter Cushing, I knew very, very tangentially. Nigel Stock I knew better. I perhaps just felt that he was a rather cold person, which may not be true at all, but I have to say that, for me, he didn't represent the most exciting opportunities. He obviously knew the character extremely well and he did it very well, but he wasn't an actor who excited me terribly. Perhaps there was a sort of coldness about his performance, which may have been right, but it didn't somehow work with Nigel particularly.'

Cushing's aloofness made things difficult, especially when the script changes went against his memorised line readings. Donald Tosh recalled one incident during filming. 'If I had to change a line, Peter would say, "Oh no, I can't take any more. It's too late. I can't make any more changes!" So, we said, "Okay, Peter, you say it your way, we'll get round it and shave something else." Nigel Stock would take on anything. He just got on and did it, he didn't mind. Cushing was the star, he had to carry the whole series, that was why he was there. He was the star.'

There was one instance when Cushing refused to say a certain line to the annoyance of writer Stanley Long and director Viktors Ritelis, who was all for editing around it. Donald Tosh finally took matters into his own hands, 'I went storming out the gallery, down onto the floor and accused Peter of unprofessionalism in front of the entire cast and crew. He was shocked to the core. He'd probably never been spoken to like that, or certainly not recently. I said, "I know you don't want to record this line, but we will record it once, if we have to pay overtime to everybody for the next week." Peter sailed through the rest of the scene, said it very quickly and it was all over and gone and wrapped and we all breathed a sigh of relief.'

The series wrapped in November 1968, and proved successful with audiences, but Cushing was unhappy with the series and his performance, so it was a return to Hammer to play another signature role.

Frankenstein Must Be Destroyed (1969) was a cynical addition to the series. Hammer could no longer fight the change with regards to violence in British horror, so it comes as a surprise that the film was directed by Terence Fisher, who had been inactive for some time after breaking his leg following a car accident. It was also Cushing's first Hammer film to be shot at Stanmore, and he missed the family atmosphere of Bray Studios.

Bert Batt's script makes the Baron completely evil. It is Cushing's most frightening performance in the role. 'Frankenstein's character has always been altered to meet the requirements of the script,' said producer Anthony Nelson Keys, 'but he's always a very charming fellow as played by Peter Cushing. He's a man who could charm the pictures off a wall and yet uses that charm for his own ruthless ends.'

'He's not an evil man,' Cushing said of the Baron, 'he's a sad man.' Always impeccably dressed and polite, Frankenstein now functions as a civilised sadist who is ready to kill anyone who gets in the way of achieving his goal of creating life, but forgetting the meaning of what life is all about. This is apparent when he damages the lives of a young couple brilliantly played by Veronica Carlson and Simon Ward.

Frankenstein has no redeeming features, but remains the film's focal point, and Cushing's magnificent performance must have had a lot to do with getting the Sherlock Holmes TV series out of his system.

From the blood-spattered opening scene to the burning climax when he comes face to face with his creation, an outstanding performance from Freddie Jones, the film pulls no punches in terms of visual and psychological violence, especially with the emotional collapse of Veronica Carlson's Anna Spengler, which includes an infamous scene that nobody wanted.

On a rare visit to the set, James Carreras complained about the lack of sex in the film and insisted on adding a rape scene between Anna and the

Baron after everything else had been shot. Carlson was outraged. 'I thought the world of Jimmy Carreras, but it was an error. I couldn't refuse to do it. I felt so impotent.'

'Peter didn't want to do it,' she added. 'He took me out to dinner one evening to discuss it, but it didn't make the scene any easier. I couldn't refuse to do it. Terence Fisher was very understanding but it was totally humiliating. Every alternative was more vulgar than the last. My reactions to Peter Cushing are false after the scene was inserted – it gives my character no credence and makes me as an actress look the fool.' Once the unhappy Fisher shouted 'cut', he stormed off the set.

Frankenstein Must Be Destroyed is up there with *Corruption* in terms of cinematic nastiness. It was also Cushing's last great Hammer performance.

The director of *Corruption* raised his head again for Cushing's next film, *Incense For The Damned* (1970). Based on Simon Raven's 1960 novel *Doctors Wear Scarlet*, this was originally Terence Fisher's pet project, but shortly after completing *Frankenstein Must Be Destroyed*, he was involved in another car accident. He eventually sold the film rights to Robert Hartford-Davis.

Raven's ponderous novel is filled with psychological symbolism, indicating that vampirism is a sexual mental illness. It is a difficult book to adapt to the big screen, and this version is nothing short of awful.

The story concerns Richard Fountain (Patrick Mower), a brilliant Oxford scholar destined for a great academic career. Suffering a mental breakdown, he disappears on a trip to Cyprus. When his two closest friends (Alex Davion and Johnny Sekka), his fiancée Penelope (Madeline Hindle) and British Embassy official Major Longbow (Patrick MacNee) visit Cyprus, they learn that he has been seduced by a beautiful woman (Imogene Hassell) into joining a vampire cult that is the centre of a police investigation into a series of ritual murders of several young women.

Second billed behind Patrick MacNee (they share no scenes together) as Richard's overbearing mentor and future father-in-law Dr Goodrich, Cushing has a tiny role. He briefly appears early on at a dinner party discussing his future son-in-law's situation but dismisses it as nothing.

Cushing's next scene takes place during a disturbing climax where a seemingly cured Richard succumbs to the same issues that prompted his disappearance and breaks down during a university dinner given in his honour, accusing Goodrich and the other 'doctors in scarlet' of controlling his mind and repressing his feelings. Richard then kills his fiancée and takes his own life.

Like Frankenstein, Goodrich is a civilised sadist, pushing his protégé to achieve the impossible and mapping out his future career and marriage. There is some slight redemption at the end when, acting as coroner, and protecting the University's reputation, he confirms Richard and Penelope's deaths as consensual. The realisation of his actions and the resultant tragedy will haunt Goodrich forever.

Incense For The Damned might have had something going for it had Terence Fisher directed, but in Hartford-Davis' hands, it is an incoherent mess that looked like two films unsuccessfully spliced together.

Not all of it was Hartford-Davis' fault. While shooting on location in Cyprus during May 1969 (there was no globetrotting for Cushing, who filmed his scenes at Oxford University), the funds ran out leaving him with an unfinished film. On his return to London, Hartford-Davis and his editor cobbled together the existing footage and included a voice over narrative explaining what was going on. The finished film wasn't seen in cinemas until 1976.

Incense For The Damned was eventually released in the United States as *Bloodsuckers* and faded into obscurity amidst internal problems and lawsuits that prompted Robert Hartford-Davis to have his name removed from the credits.

Cushing's next few films consisted of cameo appearances, the first of which was *Scream And Scream Again* (1969), a co-production between Amicus and American International Pictures.

Based on Peter Saxon's 1966 novel *The Disorientated Man*, production began in May 1969, and was historic for bringing together Peter Cushing, Vincent Price and Christopher Lee for the first time. Sadly, the producers botched up a wonderful opportunity.

'We wanted the three top horror stars in one film,' enthused Milton Subotsky. 'Vincent Price was under contract with AIP for £75,000 a picture, so I negotiated a deal to use Vincent for £40,000, which meant I could pay Christopher and Peter a lot of money for relatively small roles. Christopher was on the film for three days and Peter was on for one day I think.'

Scream And Scream Again was never designed as a showcase for the horror legends. Price and Lee were already contracted to the picture, and days before shooting began, AIP producer Lewis Heyward added Cushing to the cast. The actor had no recollection of the film and didn't meet Price or Lee during the shooting.

Compared to a bored looking Lee and a bewildered Price, Cushing walks away with the acting honours with his few minutes of screen time. Playing Major Benedek, a senior official of an unknown Eastern European fascist state, he invests the character with a steely resolve when he tries to demote party enforcer Konrad (Marshall Jones) for committing acts of torture. It's a typically forceful performance where he turns a throwaway role into a well-rounded character.

Cushing's next film is nothing to write home about, but he enthusiastically accepted his guest appearance as one of the stars was a huge fan of his work.

'The indefinable and extraordinarily talented Sammy Davis Jr asked me if I'd do him a favour by appearing for a few seconds in his 1969 production *One More Time* which would involve only a morning's work. He had already shown such kindness and hospitality to Helen and me – first night tickets for his show at the Palladium, dinner afterwards at the White Elephant Club, and endless appreciation for the enjoyment my performances had given. I happily agreed and he took us both out to lunch when my stint was finished. A fortnight later twelve bottles of champagne and a colour television set were delivered, with a note from Sammy and his director Jerry Lewis. Moreover, when Helen was so ill, he sent her a large bouquet of flowers.'

Also on board was Christopher Lee. 'Sammy was a tremendous fan of Hammer films. He'd seen every one of them and knew every part I played. We became pretty close friends, and when he did *One More Time*, he did ask me and Peter if we would do this as a favour for him, just for the fun of it – and we did. Sammy was one of the great personalities of show business, and one of the most talented. I always got the impression that Jerry Lewis really thought this cameo was gilding the lily a bit. He felt this was not really a necessary part of the story that he was directing, but he gave in to Sammy because Sammy said, "This is what I want, and I am insisting."'

Despite the reservations, Lewis, who directed the picture, had nothing but admiration for Cushing and Lee. 'They're marvellous actors and real gentlemen. It was a pleasure to work with those fine men.'

One More Time is appalling. A sequel to the crime comedy *Salt And Pepper* (1967), which also starred Davis and fellow Rat Pack swinger Peter Lawford (they acted as producers on both movies), the film is indifferently handled by Lewis, and looks more like a vanity project for all three stars, complete with a flimsy plot and mistimed jokes.

The horror stars only have one scene, and it takes a long time in coming. It remains the film's only highlight, which isn't saying much.

What happens is, Charlie Salt (Davis) and Chris Pepper (Lawford) are living in an ancestral home belonging to Pepper's deceased twin brother Lord Sydney (also Lawford). One day in the family library, Charlie finds a secret passage that takes him down to the cellar. He comes across a laboratory inhabited by a gibbering Frankenstein type monster (who looks like Dudley Sutton in heavy makeup) and a beautiful woman strapped to a table. There are also two dark, nattily dressed figures in the background.

As the camera zooms in, the dark figures are Christopher Lee's Dracula (holding a glass of something that clearly isn't red wine) and Peter Cushing's Baron Frankenstein.

'Aha, we have a visitor,' says Frankenstein as he turns to Dracula, who then bares his fangs and asks, 'Won't you join our little party?' Davis, being a Hammer horror expert makes a quick exit back to the library!

Cushing fared better on TV as a guest on *The Morecambe And Wise Show*, playing King Arthur in one of Ernie Wise's plays and having his dignity ruined by Ernie and his partner Eric Morecambe, both in fine form. It also led to a long running gag between the three performers regarding the fee Cushing was supposed to get from Eric and Ernie. After almost getting sawn in half in a magician's coffin ('You'll get your cut') and being blown up by a booby-trapped wallet, Cushing finally got his money in 1979!

Cushing spent the remainder of 1969 looking after Helen. He still needed to work, and his next assignment, *The Vampire Lovers* (1970), was the only co-production between Hammer and American International Pictures. The first of the company's 'Karnstein Trilogy', Cushing has another cameo as General Speildorf.

The Vampire Lovers, an adaptation of J Sheridan LeFanu's 1871 novella *Carmilla*, marked another change of direction for Hammer. To bolster the company's dwindling fortunes, the introduction of full-frontal female nudity and lesbian love scenes became the new selling point at the box office. It turned out to be one of Hammer's better films, ably directed by Roy Ward Baker, who found it, 'fun to make'.

'From the beginning,' Baker added, 'I was determined not to make an exploitation movie about lesbian vampires. I wasn't going to be funny about the subject. It came off better than people expected simply because the characters were simply treated as lesbians and that was it. You've got to take these films seriously while you're making them. You've got to make it seem real. Once again, we had a very good cast, with people like Peter Cushing. Peter was great. It's the first time I had worked with him.'

The Vampire Lovers was a huge hit that made a horror star out of Polish/German actress Ingrid Pitt, who became lifelong friends with Cushing, and recalled their meeting in her autobiography.

'I met Peter Cushing for the first time on the set of *The Vampire Lovers*. I was having my wig fitted when the hairdresser warned me that Cushing was doing terrible things to me on the set at that very moment. In spite of the red light, I stormed into the studio and saw, way over in the distance, a man holding something like a cabbage in one hand and swinging a sword in the other. "Swish" it went, and I realised I just had my head cut off. The censors cut this scene from the film, but it was a hell of a way to stage an introduction. I let out a yelp and Peter rushed over and introduced himself. "My dear, how awful to meet like this," I forced myself not to come up with a smart-arsed reply like, "I feel a bit cut up too."'

'We became great friends after that. On my father's hundredth birthday I had champagne brought to the set to celebrate. When Peter heard what the party was about, he invited me to dine with him and his wife Helen in the Thatched Barn. After the maître d' brought a cake covered with candles, on which was written in icing sugar "For Ingrid's Papa".'

Cushing has a well-established early scene as an elegant dinner party host. Resplendent in his military uniform, he is every inch the debonair officer and gentleman as he is introduced to the mysterious countess (Dawn Addams) and her beautiful daughter Marcilla (Ingrid Pitt), who turns out to be the vampire Carmilla, and soon enough gets her fangs into the general's daughter Laura (Pippa Steel).

Absent for most of the movie, Cushing turns up towards the end as part of a team of vampire hunters led by Baron Hartog (Douglas Wilmer) who previously destroyed the Karnstein vampire family but was unable to find Carmilla. When she is finally staked in her coffin, it is the devastated general who slices off her head.

Boasting an excellent cast of Madeline Smith, Kate O'Mara, George Cole, Ferdy Mayne and Jon Finch, *The Vampire Lovers* is a lavishly mounted production. Despite good performances, it makes dull viewing; even the female nudity is tame by today's standards.

There is a certain resonance in Cushing's performance. Helen was dying and this is reflected in his performance as the General deals with the loss of his daughter. Seeing the inevitability of his wife's passing, this was the first of many film roles where his character has lost a loved one.

In July 1970, Cushing was set to play schoolteacher Giles Barton in the second Karnstein film, *Lust for a Vampire* (1970). Unfortunately, both he and Terence Fisher were forced to drop out. Jimmy Sangster, who had just returned to Hammer after living in America, stepped in as Fisher's replacement.

'Terry Fisher was supposed to direct it, but had an accident,' said Sangster, 'so they asked if I'd do it. I was still cutting *Horror of Frankenstein* (1970) and I foolishly said yes. I loved directing. I didn't enjoy directing *Lust for a Vampire*. I came into the picture about two weeks before we were due to start shooting. The script had been finished – it was a good script. The producers were there, the picture had been cast and all the set had been built, so you became nothing more than a traffic cop. You had very little creative input.'

Then Cushing had to drop out. Ralph Bates, a good friend of Sangster, stepped in at the last-minute. Bates previously played the Baron in *Horror of Frankenstein* and met Cushing during a press conference where the veteran actor happily passed his mantle over to his younger protégé. Bates was happy to take over although he was too young for the role.

Lust for a Vampire is a bad movie, even by Hammer's standards. Sangster and Bates do their best, but the lack of a happy centre is obvious. There's no reason to assume the film would have been any better with Cushing and Fisher, but it couldn't have been any worse than the garbage that was released to the public.

22: Marking Time In Blighty

Another cameo followed in *The House That Dripped Blood* (1970), the first of three Amicus anthologies that reflected Cushing's emotional state. Helen had become so ill, he wanted to cancel his contract to spend time with her. Aware that his deal with Columbia would fall through if Cushing dropped out, Milton Subotsky held him to the terms of his employment.

Cushing's episode, 'Waxworks', has him playing Philip Grayson, a retired stockbroker who rents the house of the title, but his obsession with a waxwork figure that resembles a long-lost love (it doesn't) leads to his death at the hands of the jealous proprietor of the wax museum (Wolfe Morris) and his head put on display.

Director Peter Duffell wanted more than an excuse to have Cushing beheaded. 'I decided to try and give the story a little resonance on the strictly human level by building up the loneliness of the character, taking refuge from the disappointments of life in his books music and memories, and by the unhappy love for the unattainable dead girl. I would like to have gone much further in this direction, but I was not allowed to.'

Duffell rewrote Robert Bloch's script to allow Cushing to develop that side of his character, and the actor responded with a sad and moving performance. 'There is a loneliness in his role and a sadness in him at the time,' observed Duffell, 'which I think is mirrored in the film.'

Duffell enjoyed working with Cushing and saw many of the great qualities he possessed. 'Peter, I always found, during what was, after all, a fairly short relationship on the movie, an extremely gentle, kind and sensitive person. There was I think, a slight air of sadness about him at the time which subsequently became very clear because at the time when his wife whom he deeply loved very much and to whom he was totally devoted, was dying. I didn't know that until after the film was over. But in retrospect, I realise that possibly some of the slightly indrawn quality of Peter must have been due to the enormous personal stress he was feeling at that time.'

Remaining with Amicus for his next assignment, Cushing was elevated to a starring role. It was the studio's first period horror, but not one he rated highly. 'I don't think it was one that I would put at the top of my list of achievements.'

I, Monster (1970) is an interesting, but flawed adaptation of Robert Louis Stevenson's novella *Strange Case Of Dr Jekyll And Mr Hyde*, and starred Christopher Lee in the dual roles, although the names were changed to Dr Charles Marlow and Mr Edward Blake. Milton Subotsky admitted he would not have got the financing if the famous names had been retained.

Subotsky's screenplay explores the psychological angle of Jekyll's experiments, but his decision to shoot it in 3-D, prompted Peter Duffell and Freddie Frances to turn the film down. Stephen Weeks came on board although he too had serious doubts about whether the process would work.

Subotsky's script doesn't cut the mustard, but he effectively adds an interesting premise of Dr Marlow slowly changing physically and mentally instead of turning into a monster straight away, allowing Christopher Lee to develop the character further. The first incarnation of Mr Blake has little more than a toothy grin and a spring in his step, but as the film progresses, Marlow becomes more grotesque and twisted. Lee gives one of his best horror performances, even though he felt the 3-D process, 'was a disastrous mistake.'

Cushing has the less rewarding role of Marlow's friend and lawyer Frederick Utterson and gives a flat performance. 'Not the best film I've ever worked on,' he lamented, further agreeing with Lee that the 3-D process was 'a mistake.'

The situation wasn't helped by Cushing sharing several scenes with Mike Raven, a former Radio One DJ and occult enthusiast who fancied himself as a horror star, having already previously appeared in *Lust for a Vampire*. Sharing above the title billing with Lee and Cushing, Raven gives a wooden performance as Mr Enfield.

Stephen Weeks enjoyed working with Cushing and Lee. 'They were it. In those days in Britain you could say, "I have Christopher Lee and Peter Cushing in a creepy story," and you would therefore have the money. They were the Tom Cruises of their day! They were British stars that were bankable.'

The shoot for *I, Monster* went behind schedule, finally wrapping in late October after six difficult weeks for an emotionally drained Cushing.

Realising the futility of the 3-D process, Subotsky finally abandoned it, scrapping several key scenes in the editing room because they were unworkable.

When *I, Monster* was released in November 1970, the distributor, British Lion, did little in the way of promotion and the film bombed. Had Subotsky abandoned his 3-D idea and let Stephen Weeks do his job, it would have been a better picture.

Away from the personal pressures, Cushing got some respite by returning to the hilarity of Morecambe and Wise for their Christmas show. This time the actor steps out of a grandfather clock demanding his money!

In January 1971, Cushing returned to Hammer for his next film, playing archaeologist Professor Julian Fuchs in *Blood From The Mummy's Tomb* (1971), an adaptation of Bram Stoker's 1903 novel *The Jewel Of Seven Stars*. Seth Holt was scheduled to direct.

Cushing's first day's shooting was also his last. 'I started a film for Hammer at Elstree. At the end of the first day, Joyce rang to say Helen had been taken to Canterbury Hospital for a check-up, where she would be kept in for a few days.' As it turned out, Helen suffered a relapse, the emphysema finally taking its toll on her fragile health.

After discussing the situation with the doctor, it was agreed that Helen could go home, although she would need constant nursing. 'Whilst I prepared for the journey, I arranged for a day and night nurse, and then rang John Redway, asking him to cancel my participation in the film.'

Cushing joined his wife in the ambulance for their final journey home. Although she improved a little in familiar surroundings, she passed away on 14 January 1971, with her loyal husband by her side.

Filming *Blood From The Mummy's Tomb* continued with Andrew Keir replacing Cushing. The situation got worse during shooting when Seth Holt suffered a fatal heart attack, leaving Michael Carreras to step in as director.

Helen's health also prevented Cushing from playing Dr Vesalius opposite Vincent Price as *The Abominable Dr Phibes* (1971); he was replaced by Joseph Cotton. Tigon also wanted him for the stylish folk horror *Blood On Satan's Claw* (1971). The role went to Patrick Wymark.

Already in a state of shock following Helen's death, Cushing became suicidal, but deep down he knew he couldn't do it, and thanks to the many letters Helen had left him, following her passing he found the strength to carry on.

Away from work, Cushing became a recluse, cutting himself off from his circle of friends. 'He did not really want to see me either,' said loyal secretary Joyce Broughton, 'and frequently when I had journeyed over 50 miles to see him at Whitstable, he would make it abundantly clear that he wanted to be left alone.'

Had Cushing opened up to his friends and colleagues, it may have led to reconciliation with his brother David, from whom he had been estranged for many years. According to Christopher Lee, 'He told me that his brother's wife didn't approve of and wouldn't have anything to do with him, so he hadn't been in contact with his brother for many years. It seemed very sad indeed.' David Cushing died in 1987.

Cushing remained open about his feelings of reuniting with Helen. 'I positively look forward to death. I just hope it will come quicker, so I can see her again as soon as possible.' As touching as his sentiments were, it wasn't a great recommendation for film producers who would be reluctant to use him in any forthcoming projects, thus limiting his job offers.

With Helen's death, Cushing let all his various hobbies go, although his friend, the artist Edward Seago encouraged him to continue painting. Now the focus was on work to help him cope with his grief. Two months after Helen's death, Cushing returned to work on Hammer's third Karnstein movie, *Twins Of Evil* (1971), which Wayne Kinsey felt was, 'the release that Cushing needed from his grieving.'

Cushing plays Gustav Weil, the leader of a band of black-robed, misogynistic, vampire chasing puritans who spend their evenings riding the countryside, abducting and burning pretty girls who just happen to be in the wrong place at the wrong time – all in the name of God. It does make one wonder if there were any girls left in the area after the puritans finished their work.

Weil's organised lifestyle is disrupted by the arrival of his orphaned nieces, played by real life twins and *Playboy* models Madeline and Mary Collinson. Despite the English sounding names, the twins were Maltese, and their voices were dubbed. The film's title is a bit of a cheat as only one of them is evil.

Cushing spends most of his time shouting at the top of his voice and stomping around in a constant bad mood; it's as if the only fun he has in life is lynching innocent young women. His thunderous presence adds weight to a depressing chiller.

Otherwise, he gives another flat performance. Now painfully thin, there is no life in his eyes other than the tears that would well up at any moment. If there is any audience sympathy for his character, it owes more to Cushing's fragile state of mind, not his joyless acting.

From Hammer to Amicus for his next assignment, which began in September 1971. It was a return to the anthology format, and for Cushing, the performance of his career.

Tales From The Crypt (1972) is an adaptation of some of the celebrated ghoulish stories from E C Comics who produced titles such as *Haunt Of Fear*, *The Vault Of Horror* and *Tales From The Crypt*. They were a big hit with many American youngsters, among them Milton Subotsky, whose dream was to bring the tales to the big screen.

'When I read *Tales From The Crypt* in the Ballantyne paperback reprint,' said Subotsky, 'I remember reading it before, a long time ago. I went after Max (Rosenberg) to get the film rights to it. But it was very difficult, because money didn't interest Bill Gaines, who owned them. He was more interested in seeing a good film made from the material. The fun of it interested him. I kept coming back to Max from time to time, and finally he met with Bill Gaines, and they were able to work out a deal.'

Part of the deal was to stay close to the original material. Subotsky chose five tales and wrote the script in accordance with the stipulation.

As with most Amicus portmanteaus, it boasts an excellent cast of Joan Collins, Ian Hendry, Richard Greene, Patrick Magee, Barbara Murray and Nigel Patrick, with Ralph Richardson as the Crypt Keeper. Returning too as director after a long hiatus from Amicus was Freddie Francis.

Cushing declined his original role because he was more interested in another character close to his heart. 'I was attracted to the part of this little old man Grimsdyke, but generally it was a non-speaking part – all the commentary was done as a voice-over. I said that in the normal way an audience would not accept a solitary man talking to himself, but here was a special case, and if they would give him some dialogue, I would take the part. You see my dear wife had died not long before this and I used to talk to her when I was alone and to her photograph. So, I knew I could make the part convincing because it was something I did myself. And that was how the part evolved, and it became instinctive to me.'

Grimsdyke is an elderly dustman living in an affluent village. A lonely widower, he is a kind man who takes in stray dogs and makes toys for the local children, to the disgust of his snooty neighbour (Robin Philips), who wants to buy the house as it has some land value.

The neighbour starts a hate campaign, blaming Grimsdyke's dogs for destroying another neighbour's garden, getting him sacked from his job (and losing his pension), spreading rumours about him that stops the children from coming. Finally, he sends cruel Valentine cards from the villagers, which breaks the old man's heart and drives him to suicide.

Being an Amicus fairy-tale, the neighbour meets a nasty end. Grimsdyke was a spiritualist who was in regular contact with his dead wife. A year after his death, his rotting corpse rises from the grave to exact his well-deserved revenge.

For the first time in his career, Cushing plays a monster. It was Roy Ashton who created his appearance. 'Roy Ashton, a dear man of gentle disposition and an expert makeup artist, took care of that department,' Cushing recalled. 'The moment when the character emerged from his grave, having spent quite a spell underground, was scheduled for shooting immediately after lunch, up to which time I had to look normal. Roy kindly gave up his hour's break in order to get me ready for resurrection.'

Roy Ashton explained how he created Grimsdyke's decomposing look. 'The makeup was applied to Peter Cushing's face with pieces I had previously prepared from laminated paper to suggest the severe wasting of features. To accentuate the skull-like appearance I fabricated shapes and built them up around each eye. Within those, I simply fastened a piece of an old black costume my wife used to have since matt black doesn't photograph and he should appear to be sightless. Peter could still look through the nylon, but we couldn't see his eyes beneath the fabric. I brought the hair forward and made it very lank and filthy looking. This was an operation you can do in a few seconds with grease paint, dirt and various bits of rubbish. A slight growth of beard combined with prominent teeth to complete the effect.'

It is impossible to watch Cushing's performance without feeling his heartbreak. Now visibly aged, and looking like everybody's favourite grandfather, he bestows a true heart and soul to a character that was originally a non-speaking, non-entity.

Cushing initially wanted a photo of Helen to appear in the film, but following a discussion with Freddie Francis, another was used instead, but her name remained. Cushing's reactions to the photo echoed his raw emotions, especially during the Ouija board scene where his wife gives him a warning. 'It was like I felt Helen's presence.' This makes uncomfortable viewing because the audience also feels his real-life pain and heartbreak.

Tales From The Crypt was Amicus' most financially successful film with Cushing giving his finest performance. 'It was a real delight when the picture got such a wonderful press and people actually wrote to me saying how sympathetic they found the part. I even won an award for it in France, which was doubly satisfying for something that was created out of nothing.'

The award came in April 1973, when Cushing went to Paris as a guest for the Second International Horror Festival. Organised by Alain Schlockoff, Cushing received the *Licorne D'Or* award for his performance in *Tales From The Crypt* and a lifetime achievement award for his services to horror.

Rising from his seat to collect the award, Cushing was overwhelmed by the standing ovation he received from the audience. According to one fan, 'Peter Cushing won two medals, one as Best Actor: another especially for his work in *Tales From The Crypt*. He was very emotional and made a speech in French. It was so kindly said that the audience wildly applauded him. I certainly saw tears in his eyes. Yes, Cushing is one of the most co-operative actors that I've met. He answered hundreds of questions, autographed stills, always smiling, even after one in the morning.'

After Paris, Cushing was off to Nice and the French Riviera for an episode of the Lew Grade's ITC crime series *The Zoo Gang*, starring Cushing's old mates John Mills and Barry Morse. The series focused on four former resistance fighters, played by Mills, Morse, Brian Keith and Lilli Palmer, who reunite on the Riviera 30 years later to fight modern-day criminals.

In the episode entitled 'The Counterfeit Trap', Cushing plays Judge Gaultier, a free spending French magistrate who falls into debt. To keep his young wife (Jacqueline Pearce) in the lap of luxury, the judge gets involved in a smuggling ring. The episode was directed by John Hough, who worked with Cushing on *Twins Of Evil*.

Cushing was back with Hammer in September 1971 to shoot *Dracula AD 1972* (1972) at Elstree Studios. Returning as Van Helsing, he reunited with Christopher Lee, who donned the Dracula cape once more.

Michael Carreras had returned to Hammer at his father's request to run the company. To breathe new life to the dying genre, he brought the Count into the 20th Century after striking a deal with Warners to produce two modern day Dracula pictures.

Michael Carreras saw the potential in updating Dracula following the success of several independently made American vampire flicks *Count Yorga, Vampire* (1970) and its sequel, *The Return Of Count Yorga* (1971), and the USA TV horror-based soap opera *Dark Shadows* (1966-1971) which had at the time resulted in two films *House Of Dark Shadows* (1970) and *Night of Dark Shadows* (1971).

However, Carreras also had to bring back the increasingly disillusioned Lee. 'How they managed to drag Christopher Lee back for this one I do not know,' recalled Wayne Kinsey. 'We have already witnessed his growing disenchantment with the character, vowing that [each film] would be his last. Yet he came back for more.' The reason for Lee's decision has a lot to do with being out of work for a few months after several film projects fell through.

The idea sounds promising since Dracula, like Sherlock Holmes, was a man of his time, but despite the cult following it received many years later, *Dracula AD 1972*, written by Don Houghton, is a depressing effort that wastes the horror legends, especially an ill-at-ease Lee. Thanks to the script's lack of originality, Dracula is confined to a disused gothic church, leaving his disciple Johnny Alucard (Christopher Neame) to go out and find him victims.

Peter Cushing fares slightly better than Lee, and their opening scene together remains the film's highlight. Ostensibly showing the conclusion of an unseen adventure/battle between Van Helsing and Count Dracula, they battle one another on Dracula's coach, which then crashes, leaving the Count impaled on a broken wheel as he and Van Helsing expire from their wounds. The opening scene is so well staged; one wonders what kind of story it was that led to the protagonists' final confrontation.

Fast forward 100 years and Cushing is playing Van Helsing's descendant. This was originally intended to be the father of Jessica Van Helsing (Stephanie Beecham), but because Cushing looked much older than his 58 years, he became her grandfather.

Cushing does well with the role, but only just. The modern day Van Helsing is just as fanatical about vampires as his ancestor. It might have worked better if the character had been more of an unbeliever who realises that vampires are real after encountering Dracula. Yet Cushing is so convincing in the role, the whole thing works to the film's advantage.

Unlike Lee, who felt 'the hippy idiom was already out of date when the film was made,' Cushing was more enthusiastic. 'I think it's going to be nothing short of genius to present Dracula in such a new way,' and finding the script, 'particularly good.' As always, working with Lee remained a positive experience.

Van Helsing's office has the same photo on display of Grimsdyke's wife previously seen in *Tales From The Crypt*, indicating that the professor is a widow, which makes his relationship with Jessica more poignant, especially when Dracula has set his fangs on her. Once again Cushing plays a character dealing with potential loss as he battles to save an important person in his life.

These strong emotions are touchingly reflected in Van Helsing's relationship with Jessica. Stephanie Beecham does well in the role and had fond memories of working with Cushing. 'I felt a touch of friendship with him that one is always grateful for. When you're with someone who is as kind, as well meaning, as beautiful and generous as Peter Cushing, you feel very privileged.'

Dracula AD 1972 has some good moments, and Alan Gibson's direction is competent. The performances are acceptable with Christopher Neame taking the acting honours as the decadent Johnny Alucard. Michael Coles is equally effective as the sceptical but understanding Inspector Murray, whose disbelief regarding Van Helsing's theory on vampirism is equal to his respect for the scientist. Coles' scenes with Cushing are such a joy to watch one regrets that no further films were made featuring the characters.

Following *Dracula AD 1972*, the Cushing/Lee association continued in Spain with one of their most enjoyable films.

23: Horror Express (1972)

Cushing and Christopher Lee in *Horror Express*.

'Monster? We're British You Know!' One cannot mention *Panico en el Transberiano,* or *Horror Express* (1972) without repeating Cushing's immortal line, which is the sub-title of John Connolly's excellent book about the film. It was also an important period in Cushing's life, personally and professionally.

Still dealing with the loss of Helen, Cushing found himself in an awkward situation: Christmas was coming, and it would be his first without her. This coincided with an offer to star in a Spanish film being shot over the festive season.

Prior to *Horror Express*, Cushing made cameo appearances in two British films shot back-to-back. Directed by Jimmy Sangster, *Fear In The Night* (1972) co-starred Judy Geeson, Joan Collins and Ralph Bates. Geeson plays a character battling mental illness who is driven by her husband (Bates) and his lover (Collins) into killing the latter's husband (Cushing). Being a Hammer thriller, the tables are quickly turned.

As the unusually named Michael Carmichael, headmaster of an exclusive boy's school, Cushing plays another character dealing with bereavement. The school closed following a fire that killed several boys, resulting in Carmichael losing his arm and his sanity. The school is now an elaborate convalescent home for the headmaster to live out his fantasies of teaching again with Bates acting as his nurse. Cushing only has a couple of scenes, which he plays very well.

The other film was *Dr Phibes Rises Again* (1972) with Vincent Price reprising his role as the disfigured musical genius. Retaining his moustache from *Fear In The Night*, Cushing guest stars as the captain of a ship sailing to Egypt with Phibes on board. When archaeologist Harry Ambrose (Hugh Griffith) is thrown overboard in a large whiskey bottle, the captain questions his associate (and Phibes' nemesis) Darius Biederbeck (Robert Quarry). It is Cushing's only scene, but he has a good joke when he asks Biederbeck, 'I suppose he never touched the bottle?' A not so discreet reference to Griffith's notorious heavy drinking.

Cushing shot his scene at Elstree Studios and wasn't part of the cast and crew that set off to Ibiza for the location work: he had already packed his bags for his own journey to Madrid to start work on *Horror Express*.

'Cushing disliked overseas filming,' said David Miller, 'but his intention was clearly to be as far away as possible from familiar things for his first Christmas without Helen. When he got to Spain, however, he was ready to come straight home again.'

Arriving in Madrid Airport on 13 December, Cushing met the film's producer Bernard Gordon for the first time. 'He was slender,' recalled Gordon, who only knew the actor by reputation and admitted he had never seen any of Cushing's performances because he disliked horror films. 'Not tall, very fair, with delicate features, not what I expected from one of the world's leading actors of horror films. No Frankenstein monster he.'

'Cushing was, in fact, quite tall,' said Connolly, 'but more to the point, he had never played Frankenstein's creature, only its creator. Gordon published his memoir in 1999, but it seems that after almost thirty years he still hadn't bothered to find out much about his leading men in the best film he ever produced. Then again, Gordon can be forgiven some residual ambivalence toward Cushing.'

On the way to the hotel, Cushing immediately told Gordon that he wanted to return to England. Connolly notes: '[Cushing said] he had only travelled to Spain because Ben Fisz, Philip Yordan's partner at Scotia International, insisted that Cushing inform Gordon in person of his refusal to work.'

'He was extremely polite and gentle,' recalled Gordon, obviously reeling from the shock of Cushing's decision. 'He had approved of the first draft of the script, but when he later read the final draft, he didn't like it and didn't want to go to work on it.' Cushing was supposed to start filming the next day, and Gordon needed to know the reasons for his refusal to take part. The actor signed up for *Horror Express* on the strength of the first draft of the script, he told Gordon, 'When I read the final one, the one you're shooting, I told Mr Fisz that I didn't care to work on the

23: Horror Express (1972)

film.'

'Given how poor the first draft had been,' observed Connolly, 'one can conclude that Cushing had latched onto this as an excuse to return home and continue mourning his late wife.'

Production had already started on 6 December 1971 at Estudios in Danganzo, Madrid and with Cushing standing firm, Gordon was now stuck with a massive headache. 'Gordon managed to get Cushing to the studio,' said Connolly, 'and called Ben Fisz in London. Fisz pointed out that Gordon was the producer, and Fisz had fulfilled his duty by getting Cushing to Spain. It was up to Gordon to convince him of the necessity of adhering to his contract.'

Gordon turned to Christopher Lee, who had been working on the film a week earlier, to sort out the crisis.'

'Don't be concerned about it,' Lee reassured Gordon. 'We'll meet after work at the hotel, and it will all work out.' Lee also told Gordon that Cushing was always nervous when taking on a new role and his reluctance to commit himself to a film was a part of his established routine.

According to Mark Miller, 'Lee, Cushing and Gordon got together in the hotel's sitting room. Lee immediately began a verbal filibuster of anecdotes designed to place Cushing at ease and not give him a chance to mention his intended desertion, Lee adding simply, "Okay, Peter, see you at work tomorrow," and Cushing was over the crisis without saying a word. Such was the power of a long, trusting friendship and collaboration.'

A week into the production a much happier Cushing apologised for his behaviour. 'He really did like the script now,' said Gordon, 'and he did like the way the film was going and was sorry for having been difficult.' By that time Gordon had become aware of Helen's death.

'This was a considerable oversight on the part of Gordon and his colleagues,' Connolly said of the situation. 'Being a producer is undoubtably a difficult job, but to be unaware of the personal circumstances of one of your lead actors, especially when they involve such a painful bereavement, appears careless to an unusual degree. Ben Fisz was responsible for casting the leading roles in London and should have alerted Gordon on the extent of the actor's grief, which was widely known to the British community. To Cushing he should allow some latitude; he had signed on for *Horror Express* after Helen's death, perhaps believing himself ready to work abroad again, but when it came time to leave, he must have realised his mistake.'

Horror Express illustrated the deep friendship between Cushing and Lee, who acted as his unofficial interpreter throughout the shoot. 'I adored doing that,' recalled Cushing. 'We did that in Spain and Christopher was so kind because it was one of the first things I did after I had undergone a personal trauma. It was an enjoyable film to make, and Christopher was marvellous during it because he's so good with languages – he speaks about ten, bless him. It's very tricky working in a foreign country when you're so used to English ways. I can hardly speak English, much less Spanish, but they were all so sweet during the making of that. It took a little more time, naturally for the Spanish to get across to me what they were after – and vice versa – but Christopher was, as always, a tower of strength. It was indeed a very happy film to make. He and I had some nice exchanges of dialogue. We always work on those together, with the director of course.'

Many fans regard *Horror Express* as the definitive Cushing/Lee collaboration because it showcases their on-screen chemistry to full advantage. They have equal screentime and brilliantly play off each other with great humour.

Although not based on an H P Lovecraft story, *Horror Express* is firmly rooted in the reclusive writer's Cthulhu Mythos world. It begins with an expedition to Manchuria in 1906 by eminent British anthropologist Professor Sir Alexander Saxton (Christopher Lee), who finds a well-preserved fossil of a primitive man.

Saxton is returning to England with his discovery on the Trans-Siberian Express from Shanghai to Moscow. Also on board is friendly rival and colleague Dr Wells (Peter Cushing) and his associate Miss Jones (American stage actress Alice Reinhart). Saxton is so protective of his find, that it arouses his colleague's curiosity.

The train is crammed with an assortment of characters straight out of Agatha Christie. Joining Saxton and Wells is Count Petrovski (Georges Rigaud), an expert on metals, who is travelling with his pretty young wife (Sylvia Tortosa), a Marta Hari type spy (Euro horror star Helga Line), who is after the Count's secret, a rocket scientist (Angel de Pozo), a suspicious Russian police inspector (Julio Pena) and the count's spiritual advisor (Alberto de Mendoza), who came straight from the Rasputin School of Mad Monking. Only Hercule Poirot is conspicuous by his absence.

The fossil quickly defrosts and breaks out of its crate. The story is, that the creature is inhabited by an alien, who can absorb the memories and intelligence of its victims through their eyes. It's ability to escape its confinement came courtesy of a crooked locksmith it managed to despatch before the train set off. The alien can also take possession of another human, and Inspector Mirov becomes the new host after the policeman guns it down.

Joining forces to solve the mystery, Saxton and Wells are up to their necks with mysterious deaths and hysterical passengers as the alien tries to accumulate enough knowledge to build a spaceship so it can return home, but its efforts are thwarted when the train is boarded by a detachment of Cossacks led by Captain Kazan (Telly Savalas). Throw in a couple of autopsies and a few reanimated zombies, and Hercule Poirot was wise not to board the train.

Horror Express came about at a time when Spain was enjoying a productive period of filmmaking that began in the late sixties and was spurred on by the horror antics of filmmaker Jesus Franco and *El hombre lobo* himself, Paul Naschy. By securing Britain's top genre headliners, *Horror Express* was a step forward for the Spanish horror film industry.

The story originated during the summer of 1971. Working as producer on the spaghetti western *Pancho Villa* (1971), Bernard Gordon procured two scale model trains and 1,000 metres of rail track, previously used for the historical epic *Nicholas And Alexandra* (1971). The trains, languishing in Madrid's 70 studio complex, were put to good use in *Pancho Villa*.

Gordon then joined forces with fellow American producer and friend Philip Yordan. With the models in his possession, Gordon admitted he had to, 'Think about what the hell we could do to use this train to get going on another picture. I came up with *Horror Express*, and from there we built up a story.'

Yordan's London based Scotia Films, entered a deal with Spain's Granada Films and Britain's Benmar Films. 'Scotia's affairs were complex,' said John Connolly, 'involving backers in the UK and the US, but also had a line of credit with Banco de Bilbao in Spain, and the company was always hustling. It couldn't afford to let studio space in Madrid lie dormant for any length of time and believed it was better to be making poor films than no films at all.'

Yordan gave *Horror Express* the go-ahead with Gordon as producer. This came at the right time because the Spanish studio where the film would be shot had been reorganised to reduce expensive overheads. According to Connolly, 'Gordon budgeted *Horror Express* at just $300,000, riding to $350,000 once salaries of the British and American stars were taken into account, Gordon was now in sole charge in Madrid, a situation that caused difficulties with the Spanish authorities, because Spanish law did not permit foreign ownership of any media, film studios included.' To avoid any issues Gordon maintained a low profile throughout the shoot.

Arnaud d'Usseau's first draft of the script lacked sufficient action and horror to sustain a movie, so Julian Zimet was brought in for further rewrites. It was Zimet who added the reanimated fossil and the alien.

Gordon approached Freddie Francis to direct, but problems with Milton Subotsky on *Tales From The Crypt*, his reluctance to work in Europe following the disastrous *Vampire Happening* (1971), and his annoyance at being pigeonholed as a horror director, prompted him to decline. The assignment then went Eugenio (Gene) Martin, who directed *Pancho Villa*, which was part of a three-picture deal he had with Philip Yordan.

'When I made *Horror Express*,' recalled Martin, 'I was under contract with Philip Yordan, although he had somebody else (Bernard Gordon) fronting this project, and the picture was an Anglo-Spanish co-production. That's how Peter Cushing and Christopher Lee came to be involved.' Telly Savalas was also under contract, hence his brief appearance in *Horror Express*.

Dissatisfied with *Pancho Villa*, Martin made it clear at a producers' meeting in London in September 1971 that he would accept the assignment if he could work on the script. Production was delayed another week when Martin had to undergo an operation. Contrary to popular belief and the film's credits, Martin did not write the original story.

Production finally went underway. The snowy regions of Puerto de Navacerrada effectively doubled up for Manchuria, and the opening scenes at Shanghai Station, brilliantly capturing the hustle and bustle of turn-of-the-century rail travel, was filmed at the Delicias Railway Station in the centre of Madrid. Everything else was filmed at the Estudios 70 complex.

For the scenes at Shanghai Station, Gordon used a real train, which allowed the audience to think that the subsequent scenes with the models were also real. 'Through an arrangement with he made with the Spanish railroad,' said Mark Miller, 'Gordon was granted use of an old, wrought iron train station that had been built by Alexander Gustave Eiffel, the architect who constructed the Eiffel Tower. The actors and crew were allowed to use the station and one of the historical period trains stored there, so director Eugenio Martin was able to include an impressive shot of a turn-of-the-century, steaming iron horse pulling out of the station.'

For the spectacular climax where the train careens off a cliff taking the alien (now possessing the mad monk) with it, cheaper models were used. According to Gordon, 'the cameraman and director wanted to search all through the area of Madrid for a 300-foot cliff because the script called for it. I couldn't quite convince them that, because we were going to put a miniature train over the cliff, not a full size one, a 300-foot drop would be out of order, not to mention the fact I didn't have the money for all that nonsense of looking for locations.'

Plundering the discarded props from *Pancho Villa*, a sentry tower was redressed by art director Ramiro Gomez Guadiana who placed a matte painting of the cliff edge between the sentry tower and the camera. The resulting shots of the wooden duplicate train flying off the cliff edge are visually stunning and look more expensive than the budget allowed.

The impressive visuals are thanks to the excellent camera work of cinematographer Alejandro Ulloa, who previously worked with Martin on *Pancho Villa*. 'He is very good and very fast,' said Martin, 'and lights things in a way that makes colours pop and creates beautiful shades between light and shadow. Without the work of Gomez and Ulloa, *Panico en el*

23: Horror Express (1972)

Transberiano would be a poorer film.'

The train's interiors are equally impressive. According to Cushing, 'all they had in the studio in Spain was a carriage in one sound stage and a carriage in another sound stage, so we worked in one which was dressed up as the guard's van, and the other would be dressed up as, say, the dining car, and when we were finished in the guard's van we went and did all the scenes in the dining car. In the meantime, they altered the guard's van into something else.' The carriages were built on springs giving them movement as if the actors were on a real train.

Christopher Lee found Estudios 70, 'the most appalling studio, if you can call it that: an absolutely ghastly little studio out in the middle of nowhere, just a couple of large shacks with some offices attached. The commissary of the restaurant was quite unspeakable. The food was the worst I've ever had anywhere in the world on all the films I've made. I became extremely unwell as a result of eating it.'

Working on *Horror Express* was the only time Cushing upset Lee. 'Only once did he say something that brought me up short. It was on the set of *Horror Express*. The train in question was meant to be the Trans-Siberian Express, but our location was just outside Madrid, in an unspeakable studio in Daganzo. The food was deadly, salmonella the principal source. Peter never used the restaurant. He always ate the same meal, day after day, year after year, either because Helen liked it, or because he thought it was healthy: apple and cheese. Afterwards he would smoke a cigarette wearing white gloves, because the stain might show up on the screen, and because Helen didn't like him smoking. So, I found him in our so-called dressing room. "I can't stand this anymore," I said. "Oh, what is that dear fellow?" Then I went into a tirade about the food. "I feel I'm going to die of this frightful food. This is a ghastly studio." A massive whinge. He looked at me and peeled his apple. He just said, "Well, there's no good bellyaching about it, you know." That was about as severe as he could be. Coming from him, it was devasting.'

Filming paused for Christmas, and this was the time Cushing feared the most, but once again Lee was on hand to save him from this potential nightmare.

Lee arranged for his wife Gitte and daughter Christina to fly to Madrid, and Cushing joined them at their hotel on Christmas Day. If there was a time where their friendship was at its most personal, it was their time on *Horror Express*.

For Lee, this Christmas was very personal. Bernard Gordon hosted a Christmas dinner for the cast and crew, and to his surprise, he saw Lee's 9-year-old daughter Christina jump around manically on the dance floor without any intervention from the parents. 'I thought it was rather surprising,' he recalled, 'that Christopher, who was not an insensitive man, and his wife Gitte didn't interfere at all. They just let the little girl carry on and sort of take over. Later I found out why and was rather touched. It was because she had been born with her feet twisted backwards and had been through many operations in Switzerland. This was practically the first time she was able to get around freely and function so well on her feet and they were delighted to see her doing it.'

The filming of *Horror Express* went smoothly, but not without incident due to the language barrier and the usual cultural clashes that came with making a movie in another country; Gordon had a few problems getting Martin to motivate his crew to work until noon.

'We were doing quota pictures, so we had to have a Spanish director which is why we didn't have an American or English director even though the films were English language ones. Eugenio's English was very good; he was very capable, professional and co-operative, but as I say, he was hired principally because of his nationality. We were satisfied with his work and his performance, with one exception. He couldn't get his crew or anybody else moving before midday. Then he would rush like hell to get the work in for the day and go overtime. The crew would get pretty annoyed at how late they had to work, although they didn't mind how late they would get started in the morning, that was just a constant battle that I had. I was up against a cultural conflict. I was so disturbed that I would insist on a production meeting after work each day to know exactly what shots were going to be set up first in the morning so I could try to see that the lights were ready by the time everybody got to work. But it was a losing battle for me. It's just not the way they function.'

Although Lee spoke fluent Spanish and helped Cushing communicate with the cast and crew, he had his own experience with the language barrier during filming.

'I've worked in most countries of the world where films are made, and I find a good technical crew is a good technical crew wherever. Their approach varies from country to country, and working conditions vary, but basically, they all aim for the same result, quality. Obviously, culture is different also, food is different, facilities less advanced in some countries than they are in others, and the language is different. But our Spanish director spoke pretty good English, and some of the Spanish cast in that particular film did speak English passably also, but some of them didn't. They still had to try their best to learn their lines phonetically in English, which is extremely difficult, just as I would if I were asked to do a film in Japanese so that someone else who speaks that language proficiently could dub the voice properly afterwards. But I don't remember any problems on that picture.'

Because most of the supporting cast spoke English, it was easier for the voice actors to dub them after the film was completed. George Rigaud retained his voice while Alberto de Mendoza and Julio Pena were dubbed by Robert Rietty and Roger Delgado. Sylvia Tortosa, Helga Line and Alice Reinhart were revoiced by English actress Olive Gregg.

Production wrapped mid-January for Cushing and Lee to return to Britain for another Lovecraft inspired chiller *The Creeping Flesh* (1972) for Tigon Films. However, a scene had been missed on *Horror Express* and, considering his reluctance to go to Spain in the first place, Cushing was all for returning to complete it.

The scene had Dr Wells performing an autopsy on one of the alien's victims. The producers just needed his hands, and ever the perfectionist, Cushing was willing to return and complete the scene: he even refused a fee to do it. The budget, however, didn't stretch towards flying the actor back and so Gordon used someone else.

The negative was flown back to Britain for editing, and the soundtrack was recorded by American composer John Cavacas. Inspired by the creepy whistles and guitar twangs of Ennio Morricone's spaghetti westerns, Cavacas' score opens with a familiar whistling theme similar to Sergio Leone's *A Fistful Of Dollars* (1965). 'That was a brilliant idea,' thought Eugenio Martin.

The completed print was finally ready for distribution in October 1972, but an agreement hadn't been reached in England and apart from a couple of trade shows, *Horror Express* was left with no distribution deal. Eventually Ben Fisz and Philip Yordan released the film Stateside through Scotia International.

Problems within Scotia occurred late on when the company's associate Robert Marbor, a real estate developer who had been involved in the Scotia production of *Royal Hunt For The Sun* (1969), was unable to pay back a $150,000 loan advanced towards the production costs of *Horror Express* to the Banco de Bilbao, which was secured against the negative of the film.

'Because of the nature of Spanish co-productions,' observed John Connolly, 'the signatories of the loan were Gordon's nominal co-producer Gregorio Sacristan, and the film's accountant. Since these two gentlemen had no desire to be stuck with the bill from Banco de Bilbao, they seized the negative from the laboratory in Madrid.'

In October 1972, *Horror Express* was screened at the *Fifth International Festival of Fantasy and Horror* at Sitges, where it won an award for best screenplay. The film was then picked up for British distribution by Gala Film Distributors. Following a UK trade show in March 1973, *Horror Express* finally got an official UK release in June 1974 as part of a double bill with the Blaxploitation crime flick *The Godfather Of Harlem* (1973).

'*Horror Express* would cover its $350,000 budget in Spanish ticket sales alone,' said Connolly, 'but was never the hit it might have been. Nevertheless, its reputation has only grown in the decades since its release and has built a sizeable cult following.'

'It went down well abroad,' said Eugenio Martin, 'but nobody thought much of it here. The Spanish critics reviewed it following their usual negative criteria.'

The critical response was mixed. There was praise from *Cinemaforme* when they wrote, 'Using the immortal Peter Cushing and Christopher Lee as indispensable elements in the fabric, Martin has succeeded in making a very interesting film, in which the atmosphere is a marvel of realism. The two "sacred monsters", Cushing and Lee, are surrounded by a highly effective ensemble in which Alberto de Mendoza's mystical character is a stand-out,'

Although finding the film, 'An inferior reworking of *The Thing From Another World* (1956),' *Time Out* found much to enjoy. 'From their first greeting of, "Well, well, look who's here!" Lee and his arch-rival Cushing, at their most urbane, ensure that it remains watchable, while the express train setting keeps it all moving at a better speed than it perhaps deserves.'

Screen International also appreciated Cushing and Lee's presence. 'It's a gothic horror on wheels, lightly sprinkled with in-jokes for the benefit of British audiences who can understand the understated wit. Christopher Lee and Peter Cushing portray stiff upper-lipped Englishmen coping with a lot of hysterical foreigners.' *The Sunday Times* wrote, 'The supernatural and medical horrors are enjoyably absurd, and it is always a pleasure to see Peter Cushing and Christopher Lee together.' *The Sunday Telegraph* also praised their performances. 'Both Lee and Cushing have developed a dapper way of saying an idiotic line straight, while still communicating the joke of it to the audience.' For the *Monthly Film Bulletin*, 'as bad horror films go, it isn't all that bad.'

Variety on the other hand felt the film could have been developed better. 'Though the picture does attain some nice horrific moments and builds up the tension quite nicely, the sci-fi angle is too laboured, while the transfer of evil powers by glowing eyes is too childish for sophisticated audiences.'

The Observer wasn't overly impressed. 'You would need to be fanatically devoted to Cushing and Lee to get much more than a hollow laugh and a snooze out of *Horror Express*.'

Horror Express is a rollercoaster of a movie, even if it's far from perfect, especially with the science fiction angle. The alien possessing the fossil is comprised of pure energy that can transport itself from one animal to another, which begs the question why such an alien would need to build a spaceship to return home. It also seems too much of a coincidence that the passengers include a rocket scientist and a Count who has knowledge of metals, which are perfect for the creature to construct its ship.

That said, *Horror Express* runs at a cracking pace. Eugenio Martin keeps things ticking over and the claustrophobic tension is well sustained. The thrilling climax brings everything to a satisfactory conclusion.

And there's Cushing and Lee in top form and having lots of fun with the material. Although the characters are thinly sketched, the actors get some great opportunities to feed off one another. At first, we see them as rival scientists with Lee's bad tempered Professor Saxton having little time for his playful colleague Dr Wells. They simply nettle one another, until the monster goes on the rampage, and then they team up to find out who is behind the killings as well as becoming spokespersons for the panicking passengers.

Their partnership is finally sealed with the film's most famous scene. Inspector Mirov (now possessed by the alien) is discussing the situation with Saxton and Wells, who have advised all the passengers to stay in pairs. Seeing that the scientists have joined forces, Mirov says, 'The two of you together, that's fine. But what if one of you is the monster?' The scientists react with astonishment, prompting Wells to say, 'Monster? We're British you know!' Saxton smiles silently in approval.

Cushing's performance in *Horror Express* is more remarkable considering the emotional trauma he was going through. After playing several bereaved characters, his sense of fun had returned as he charms the impossibly beautiful Helga Line and revels in the banter he shares with Lee. It seemed being away from all things familiar did more good than staying at home. Working in a new environment with different actors energised his performance.

Lee also has a great time as Professor Saxton. His haughty scientist soon mellows in the face of the unfolding dangers. He even becomes heroic when he risks his life to save the countess from the alien. It makes a pleasant change to see Lee play a good guy, and it shows with his enjoyable performance.

Cushing and Lee are well served by the strong supporting cast of Euro horror veterans with Albert de Mendoza having a fun time as Pujardov. Julio Pena (who died shortly after completing *Horror Express*) is equally effective in what turned out to be a dual role, and Sylvia Tortosa makes a suitably dewy-eyed countess, even though she's no match for the seductive Helga Line.

Line provides a perfect foil for Dr Wells, who clearly has his naughty eye on her. Annoyed with having to share his berth with Saxton, when his colleague is arrested and placed in solitary confinement, he could now seduce the female spy, only for his fun to be ruined by Mirov who requests he performs an autopsy on one of dead soldiers.

Wells has no choice but to ask his assistant, the cigar puffing Miss Jones, for help. Looking at the beautiful Miss Line seated in the dining carriage, she responds with, 'Yes, well at your age I'm not surprised.' Alice

Reinhart has a great time as Cushing's assistant. A veteran of the American stage, Reinhart worked extensively on radio on both sides of the Atlantic, making it surprising that her voice was dubbed in *Horror Express*.

There is another star in the film, and his name was billed over Cushing and Lee on the various American releases. With his trademark shaved head, Telly Savalas is great as Captain Kazan. Swigging vodka, putting everyone on the train under arrest, babbling nonsense, and happily playing the role for laughs. It's a fun cameo and Savalas chews the scenery with good humour. He also enjoyed working with Cushing and Lee, who he described as, 'two very bright, erudite, interesting men.'

This leads to the thrilling climax when the alien (now possessing Pujardov), finishes off Kazan and his men. Later, after Saxton confronts Pujadov for answers, the alien uses its powers to reanimate the Cossacks as white eyed zombies. The actors were really working blind during the climactic dual with Saxton as he saves the Countess.

Eugenio Martin enjoyed working with the three stars. 'Christopher Lee and Peter Cushing were two very good actors in their own way, and Telly Savalas was a very good actor in his. Lee and Cushing were both very orthodox and disciplined, incredibly professional, who could do seven identical takes of a single shot because they knew what they had to do, and they knew that they were doing it well. They never made mistakes in their lines or their next blocking, they were always ready, they never showed anyone else's work down. They hit their marks, knowing exactly what fans of the Gothic expected of them. Savalas was the opposite: an impulsive, emotional actor, a lover of improvisation, someone who enjoyed finding new things in each take, in order to react spontaneously. I enjoyed working with Savalas more: as a director of actors, I found him more inspiring.'

With *Horror Express* completed, Cushing and Lee returned to England to star in their next film.

24: Back To Blighty

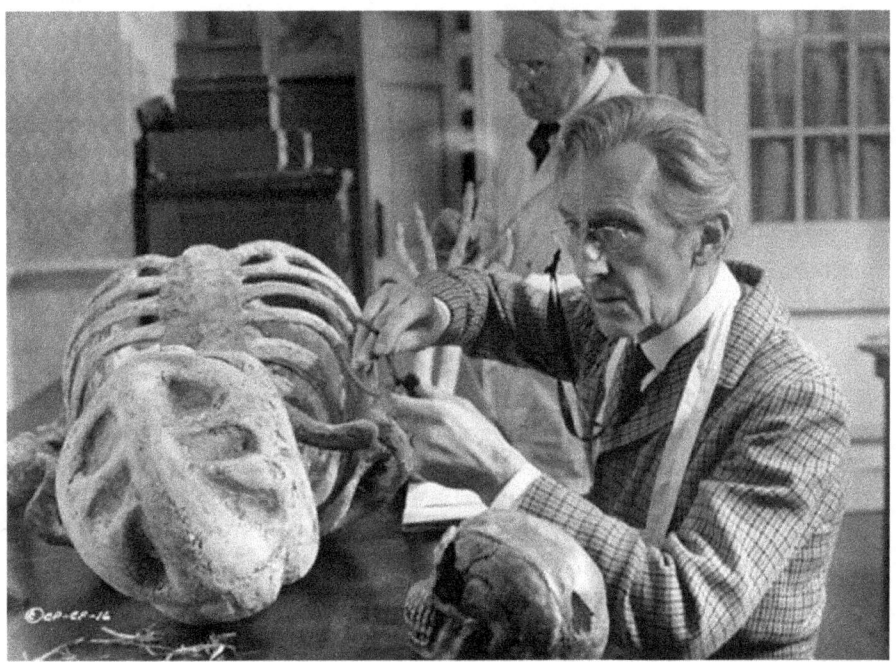

Cushing in *The Creeping Flesh*.

Directed by Freddie Francis, *The Creeping Flesh* is something of a companion piece to *Horror Express* as it also ventures into Lovecraft's Cthulhu Mythos universe (without actually being explicit about it). The tone is much grimmer, and once again, Cushing plays a bereaved widower.

The Creeping Flesh was the brainchild of producer Michael Redbourn. He secured the rights of the project in January 1971 but didn't start any preparation for a year because he wanted to get the right people, and that included Cushing, Christopher Lee, Freddie Francis (replacing Don Sharp) and producer Norman Priggen. Considering Francis' reluctance to make further horror films, securing his services was quite a coup.

Redbourn approached Tony Tenser at Tigon Films to bankroll the property. 'From Tenser's perspective,' observed writer John Hamilton, 'Lee and Cushing made the film a bankable proposition, at least in the UK where they were at that point thought of as being part of an elite group of stars whose mere presence could guarantee box-office receipts. Veteran cinematographer Freddie Francis had a reputation for quality work in the genre and more importantly from Tigon's perspective for delivering his films on time and within budget. Tenser agreed to acquire the UK rights through Tigon in exchange for a financial stake. World Film Services would retain the overseas rights as well as owning the picture itself. Tenser of course took the executive producer credit but was content with the package as it stood and called for no script or cast changes.'

Cushing was assigned the pivotal role of Professor Emmanuel Hildren, a scientist who returns to England with a unique fossil from New Guinea. Lee has the smaller role of Emmanuel's unscrupulous half-brother James. By 1971 Lee was allegedly Britain's highest paid actor, and to secure his services, he received top billing, even though Cushing had the bigger role. 'Despite the disparity of the role,' said John Hamilton, 'Lee's status had by this time all but eclipsed that of his long-time friend, so he was assured both top billing and the larger pay packet.' Lee was paid three times as much as Cushing, although both actors received a percentage of the profits.

Production began in January 1972 at Shepperton Studios. Told in flashback from a white cell, Cushing's Emmanuel brings a magnificent skeleton, discovered by him in New Guinea in 1894, back to his Victorian home where he is greeted by his beautiful daughter Penelope (Lorna Heilbron) before continuing his work in his laboratory.

At first glance everything seems pleasant, but something isn't quite right, and as things progress, the real skeleton of the story is not the fossil but the one that exists in the professor's own closet. We later learn that Penelope has been left to run the household with insufficient funds while her father travels the world. Emmanuel clearly loves his daughter, but there's a thin barrier between them.

Things take a turn for the worse when Emmanuel receives a letter from his half-brother James (who runs the local asylum) informing him that his wife, a long-term inmate, has died. For many years Emmanuel has never spoken to Penelope about her mother, who she thought had died many years earlier.

The meeting between Emmanuel and James is vintage Cushing and Lee, and this time they are sparring partners, which Lee felt generated a better atmosphere. James is working on a treatise on mental disorders and, like Emmanuel, is hoping to win the coveted Richter Prize. James coldly tells his sibling, 'Things have changed. It was always you who was destined for great success, whereas I was only the poor, hard-working half-brother, whom you had to put up with. Now it is I who am the success. I intend to win that Richter Prize, Emmanuel, and the prestige that goes with it.'

Emmanuel's wonderful return home is now an emotional anti-climax that makes the skeleton secondary to the events that have taken place. This soon changes when Emmanuel splashes water on one of the skeleton's fingers.

Flesh grows on the finger, and Emmanuel realises that he may have found the remains of an ancient god known by the New Guinea natives as the 'Evil One' and is reputed to return when the sky gods 'weep', meaning rain.

Chopping the finger off, Emmanuel thinks he may have found a way to prevent what he calls 'the disease of evil'. He develops a serum that he believes can cure humanity of all forms of evil, including insanity.

Worried that Penelope may inherit her mother's insanity, Emmanuel rashly injects her with the untested serum, but instead of curing her (she showed no sign of insanity, only anger) she turns evil, or at least nasty, and runs amok in a local tavern where she murders someone and ends up at her uncle's asylum.

After a failed blackmail attempt, James steals both Emmauel's research and the skeleton. When it starts raining, the reanimated creature returns to Emmanuel's home to retrieve its finger.

The Creeping Flesh is an interesting character study that shows far more depth and intelligence than most recent British chillers. Freddie Francis' stylish direction manages to weave the complex plot together with some clarity, building things up to a suspenseful and satisfactory climax that includes a surprise twist ending which leaves a lot of unanswered questions, mainly the validity of Emmanuel's story.

Cushing gives one his best performances with Lee adding solid support. Special mention to Lorna Heilbron as Penelope: her degradation from beautiful, devoted daughter to feral lunatic is brilliantly realised.

Heilbron was highly impressed at Cushing's attention to detail. 'He came the first day on the set with his script covered, literally covered, with notes he had written about what he felt his character would do or be feeling at any particular time. He also knew down to the last detail what props he would require and had obviously chosen his costumes with immense care. Within the careful forethought he was very flexible so that if an actor gave him something unexpected, he would respond to this and was willing to go with what was happening now. He was charming, courteous and clever, and was dearly liked and admired by everyone.'

Arriving at Shepperton Studios on 6 April 1972 for a two-day shoot, Cushing returned to Amicus for their next portmanteau film, *Asylum* (1972). Scripted by Robert Bloch and directed by Roy Ward Baker, *Asylum* consisted of four creepy tales, and as usual Milton Subotsky had hired an excellent cast that included Robert Powell, Patrick Magee, Herbert Lom, Richard Todd, Sylvia Sims, Brit Ekland and Charlotte Rampling.

Cushing appeared with old friend Barry Morse for the second tale, 'The Weird Tailor'. Dressed as a bowler hatted city gent, Cushing's Mr Smith pays a visit to a down-on-his-luck tailor (Morse, narrating the tale from his padded cell), and commissions him to make a magical suit, which is designed to bring his son back to life. Once again Cushing plays a character dealing with bereavement, and gives another heartfelt, but dignified performance.

Much like *The Creeping Flesh*, the beauty of *Asylum* is the ambiguity of the stories: are they genuine or the ravings of four mental patients? Once again, the viewer is left to decide.

Shortly after completing *Asylum*, Cushing went to Pinewood for his next film, working once more with Christopher Lee. In 1970, Lee and Hammer producer Anthony Nelson Keys formed Charlemagne Productions Ltd with the intention of producing more worthwhile British films.

Lee and Keys acquired the rights to the Dennis Wheatley novels, *The Haunting Of Toby Jugg*, *To The Devil, A Daughter* and *The Satanists*, all of which had been unfilmed Hammer projects. They also secured the rights to two John Blackburn novels, *Bury Him Darkly* and *Nothing But The Night*, and an original screenplay by Robin Squire called *Portrait Of Barbara*.

Lee and Keys approached Rank with *The Haunting Of Toby Jugg* and *To The Devil, A Daughter*, but they were rejected in favour of *Nothing But The Night*. Lee was happy with the decision because the novel's two main characters would make perfect roles for him and Peter Cushing.

Nothing But The Night was far from the personal film Lee envisaged. According to Mark Miller, 'Rank financed it and made most of the important decisions, including those regarding budget, script and director. The one suggestion Lee and Keys made that Rank readily agreed to, however, was the casting of Peter Cushing in a leading role opposite Lee. Regrettably, not many of the other decisions were wise. As a result, Lee and Cushing are wasted in what should have been one of their best films.'

Cushing was enthusiastic to be working with Lee once more. 'It's a psychological thriller, I play a pathologist, which I have never done before, and Chris is an ex-army officer with Special Branch Connections. I am happy to say that Hammer Films are not at all disturbed, in fact they are bending over to help us. It will be the third consecutive film I've made with Chris in three months. We've become a sort of Laurel and Hardy act.'

Nor did Cushing feel intimidated by Lee's role as producer. 'We're too good friends for that. The only thing that makes me nervous is myself. I never feel I'm getting what I'm aiming at.'

Production began on 17 April 1972 with Dartmoor doubling up for the Scottish Coast. When several trustees of the wealthy Van Traylen Orphanage die mysteriously, leaving their fortunes to the orphanage, the sinister nature of their deaths piques the interest of Special Branch's Superintendent Charles Bingham (Lee) and his close friend, pathologist Sir

Mark Ashley (Cushing). As the investigation unfolds, it seems the orphans themselves are responsible.

Nothing But The Night has an intriguing premise, but the end result should have been better than it was. Brian Hayles' contradictory script, budget restrictions imposed by Rank, and Peter Sasdy's confused direction undermined the film's effectiveness. Lee was unhappy when it bombed at the box office, and blamed Rank for not promoting the film. *Nothing But The Night* remained his only effort as producer.

Better suited to off-beat roles, Lee is ineffective when it comes to playing policemen, civil servants and other more straight-forward characters. The role of Bingham is boring and Lee gives a boring performance.

Cushing fares slightly better. The original character of Marcus Levy (changed to Sir Mark Ashley) was a widowed concentration camp survivor, a role which would have enabled him to channel his grief with an excellent performance, but on screen, he comes across as unsympathetic and quite bad tempered.

While Charlemagne was planning a second, ultimately unfilmed project, Lee received the role of a lifetime. *The Wicker Man* (1973) is regarded as one of the greatest British chillers ever made, and Lee's turn as the Pagan Lord Summerisle remains his finest horror performance.

Lee wanted Cushing to play the repressed Christian policeman Neil Howie. 'Christopher wanted me for the part that Edward Woodward played, the policeman, but I couldn't do it because I was involved in something else.' Woodward later admitted that 'if I were Christopher, I'd have petitioned for Peter Cushing to appear in the film.'

It is fair to say that Cushing was too old to play Howie and now a deeply religious man, it is unlikely he would have been comfortable with the film's Pagan story. He might have made an interesting Lord Summerisle as the character's age would not have been an issue, or possibly Lyndsey Kemp's pub landlord or Russell Walters' creepy harbour master.

Instead, he was back with Amicus for *And Now The Screaming Starts* (1973). Working again with Roy Ward Baker, Cushing made up a strong cast that included Herbert Lom, Patrick Magee, Ian Ogilvy and Stephanie Beecham. Production began on 17 July 1972 at Shepperton Studios with location work taking place at Oakley Court.

Despite his top billing, Cushing turns up halfway through the film as psychiatrist Dr Pope and sports an awful bouffant wig which, he admitted, 'made him look like Helen Hayes.'

With Stephanie Beecham's beleaguered heroine constantly wailing, the film should have been renamed *And Now The Screaming Never Stops* because that is exactly what she does. There's little to scream about. Its well-made, competently directed and looks impressive thanks to an increased budget, but it's routine stuff, and Cushing's role is basically another well played cameo.

And Now The Screaming Starts didn't get a proper release until the fall of 1974, and received a lukewarm response. *The Exorcist* (1973) had already reinvented the genre that Hammer, Amicus, AIP and Tigon had built their reputations on, and brought about the terminal decline of the British horror market.

'I wouldn't go see *The Exorcist* than I would go and see a blue movie,' said Cushing. 'It would turn me sick to my stomach. I believe good movies should be made to entertain, not make you sick to your stomach. I don't like profanity. The language and some of the things the possessed child does in the movie would turn my stomach. The film is too explicit and blasphemous, and I can't bear blasphemy. In the films I make, the power of good triumphs over evil, and there is nothing profane.' Cushing went as far as telling Christopher Lee not to watch it.

British horror films were still being made at an alarming rate, and Cushing, retaining his wig from *And Now The Screaming Starts*, returned to Hammer to reprise his most famous role one last time.

Frankenstein And The Monster From Hell marked the end of an era. As well as being Cushing's final performance as the Baron, it was also Terence Fisher's swansong. 'I didn't sleep at all the night before I started directing the film, wondering if I was going to make a good job of it, I think any creator feels the same way.' Sadly, the production looks grainy, dour and threadbare.

Fisher remained committed to the project. 'The real task of the fantasy film director is to bring integrity to his film making. I always ask for a similar response from my actors, and I rarely fail to get it, especially from Peter Cushing.'

Based on a script by Anthony Hinds (his last for Hammer) and a cast that included Charles Lloyd Pack, Peter Madden, Patrick Troughton, Madeline Smith and Shane Briant, *Frankenstein And The Monster From Hell* proved to be a fitting end to the series.

Cushing remains impressive as ever in the role that made him a star. The once handsome, elegant and idealistic Baron has descended into madness. Working as a doctor at an insane asylum, he continues his work, but is as much a patient as he is the physician. His goals are twisted, and he has lost his ability to reason. Forgotten by medical science and his theories cast aside, his desire to create life has become little more than the rantings of a madman residing in an institution.

Cushing kept the wig for an appearance in Anglia Television's anthology series *Orson Welles' Great Mysteries*. The series consisted of several macabre tales each one introduced by the cigar chomping Welles.

24: Back To Blighty

With an excellent John Barry score, the series boasted an outstanding cast of Christopher Lee, Patrick Magee, Eli Wallach, Donald Pleasence, Cyril Cusack, Simon Ward and Jane Seymour.

'La Grande Breteche' has Cushing playing Count de Merret, a nobleman who learns that his wife Josephine (Susannah York) is having an affair with a young Spanish army officer. Confronting his wife and forcing her to swear on her crucifix that her lover is not hiding in the closet, he proceeds to have it bricked up. 'Le Grande Breteche' is the most memorable episode with Cushing in fine malevolent form. Directed by Peter Sasdy, this collaboration is far more satisfactory than *Nothing But The Night*.

Frankenstein came to a dignified end, but the same cannot be said for Hammer's other nobleman. *The Satanic Rites Of Dracula* (1973) is notable for being the last horror teaming of Peter Cushing and Christopher Lee.

For Lee, it was time to hang up his fangs. 'I will not play that character anymore. I no longer wish to do it, I no longer have to do it, and I no longer intend to do it. It is now a part of my professional past, just a role I have played in a total of 124 films.'

Cushing was sympathetic with his friend's decision. 'I think he showed great courage when he sought different characters to play in Hollywood, he wanted to cast off the mantle of the Count that had shackled him.'

Directed by Alan Gibson and written by Don Houghton, *The Satanic Rites Of Dracula* doesn't explain how the Count was revived from the previous film and how he managed to amass a fortune as reclusive industrialist D D Denham within the space of a year. Dracula plans to unleash a new strain of bacteria on the world with the help of several senior scientists and government officials who are also his followers.

Dracula's antics come to the attention of British Intelligence, who enlist Inspector Murray (Michael Coles) and Professor Van Helsing (Peter Cushing). Stephanie Beecham was not available to play Jessica, and her hippy character underwent a radical rethink when she was replaced by the prim and proper Joanna Lumley.

Production began at Elstree Studios in November 1972 with William Franklyn, Richard Vernon, Patrick Barr and Freddie Jones making up a strong cast. Houghton's sluggish script is more 007 than Hammer, and while it is an improvement on *Dracula AD 1972*, it remains a depressing experience that doesn't have the camp value of its predecessor.

Lee has next to nothing to do. He makes his first appearance midway through the movie and adopts a phoney Bela Lugosi accent when he first meets Van Helsing. The Count's silly demise in a thorn bush is a far cry from decomposing in sunlight or being impaled on a cross as in previous efforts.

Cushing still gives Van Helsing a sense of urgency, but tiredness had already set in due to his imposed work schedule.

'In the best Dracula films there must always be Peter Cushing and Christopher Lee, anything else is counterfeit,' Joanna Lumley said in her autobiography. 'If (Christopher Lee) is the eagle, then Peter Cushing is the dove. Gaunt, Mekon-looking, with haunted eyes, Peter Cushing is one of the gentlest and most generous men you could meet. Immaculately elegant, he would join us as we sat at the edge of the set on our chairs with names on them, with kindness and courtesy positively whizzing out of him. All people are equal to him, every electrician and runner and carpenter was greeted, every makeup girl made to feel like a duchess.'

William Franklyn, who had worked with Cushing in *Fury At Smuggler's Bay*, was equally praiseworthy of Cushing. 'I've seldom met a person of such generosity of spirit, humour, natural courage and non-judgemental reactions. He was an icon of the non-egotistical, totally professional and immensely companionable actor team-spirit. On a film set, Peter always wore an immaculate white glove, as if being expected to serve crumpets and pour tea. As if by magic, it disappeared the moment the perpetration for a take was sounded, and the on word "print" from the director it would miraculously appear again, with the inevitable cigarette between the first and second fingers. A nicotine-stained professor of whatever branch of horror was, to Peter, unthinkable.'

Filming wrapped in January 1973, and Lee began work on *The Three Musketeers* (1973). He was surprised by Eamon Andrews and the 'Big Red Book' for an episode of *This Is Your Life*. Cushing was on hand to pay tribute, and appearing as the final guest was Vincent Price. This was the first time the three horror legends appeared together on British television.

Warner Brothers showed little enthusiasm with *The Satanic Rites Of Dracula* when it was released in 1974 as a double bill with *Blacula* (1972). It didn't come to American shores until 1978 when Max Rosenberg's short-lived Dynamite Entertainment released it in 1978 under the title *Count Dracula And His Vampire Bride*.

After completing *The Satanic Rites Of Dracula*, Cushing guested on the children's TV series *Ask Aspel*, and was an honoured guest at the National Theatre's John Player Lecture series, where he discussed his work at great length followed by screenings of *Vigil In The Night, Dracula* and *Cash On Demand*. He spoke in detail about his Hollywood career, his work on the stage, and of course Helen, but gave little away about his time with Hammer.

After demanding his money yet again on the *Morecambe And Wise Show* in February 1973, Cushing travelled to France in April 1973 to attend *The Second International Horror Film Festival*, where he received the *Licorne D'Or* award for his performance in *Tales From The Crypt*.

Remaining in France to guest star in *The Zoo Gang*, Cushing returned to

England the following month to star in three Amicus films made back-to-back. The first movie is the best remembered because it marked his first horror teaming with Vincent Price.

Based on Angus Hall's 1969 novel *Devilday*, *Madhouse* (1974) had been on AIP's production schedule for some time. The project resurfaced in April 1973 and to keep costs down, Sam Arkoff struck a co-production deal with Milton Subotsky. With shooting taking place at Twickenham Studios, Subotsky was able to access cheaper sets mainly used for television.

Originally titled *The Revenge Of Dr Death*, *Madhouse* stars Vincent Price as Paul Toombes, a washed-up horror star whose career ended after being suspected of murdering his wife. He reluctantly arrives in London to star in a TV series based on his character Dr Death, only to find himself at the centre of several more murders.

As Toombes' best friend Herbert Flay, Cushing was a late addition to the cast when he replaced Robert Quarry, who was moved to play a different role, that of Oliver Quayle.

It was a historic moment to see Cushing and Price together on the big screen, and even though *Madhouse* is a long way off their best work, it began a friendship that lasted until Price's death in 1993, and was strengthened by the fact that Cushing's birthday was the day before Price's.

Cushing and Price have such a natural on-screen chemistry, it comes as a surprise that a horror teaming hadn't happened sooner. 'The relationship between Vincent and Peter was one of mutual respect,' observed co-star, Natasha Pyne. 'Each had a healthy objective view of their work that made their living, which helped for an easy, mutually supportive working relationship. They seemed to me very good friends.'

Cushing had nothing but admiration for Price, describing him as, 'a dear man, with a great sense of humour, strictly a professional, who cares far more about his work than he allows his public to know. I am extremely fond of him and bask in his gentle kindness and warmth.'

Price was equally in awe of his co-star, especially during their climatic fight scene. 'He's nothing like Christopher Lee because Peter is a very wiry, little fellow. But Peter is one of the strongest men I've ever known in my life. I had to do several fights with him. My God! He can throw you! Nobody warned me about this, and I was sort of battered and bruised. He's a very realistic and very serious-minded actor. I like Peter very much, and I hear from him always at Christmas. On our birthdays we send each other the funniest cards we can find. He's a gentle, sweet man. I am very, very fond of him.'

Natasha Pyne was equally fond of Cushing. 'Peter was a very dignified, quiet, sweet person. He was gentle with old fashioned manners, and he had a vulnerability both as an actor and in life which made one want to wrap him in a warm blanket and cherish him.'

Robert Quarry also enjoyed working with Cushing. 'We became good friends. The nicest gentleman and a darn good actor. It's too bad Peter got stuck in the horror category, because he is really a much better actor than that.' Concerned that Cushing wasn't eating properly, Quarry cooked him dinner at his rented Chelsea apartment during their time on *Madhouse*.

Although enjoyable, *Madhouse* could have been better in view of the once-in-a-lifetime horror teaming. A bored looking Price only shows his customary warmth when he plays opposite Cushing, who doesn't have a lot to do but at least goes into full throttle ham during their climactic fight scene, which Cushing described as a 'Titanic ding dong.'

Madhouse wrapped in June 1973 and a press screening took place in March 1974 before a general release, largely to a negative reaction and an indifferent box office performance. The names of Price and Cushing no longer guaranteed punters would see a film.

During the making of *Madhouse*, Price acted as host for a BBC radio anthology series called *The Price Of Fear*. On Price's insistence, Cushing starred in the show's most memorable episode, 'The Man Who Hated Scenes'. Here Price's host is taking a long train journey where he encounters at breakfast Cushing's timid little man; a chap who tries to avoid a scene if he can help it.

The ineffectual chap turns out to be a cuckolded husband who reluctantly takes revenge on his adulterous young wife. Price may have been the star of *Madhouse*, but it's Cushing who takes the acting honours in 'The Man Who Hated Scenes'.

Cushing's next Amicus chiller took him back to Twickenham Studios in June 1973 for what was to be the studio's final portmanteau picture.

Unable to film further E C comic stories following the critical reaction to *The Vault Of Horror* (1973), Milton Subotsky opted for new tales provided by prolific horror writer Ronald Chetwynd-Hayes. Chetwynd-Hayes' involvement came about via director Kevin Connor, who had purchased the writer's short story collection, *The Undead*. Enlisting Raymond Christodoulou and Robin Clark as screenwriters, Connor, Subotsky and Amicus producer John Dark selected four stories with Connor devising a linking story set in an antiques shop, and *From Beyond The Grave* was born.

Once again, Amicus assembled an excellent cast of David Warner, Ian Bannen, Donald Pleasence, Diana Dors, Ian Carmichael, Margaret Leighton. Nyree Dawn Porter, Ian Ogilvy, Lesley Ann Down and Jack Watson, but for the pivotal role of the mysterious Proprietor of the antique shop, *Temptations Limited*, Peter Cushing took centre stage.

The simple premise involves a customer visiting the shop and purchasing an item under the watchful eye of the cloth-capped, pipe smoking Proprietor. If the customer steals the item or cheats the old man, they meet a nasty end with the 'bumper surprise' that comes with every purchase. Even honest customers get more than they bargain!

After a succession of bereaved characters and wafer-thin roles, Cushing was back to his more humorous antics. With bushy eyebrows, moustache and thick Yorkshire accent, Cushing has a whale of a time.

The accent adds to the sardonic charm of the Proprietor as he looks in disbelief at the crooked behaviour of his customers. He also gets another priceless line of dialogue: Ian Carmichael swaps price tags on two snuff boxes and buys the expensive one for the cheaper price. Without missing a beat, Cushing happily responds with, 'I hope you enjoy snuffing it!' And indeed, he does in grisly style!

Playing the only surviving customer, Ian Ogilvy had nothing but praise for Cushing, who he regarded as, 'a man so saintly and kindly and wise that being in his presence for only a few minutes could comfort the bereaved and calm the hysteric – both of which categories seemed to be drawn to the man like ants to a picnic.'

Although *From Beyond The Grave* did well across the UK, the lack of distribution in the States killed any box office success. Subotsky planned a sequel called *More From Beyond The Grave*, but his relationship with Max Rosenberg deteriorated so badly, he left Amicus in 1975 and embarked on several lawsuits against his former partner, who filed just as many against Subotsky.

The final Amicus horror was *The Beast Must Die* which began production at Shepperton Studio in July 1973 with first time director Paul Annet stepping in after Don Sharp became unavailable.

Based on James Blish's 1950 novella, *There Shall Be No Darkness*, *The Beast Must Die* boasts a quirky voice-over saying, 'This is film is a detective story – in which you are the detective. The question is not "Who is the murderer?", but "Who is the werewolf?" After all the clues have been shown, you will get the chance to give your answer. Watch for the werewolf break.'

Not on a par with William Castle's legendary gimmicks, but still fun. Sadly it's the only highlight of this pedestrian effort that fails to do justice to a nice idea. Paul Annett wasn't happy with the werewolf break but was overruled by Subotsky.

Dropping Blish's main plot, *The Beast Must Die* owes more to Agatha Christie's 1939 novel *Ten Little Indians/And Then There Were None* and the 1924 Richard Connell short story 'The Most Dangerous Game' aka 'The Hounds of Zaroff'. Big game hunter Tom Newcliffe (Calvin Lockhart) wants to achieve the ultimate prize of killing a werewolf and invites to his isolated country estate a weird assortment of guests, all of whom has a guilty secret linked to lycanthropy.

Playing German werewolf expert Dr Lundgren, this was the first time

Cushing encountered the creature. 'I have to admit that werewolves as such are a group of beings that I have never been able to accept in films. Somehow the idea of a wolf's head on a man's body always seems phoney and rather obviously a makeup job, however brilliantly done.'

Due to budgetary restrictions, the werewolf was played by an unconvincingly made-up German Shepherd dog, who co-star Ciaran Madden described as, 'so adorable'. You can see the pooch wagging its tail as it 'attacks' Newcliffe.

This setback, along with Lockhart's weak performance, torpedoes *The Beast Must Die*. Ever the perfectionist, Cushing puts on a decent Germanic accent and a nicely wolfish look courtesy of the makeup artist.

As soon as *The Beast Must Die* was completed, Cushing went to the Far East for his next assignment.

25: The Legend Of The 7 Golden Vampires (1974)

Cushing in *The Legend Of The 7 Golden Vampires*.

The Legend Of The 7 Golden Vampires (1974) was Cushing's third overseas excursion with Hammer. It was also his penultimate film for the studio and his final turn as Van Helsing.

Achieving a knighthood and a wealthy lifestyle, Sir James Carreras decided to retire from Hammer. He had brought his son Michael back to run the company, but their relationship remained stormy and when Sir James failed to tell his son about his intentions to sell Hammer to Tony Tenser, Michael borrowed money from the ICI Retirement Fund and met his father with a counter offer, which was accepted.

Michael Carreras' tenure at Hammer was tragically short lived. According to Bruce Lanier Wright, 'The company he'd acquired was heavily in debt and had never really been wealthy, due to its heavy reliance on the deep pockets to which Sir James had provided access.'

Sir James had a contract with EMI, but upon his retirement the deal was cancelled. 'In (Michael) Carreras' retelling,' said Wright, 'EMI said in so many words that their deal had been with his father, not him, which must have been a shattering vote of no-confidence for the fledgling studio head. Michael was a very different person than his father, just as bright and certainly more creative, but he lacked Sir James' uncanny knack for salesmanship, and would be dogged with financial problems for his remaining tenure with the company.'

Cinema goers in the early seventies were in the grip of kung fu fever, thanks to the success of *Enter The Dragon* (1973). Hollywood quickly invested in movies produced by Golden Harvest and the Shaw Brothers, and television also capitalised on the new trend with shows like the serious *Kung Fu* and the cartoon *Hong Kong Phooey*, while imported series like *The Water Margin* and *Monkey* proved popular on British TV.

Carreras felt the martial arts genre would be commercially perfect for Hammer. He still had his Warner Brothers contract and sensing a potentially interesting idea of combining gothic horror and kung fu, he decided to produce a film based on that concept.

The idea came about thanks to Hammer's in-house screenwriter Don Houghton. Houghton was married to actress Pik-Sen Lim, whose father was a close friend with Hong Kong Film producers The Shaw Brothers, Run Run and Rumne. The brothers had produced several martial arts films, although stiff competition from Golden Harvest were edging them out of the market, so the idea of a co-production with Hammer seemed like a good idea.

Houghton arrived in Hong Kong in February 1973 and was promptly chauffeured to a meeting with the brothers at their studio in Kowloon to discuss the deal. Houghton met Vee King Shaw, the nephew of Run Run Shaw and in charge of production and distribution. He gave Houghton a tour of the studios, prior to the initial meeting.

Houghton was then, 'Collected at my hotel by Vee King Shaw and taken for a magnificent dinner. The party included Vee King Shaw's charming wife Linda, company accountant, Peter Wong and his English wife, Wendy. There followed a tour of Hong Kong nightclubs and nightlife.'

After enjoying the Hong Kong hospitality, Houghton was chauffeured from the hotel to the studios. 'Vee King was waiting for me, and the next three hours were spent on general discussion, questions and answers in regards to any joint or co-production schemes.'

The deal was finally made between Hammer and the Shaw Brothers. Both companies would share the production costs of two movies produced

25: The Legend Of The 7 Golden Vampires (1974)

at the brothers' Hong Kong studio. The proposed start date for the first film was scheduled for 3 September 1973.

Due to constant arguments between the producers over budgets and shooting schedules, the deal was almost abandoned. 'Shooting didn't actually commence until late in October,' said Marcus Hearn, 'and last-minute wrangling between the two sides over the precise costs each company would shoulder almost scuppered the film altogether. Hammer cast only Peter Cushing, Nordic bombshell Julie Ege, Robin Stewart and *The Vampire Lovers*' "Man in Black" John Forbes-Robertson. The remainders, including contract players David Chiang and Shih Szui, were paid for by the Shaws.'

Michael Carreras wanted to develop a series of Asian based chillers under the Hammer name. According to Deborah Del Vecchio, 'Hammer's idea to create a film based on the Far Eastern vampire lore was indeed a novel concept. It could have afforded the filmmakers a whole new medium to explore, a series of films based on various legends of the undead which prevailed around the world.'

With everything straightened out, Houghton started work on the script. The main idea was to have Professor Van Helsing travelling to the Far East to continue his vampire hunting. It was inevitable that Cushing would return to the role.

The character of Dracula wasn't supposed to be in the film, but due to the Count's popularity in many Asian countries, the Shaw Brothers insisted on incorporating the vampire into the story. Houghton hastily inserted Dracula into the script, allowing him to appear at the beginning and the end of the film. With Christopher Lee well and truly finished with the role, John Forbes-Robertson took his place.

Lee was fully aware of the project and tried talking Cushing out of taking part, feeling that the whole thing was beneath him. Ralph Bates offered to step in at the last minute should Cushing change his mind. Still grieving over Helen, he felt a change of scenery would help alleviate his depression.

The story begins in 1804, forty years before Bram Stoker was born, where a Chinese disciple named Kah (Chan Sen) makes his way to Castle Dracula. The Count then rises from his coffin to hear Kah asking for help, in subtitles since the actor had problems mastering the English language.

The coffin idea was quite novel and according to John Forbes-Robertson, 'They had a plank of wood like a seesaw, hinged in the middle. I was strapped on it and then two stagehands pulled on the part where my feet were, and my head came up and suddenly you see me rise into shot.'

'You never see him get out of the coffin,' said Roy Ward Baker, who replaced the original choice of director Gordon Hessler, 'he just appears beside the other man in the scene as if he'd just floated down. You cannot have a character like Dracula getting up, hitching his cloak, and stepping out of his coffin. That would destroy the mood immediately.'

'When I shot that first scene with the Chinese actor,' Forbes-Robertson added, 'in the script he hadn't got one word of English, and I hadn't got one word of Chinese. I said, "May I see your script?" and he showed me. I ran my hand down saying, "There's your speech. Then you stop. Then that's me." All I wanted was to hear what his words sounded like for my cue and that's how you worked.'

Kah asks Dracula to return with him to the village of Ping Kwei in Szechwan where he is the high priest. The once dominant Seven Golden Vampires have long lost their power in the village. Initially scoffing at the idea, Dracula takes possession of Kah's body and heads off on the long journey to Ping Kwei.

The best laid plans of vampires and undead didn't seem to work as a century later, Professor Van Helsing is giving a lecture about vampirism at Chunking University. Dracula's presence in Ping Kwei hasn't done much good either; the legend of the Seven Golden Vampires is now a forgotten myth: even the name and location of the village is unknown.

Van Helsing's lecture is met with scorn by the students and tutors in attendance, except for Hsi Ching (David Chiang), who is the descendent of the farmer who defeated the seven vampire lords who presided over the village. Together with Hsi Ching's siblings, all of them martial arts experts, Van Helsing's son (Robin Stewart) and wealthy widow Vanessa Buren (Julie Ege) who finances the expedition, their party sets off to Ping Kwei.

Production began on 22 October 1973 with the technical crew consisting of Hammer and Shaw personnel and Roy Ward Baker overseeing the shoot.

Although Baker thought it was a good idea, he found *The Legend Of The 7 Golden Vampires* an unhappy experience. 'There was a clash of cultures before filming was due to commence. This was another classic example of inadequate liaison, reconnaissance and planning. The advance party set off a couple of weeks ahead of the shooting date: Jean Walter, production secretary; Christopher Carreras, production supervisor; Don Houghton and I. As soon as we arrived Houghton withdrew to an office somewhere to rewrite, or complete the script, which was in a fairly rough state. So, I walked around the vast studios with Christopher. Now, we had to come to shoot the picture in the usual way: direct recorded synch sound in English. We found the stages were enormous tin sheds with no sound-proofing at all. We noticed a number of stray dogs bounding about, barking their heads off. Kai Tak airport was not far away. The answer was simple: the usual local method was to shoot everything silent, because the release of their films in the enormous territory of the Far East was to audiences who spoke several different languages. So, the actors spoke their lines in their

25: The Legend Of The 7 Golden Vampires (1974)

own way, which could then be roughly dubbed into any speech suitable for any market. These divergent approaches led to friction which was never satisfactorily solved.

'The standing sets in these studios had to be seen to be believed. They were magnificent, the best that you would expect from the Chinese design. They had been standing for years and the dust underfoot was four inches thick. Unfortunately, very little use was made in our script of these facilities, in fact I can't remember any. So, we had to build sets. The art director was Johnson Tsao, a charming man who spoke English very well and delivered some splendid settings. He was a great man to work with and made a bonus in the whole operation. What he could not supply, and neither could anyone else, were locations.'

Baker had his hands full with the locations, the Chinese actors and the fight scenes. 'The script called for a caravan crossing a desert. Hong Kong is barely three times the size of the Isle of Wight, which has a population of 125,000. Hong Kong had a population, then 25 years ago, of four million people and rising daily. The only suitable open space left was a spot on a hill right by the border of China proper. It was a few hundred yards square. The carts for the caravan were provided from stock, but the only horses available came from the Hong Kong racecourse. They did not take to being put in shafts at all.'

At least the horses were more cooperative than the actors, making things increasingly frustrating for Baker. 'David Chiang, who played the leading man, is a very good actor. He was very fluent in English, he's terribly keen to learn, and once you'd explained a word to him, he got it straight away. Apart from him, none of the characters could speak a word of English. They had to say their words in Chinese, and in any case, there were eighteen barking dogs and two thousand people all working around you on the sets and reconstructing the studio, going to the canteen and all that sort of stuff. It was absolute bedlam, and you couldn't keep them quiet. They had been making pictures this way forever, and for us to come into there and think it was all going to work like clockwork, like Pinewood, was cock-eyed.'

The martial arts sequences led to tensions between Michael Carreras and the Shaw Brothers and further testing Baker's patience. 'As far as the kung-fu was concerned, I said, "I'm going to film it with my unit. You can arrange the fight, sure, but the way they are covered and presented will be my way of doing it, as it is my picture." And the result is that those kung-fu sequences are more effective than the average kung-fu sequence in the average Chinese picture, because they're better photographed and they've been better directed and the camera being in the right place at the right moment, and the cuts are set to a pattern.'

Further tensions mounted when, on 31 October, Run Run Shaw visited the set, and wasn't happy with the way filming was going. According to Marcus Hearn, 'Run Run viewed the first rough-cut kung-fu sequence and declared it unsatisfactory, demanding that the remaining action scenes be shot by one of the company's own directors. A second unit was duly formed under Chang Cheh who, in addition, shot extra martial arts scenes for a 110 minute Far East release, giving rise to a so-called uncut version.'

With his scenes being reshot by Chang Cheh, Baker was now at breaking point. 'At one stage of the game, apparently the producers thought that the Chinese were going to take over the whole thing with another director. They had a director and cameraman lined up for it. The whole thing would have looked completely different. They were going to use different cameras and cameramen. They never had cameramen, they had lighting gaffers. They did manage to shoot one or two minutes of night scenes for me, and it was so underexposed they had to send it back to Tokyo and get it reprocessed.'

'Toward the end of the shoot, we got John Wilcox out from England, which helped.' Baker added. 'There were innumerable problems of communication between the British crew and the Chinese. If the camera operator wants the dolly to go forward a half an inch, it is useless to say to a Chinese grip, "Take me in a gnat's" matters are only made worse if you shout at him.

'The sound recordist, Les Hammond, worked under the most appalling difficulties, but he managed his relationships with the crew well. He and his two assistants kept themselves strictly to themselves, both on duty and off, discretion and dignity. I admired them greatly. I felt that the heaviest influence on the production was Chinese, as inevitably would be, but my responsibilities as I saw it was to make a Hammer picture for distribution in the English speaking markets, The sound recording team were the key to that. There was continuing pressure to abandon direct sound and post-synch the dialogue. What? All of it?'

Julie Ege was one of the observers who quickly became aware of the chaos when she arrived in Hong Kong. 'It was filmed in co-op with the Shaw Brothers, who were experts in martial arts films. Apparently, the project was expected to be a new adventure into the international film market for them. But it didn't take long after we arrived when all the cultural differences between the crews became apparent. Anyone who was used to filmmaking by British standards would be shocked to find the studio facilities in Hong Kong as big step down. The soundproof stages were a joke and I think Roy Ward Baker had fits of anger several times a day.'

'Thanks be for Peter Cushing!' exclaimed Baker, 'quiet and reserved as usual, a rock.'

Ever the trooper, Cushing worked on the film without a word of complaint. 'I made several films with Peter,' said Baker, 'and he was an absolute charmer. Before his appearance in every scene, he would check how he was dressed, what was in his pockets. Meticulous detail. He was very straightforward, but strait-laced, I'd say. A nice person who made a career by specialising, and what he did he was good at.'

'Peter Cushing was lovely, and we all enjoyed him so much,' said Julie Ege. 'He had recently lost his wife and there were rumours going around that he pretended dining with his wife in the hotel room by setting the table for two. Whenever he had time off from filming, he would visit many of the cultural sights of Hong Kong. The filming must have been hard on him. The days were long, hot and humid. We all came down with food poisoning but pulled through at the end.'

John Forbes-Robertson also enjoyed working with the actor. 'I remember saying to Peter Cushing one day, "Can they possibly get me a stand-in?" because it was so hot while they were messing around with everything and when it comes to the shot, it looks very bad. Peter later said, "John, they don't have anything like that out here!"'

The intense atmosphere between Hammer and the Shaws reached breaking point. Renee Glynn, who had worked as Hammer's continuity girl for many years, had her own unforgettable experience on her arrival in Hong Kong. 'In the studio it was a big experience, because they hardly spoke any English at all, but we had a bilingual first assistant, and we had Christopher Carreras as second. Roy Ward Baker, who I've now forgiven, was screaming at these Chinese not to spit. Screaming at them spitting is one thing, but he was screaming about them, and we were supposed to be a handpicked, well behaved, understanding at each other people's "cultures" crew, cast by Michael.

'The animosity was so great,' she added, 'that when it was Chinese New Year and Run Run Shaw had a party – and you go and you call him Uncle – only Les Bowie, the camera crew and I went, because Michael wasn't speaking to him, Roy Ward Baker wasn't speaking to him, and that was awful. They don't understand about direct sound in Hong Kong because they shoot everything mute, because they've got Mandarin, or Cantonese or whatever to record afterwards, and they all talk nonsense and so the sound man almost went insane. They wouldn't keep quiet and all that. The first film went really well, except that there were complaints about us – not the camera crew or me – about our behaviour, slighting the Chinese.'

The final edit was problematic for Hammer's editor Chris Barnes. 'Originally it was decreed that we would shoot the film, edit it and get approval by Run Run Shaw and Michael Carreras of the final cut, and then we would bring it back to do the sound, the sound effects, the dialogue and the music. Then Run Run Shaw said, "No, we would like to finish it here!" So, then we went into that sort of preamble, which opened a can of worms of enormous proportions, because they were not geared for it. They had been shooting film there silent up until we arrived, for the past ten years or so, so we were shooting sound on non-sound proofed stages. We took our own sound crew out. There was quite a bit of post synch to be done for extraneous noise and that type of thing. So, there was that to be done, which meant I had to get someone to shoot some of the artists, who had already gone back to England.'

Barnes had no choice but to use Shaw's Tokyo laboratories. 'Whilst I was in Japan, Run Run Shaw's sound department shot the FX and kung-fu noises, to the dialogues I had prepared, added music and dubbed it. I was not very happy with the treatment of the dialogue in the dub, but my main concern was the music used. We had no copyright clearing for it so no way could this be shown in Western cinemas. This I told Michael Carreras, and so Michael and Run Run got together, and they agreed that we'd come back to England, and we'd dub it, and do the music with Jimmy Bernard. By then of course, we'd gone a long time over schedule and the money, so of course it had to be limited.'

'Following its completion,' said Marcus Hearn, 'the cost to the Shaw Brothers' inhouse facilities was revised upwards from the original estimate to the tune of 800,000 Hong Kong Dollars. This would have a significant effect on Hammer, who had already taken out a substantial loan to pay its contribution to the two pictures. And the company's Hong Kong nightmare was not yet over.'

The Legend Of The 7 Golden Vampires went on general release in August 1974, with many critics feeling that combining Hammer horror and kung-fu action wasn't too successful. Alan Frank felt the film was, 'an uneasy combination of kung-fu and vampirism, designed to combine the then current popularity of martial arts movies with Hammer horror,' while Leslie Halliwell thought it had, 'Plenty of gusto, but not much sense.'

Time Out was less enthusiastic. 'It's a shame that the film should muff some of the simplest set-ups and rely for effect some rather mechanically intercut vampire attacks.' *The Sunday Times*' Dilys Powell description of the film came across as a back-handed compliment. 'Has vampires with knobs on, oriental vampires with gilt heads versus exponents of Martial Arts. It would be tedious were it not for the distinguished presence of Peter Cushing as a Dracula hunter and for some advanced exercises in the practice of vampire disintegration which has long been a feature of the genre.'

The Little Shoppe Of Horrors was more positive, 'The attempt to do something different gives the production an added freshness.' 'Doesn't take itself seriously,' said *Films Illustrated*, 'fatally I think, because both a Martial Arts drama and a vampire saga need careful stylisation and

25: The Legend Of The 7 Golden Vampires (1974)

tongues anywhere in their cheek. A sanguine chop suey with few redeeming features.'

The most memorable review came from Charles Murray of *Melody Maker*, which Michael Carreras kept as a memento. '*The Legend Of The 7 Golden Vampires* is perhaps the worst film I've ever seen. The part of Christopher Lee is played by a gent named John Forbes-Robertson, who is not over-endowed with either presence or charisma and looks like an old queen whose makeup has run. The part of Peter Cushing is played rather reluctantly and without much enthusiasm by Peter Cushing. The part of a pair of big tits with a Swedish accent is played by Julie Ege. Why do otherwise intelligent people pay money to see this garbage? I don't know. That's why I'm going to see it again.'

'Let's just say East did not meet West,' said Carreras. 'I have great admiration for Shaw and his operation and the relationship between him and us should have been successful but unfortunately, it wasn't, and nobody's blaming anybody. We just had two different points of view. When we saw the finished picture we thought the kung-fu parts of the film were much more exciting than the Dracula sequences, so we cut a version without Dracula at all, and what we had was a very good Chinese action-adventure/kung-fu frolic but unfortunately in that form it was too short, so we had to put Dracula back in.'

'The sad part of this adventure,' observed Roy Ward Baker, 'was that we were unable to take advantage of the opportunities that were at hand, which were considerable. The writer and the director should have been sent out there at least two months ahead of production, to tailor the script to the local capabilities.'

The Legend Of The 7 Golden Vampires did decent business in England and Europe and was a big hit in the Far East. Despite the insistence of including Dracula, Warners did not distribute the film in America. After Cannon Films and AIP also decided not to release it Stateside, it was eventually bought by Max Rosenberg's Dynamite Pictures, who put it out in 1979 as *The Seven Brothers Meet Dracula*.

For all its faults, and there's plenty of them, *The Legend Of The 7 Golden Vampires* is fun to watch. Roy Ward Baker does a solid job under difficult circumstances and the kung-fu action scenes are well staged. The film's most memorable moment remains the zombie soldiers rising from their graves to follow the Golden Vampires, which has a nightmarish quality reminiscent of Amando de Ossorio's *Blind Dead* series. These atmospheric touches make up for the inadequacies of a troubled production.

Peter Cushing gives his usual, impeccable performance as Van Helsing, who looks just at home in the Far East as he does in Mittel Europe, especially when demonstrating the use of Buddha to tackle vampirism. Cushing's steely resolve remains as sharp as ever.

The supporting cast aren't as effective. While not as charismatic as Bruce Lee, David Chiang is a likeable lead who works well with Cushing. He's athletic enough during the action scenes and provides a strong, intelligent presence that compliments Cushing's steadfast acting.

Shih Szu (playing the only female of the seven martial arts experts who accompany the expedition) is very pretty and shows off her kung-fu skills to great effect, but doesn't get a chance to act, and ends up the damsel in distress for the ultra-bland Robin Stewart, whose static presence isn't helped by having most of his scenes opposite Cushing.

Julie Ege looks stunning, but gives a wooden performance and John Forbes-Robertson is miscast as Dracula. Decked out in lurid green makeup, red lipstick and someone else's voice, he poses no threat to Christopher Lee. The final confrontation between Dracula and Van Helsing is ridiculous as the Count simply falls on his stake.

Legend Of The 7 Golden Vampires was successful enough for a possible sequel called *Kali, Devil Bride Of Dracula*, with Cushing returning as Van Helsing, out to destroy a vampire-inspired Thugee cult in India. Once again, Dracula would make a fleeting appearance. Nothing came of it, making *The Legend Of The 7 Golden Vampires* Cushing's final Hammer horror.

Except that the Hammer Hong Kong horror wasn't over yet.

26: Shatter (1975)

Stuart Whitman with Cushing in *Shatter*.

Michael Carreras' Hong Kong nightmare continued when he embarked on his second co-production with the Shaw Brothers, but with ill feeling existing between both parties, this would be their last collaboration.

Shatter (1975) is a martial arts action movie starring American actor Stuart Whitman. Thanks to his links with the Shaw Brothers, Don Houghton returned as screenwriter and reluctant producer.

Shatter originated from an unused script for an abortive project called *Shoot*. It had been planned back in May 1972 after Carreras made a deal with George Brown, a Canadian producer he met at the Cannes Film Festival. Houghton retooled the script and production was due to start in Canada in August 1972.

When Brown filed for bankruptcy, the project was shelved until December 1973 when Carreras joined forces with the Shaw Brothers. Houghton rewrote the script to satisfy Run Run Shaw's requirements, and renamed it *Shatter*.

Production began in Hong Kong on 17 December 1973, immediately after *The Legend Of The 7 Golden Vampires* wrapped, and retaining the same crew. Among the locations used was Kai Tak Airport.

Carreras wasn't happy about Houghton's role as producer. 'Don came out to Hong Kong with me as associate producer, because he'd written both of them and was my contact point, but it just didn't suit his personality. It was a silly thing to do, if anything it was a gesture of thank you, but he actually wanted to do the job and that wasn't good. He was actually going to produce *Shatter*, but by the time I came back from California to line up the second picture, all sorts of weird and wonderful things had happened on the first one.'

Assigned to direct was a protégé of Roger Corman's, Monte Hellman. 'I literally got a call from my agent on Thursday morning in late November and went to meet up with Michael Carreras and was hired instantly.

'I left the next day for Hong Kong, and started pre-production the following Monday, and I think we only had a couple of weeks pre-production. I had a lot of problems with the script. Don Houghton, the screenwriter, was also the producer at the time and I just found it a difficult situation. The suggestions that I made didn't fall on kindly ears.'

Hellman quickly encountered production problems with the loss of his director of photography. 'John Wilcox was the original cinematographer. He was one of my favourites. He'd done a lot of the Carol Reed films that I liked so much. He became ill during the production with liver problems and was in hospital.' Wilcox's camera operator Roy Ford took over for the rest of Hellman's shoot.

'It was an interesting time at the Shaw Brothers,' Hellman added, 'and this was one of the reasons that I had a problem with Michael Carreras. We were sharing a crew with two other productions. They were literally working around the clock in three eight-hour shifts, and we would attempt to start shooting at eight in the morning and they wouldn't show up till noon, because they were exhausted.'

Carreras was equally exhausted with what was going on. He accused Don Houghton of 'going native', and promptly removed him from the production. 'He'd just lost his way,' Carreras recalled. 'He was supposed to be doing schedules, and so on, but I don't know what he was doing.'

The problems continued when Carreras removed Hellman from the production. 'At the end of three weeks of this four or five week schedule, I had only finished half the picture because we were only shooting half a day, and so essentially, I was fired because we were behind schedule. Michael Carreras took over and I guess it took him another six months to shoot the rest of the picture.' With Carreras stepping in, Roy Ford was replaced by Brian Probyn.

With production wrapping on 15 January 1974, and Peter Cushing, who was on the production for four days, returning to the UK on Boxing Day after ten weeks in Hong Kong, his and Anton Diffring's scenes would have been shot by Hellman before his departure.

The change of director left continuity girl Renee Glynne perplexed. 'Michael Carreras replaced the director, Monte Hellman. I don't know why, he's only the biggest cult director in America. They thought he couldn't do it, and I never understood. I remember he shot the African assassination scene. They said it was bad filming and that he couldn't do it, and they didn't have a row or something: very odd. Then Michael muddled his way through.'

The plot for *Shatter* is uninspiring. The title character, played by Stuart Whitman, is a veteran assassin hired by a powerful drug cartel to eliminate the president of an East African state. With the job done, Shatter flies to Hong Kong to collect payment from the cartel's corrupt banker Hans Leber (Anton Diffring).

Shatter turns out to be a victim of a double-cross and is now on the run from various factions, including British Intelligence operative Rattwood (Peter Cushing). With the help of martial arts instructor Tai Pah (Ti Lung) and Shatter's lover Mai-Mee (Lily Li), the hitman turns the tables on everyone.

Shatter represents the tail end of the dying Martial Arts genre. Pacing and execution are sluggish, and while the action scenes are decent, Ti Lung is no substitute for Bruce Lee. Unattractively photographed, the grimy locations make Hong Kong look like a slum, although it does give *Shatter* added realism.

Stuart Whitman has a world-weary look about him, but he also gives a wooden performance. Spending several miserable weeks in Hong Kong was hardly a paid vacation for Whitman so it was a case of take the money and run. Anton Diffring is suitably slimy but has little to do.

Renee Glynne wasn't happy about Cushing's participation in the film, 'The worst thing about it was Peter Cushing playing a part that wasn't a Peter Cushing part.' At least his performance as Rattwood is an interesting departure from his usual style.

Wearing a trench coat and sucking on mints, Rattwood is a nasty piece of work who deservedly gets roughed up by Shatter. Cushing also gets some decent dialogue which he delivers with sardonic relish.

Returning to Elstree for a final edit, a new music score was added. Hammer's musical director Philip Martel thought the Shaw Brothers' original score was, 'absolutely appalling'. Carreras thought he had a hit movie on his hands and even considered a possible TV series starring Cushing and Whitman.

Shatter was quietly released in the States by Avco Embassy Pictures in March 1975 as *They Call Me Mr Shatter*, and quickly disappeared. EMI released the film in the UK in September 1977, before it also vanished into obscurity.

The few reviews *Shatter* received were negative. *Variety* found it 'dull and sloppy, though there are a few scenes of entertaining hokum. The martial arts sequences were choreographed with unusual skill, but that kind of stuff is getting stale by now.' *Variety* also praised Peter Cushing's 'Expertly cynical performance.'

Leslie Halliwell was equally unimpressed, calling *Shatter* a, 'Botched attempt to combine a thriller with the style of a kung-fu movie.'

'*Shatter* was unfortunately a bad picture,' said Michael Carreras, 'no question about it. We ran into all sorts of problems, and like all pictures that are bad, I think it was badly conceived from the start. One did all sorts of things to try and save it, but it didn't work.'

Renee Glynne was a little more positive. 'I can't see anything wrong with it, but according to Michael Carreras, it was supposed to be the worst film ever made! It was a mess, but I can still watch it and not be appalled.'

The Hong Kong films are not without interest, but the venture was a noble misfire for all concerned. Run Run Shaw had hoped the collaboration would give him mainstream respectability and Carreras thought it would give Hammer a much-needed boost. In the end it didn't work out for either party.

For Michael Carreras, the decline was terminal. Hammer's final horror film, *To The Devil A Daughter* (1975), did little to boost the company's flagging fortunes, and with debts mounting up, Hammer folded following an indifferent remake of *The Lady Vanishes* (1978).

Peter Cushing's next assignment took him to France for what was to be his most bizarre movie yet.

27: Tender Dracula (1975)

Cushing in *Tendre Dracula*.

'Peter Cushing was not one for globetrotting,' said Jonathan Rigby, 'and the progress of his career is therefore more interesting as it shows the wilting of the British horror tradition.' The actor returned to France on 11 February 1974 to work on a new film.

Tendre Dracula ou les confessions d'un buveur de sang or *Tender Dracula* (1975) was the directorial debut of Pierre Grunstein, who had previously worked as production manager or assistant director on a variety of French films. The script was supplied by a new writer, Justin Lenoir.

The plot, such as it is, has Peter Cushing playing MacGregor, a famous horror star who plays a vampire in a popular TV series. When MacGregor decides that he doesn't want to do any more horror related stuff, he uses a medical dispensation to get out of the show with the intention of playing a romantic lead in a 'Mills and Boon' type soap opera.

This gives a massive headache for the writers, played by Stephen Shandor and Bernard Menez, who concoct a plan to merge horror and romance and convince MacGregor, who is clearly bonkers, that this idea would work.

Along with two actresses (Marie played by Miou-Miou and Madeleine played by Nathalie Corval), the writers travel to MacGregor's isolated Gothic castle home for a weird weekend with their eccentric host (who walks around in bright sacramental robes), his creepy wife Héloïse (Alida

Valli) and their butler Abélard (Percival Russel).

What happens is a weird melee of live music, bathroom taps spurting blood, a dream sequence, a flashback explaining how MacGregor became a horror star, and female nudity from the actresses, all begging the question: is MacGregor a real vampire? The whole surreal experience ends with MacGregor and Héloïse walking hand in hand to a part of the castle that blasts off into space!

Pierre Grunstein was pleased to have secured Cushing's services and was in awe of the actor when he began work on the film. 'I won't say in a casual way that I was very nervous, but we let ourselves go. He let himself go and helped me follow the same route.'

Cushing had high hopes about the film. 'It is a fantasy comedy and if the French can imbue it with the usual elegance, it could be very amusing with perhaps a touch of pathos here and there. We shall see what we shall see.'

What the audience saw was a confused mess that didn't make sense. As bewildering French humour is to the English, one cannot imagine the film being remotely watchable by a Parisian crowd brought up on Jacques Tati. There are impromptu (and dreadful) songs sung by the actresses for no apparent reason, and several scenes that go unexplained, giving the impression that the whole thing was made up on the spot.

Despite the impressive gothic interiors that capture a little atmosphere, the direction is non-existent, and the supporting cast give non-descript performances, which leads to an amusing line delivered by Cushing: 'It takes more than drama courses and actors' workshops to become a high priest of horror.' This is unintentionally funny because these 'actors' were in dire need of a drama school.

The most shocking moment, and one guaranteed to give the most devoted fan something of a heart attack is seeing Cushing putting Miou-Miou across his knee and giving her a good spanking. And what makes it creepy is the fact that he seems to be enjoying it!

Tender Dracula comes across as a tribute to Cushing's horror career, in a role not dissimilar to Boris Karloff in *Targets* (1968) and Vincent Price in *Madhouse*. We see him display a scrapbook of his movie stills, along with a prominently displayed poster of *The Brides Of Dracula*. He also utters a line that unintentionally summed up Hammer's decline: 'Horror is dead, and being dead, it can no longer frighten anyone.'

For the first time in his career, Cushing goes into full blown ham acting, chewing the scenery and the dialogue with gusto and good humour. Giving a knowing wink to the audience, the actor is having fun even if he's clearly slumming it.

Also making the best of it is Alida Valli, who is best known for starring opposite Orson Welles, Joseph Cotton and Trevor Howard in Carol Reed's

27: Tender Dracula (1975)

The Third Man (1949), but this unfunny farce is way beneath their talents. Even Cushing expressed his doubts when he wrote, 'It's an odd film, I think, and might not be to everyone's taste.'

There is one moment that gives way to speculation as to whether he could play Dracula. Dressed in full vampire regalia, Cushing looks magnificent in costume, although his porcelain features were better suited to the character of Nosferatu. 'Cushing could have just easily played the batlike adversary,' said writer Danny Peary. 'If his head had been shaved and pointed ears attached, Cushing would certainly look like a vampire, as his gaunt face, pointed nose, high cheekbones and penetrating eyes resembled a bat's.' Werner Herzog's 1979 remake of the Max Schreck classic might have benefited from Cushing instead of Klaus Kinski.

Production wrapped on 29 March 1974, with Bernard Menez having high hopes about the film's success. 'In fact, this often happens, you have the impression the film you're doing may well be pointless, and surprise! The final result is much better than what you expected.'

Tender Dracula was released in France not long after completion under the title *Le Grande Trouille*. After making it to American shores in January 1975 as *The Big Scare*, the film drifted into obscurity.

Not surprisingly, critical evaluation was limited with *Variety* admitting that the film, 'seems undecided about its outlook and genre,' but admitted that the starring role was, 'played with despatch by Peter Cushing.'

Tender Dracula is Jean Rollin meeting Jess Franco and ending up more Edward D Wood. It remains one of Cushing's worst films during his long and distinguished career.

Cushing returned to England to star in two films for the newly formed Tyburn Film Productions. Founded by Kevin Francis, the son of Freddie Francis, the producer wanted to resurrect the old Hammer formula and adopt the same conveyor belt approach to filmmaking. These lofty ambitions went against the changing times for British horror and the gothic revival he envisaged never materialised.

The three Tyburn films that were produced were not very good. The first, *Persecution* (1974) met with a negative response, but undeterred, Kevin Francis went full steam into traditional Gothic horror with *The Ghoul* (1975), directed by his father and written by Anthony Hinds under his pen name John Elder. Cushing was asked to appear in the film when he was shooting in Hong Kong. Production began at Pinewood Studios on 4 March 1974.

'I played a clergyman, Dr Lawrence,' said Cushing of his role, 'who made a pledge to his dying wife that he would take care of their son despite the fact that the boy had been turned into a cannibal by a weird Indian sect. Returned to England, the unfortunate man hides the boy in his attic and has to make secret forays to get human flesh to feed him. So, you can gather, the man was not driven by ghoulish intent but out of the adoration for his dead wife.'

'As I was in the same boat, I had no difficulty in identifying myself with his emotions and state of mind. A photograph of the man's wife had a prominent position on the mantlepiece in his living room. Kevin's father, Freddie Francis, directed the picture, and I asked them both if we could use a picture of my Helen for this purpose. They thought it was a lovely idea, and Freddie made sure there was a close shot of the dear face on the screen in the final cut.'

The Ghoul is a reworking of Hammer's vastly superior *The Reptile* (1966). Set in the 1920s, it features a group of bright young things, including Veronica Carlson and pre-*Zombie Flesh Eaters* (1979) Ian McCulloch stumbling upon Dr Lawrence's residence and potentially ending up victims for his cannibal son.

Once again cast as a widower, this was one bereaved character too many for Cushing to cope with during filming.

Veronica Carlson, who played the ill-fated Daphne, saw a marked change in Cushing's appearance and manner since they had last worked together on *Frankenstein Must Be Destroyed*. 'The loss of Helen had changed Peter so much, always thin, he was almost skeletal in appearance. He had become a very solitary man and retired to his dressing room at every available opportunity. To me, it seemed a part of Peter had died along with Helen.'

Carlson was also saddened by his uncomfortable level of commitment. 'He wasn't acting at all. And he broke down and it was very difficult for all of us. We were seeing the truth and not a man acting the part. I wanted to go up and give him a hug, but you couldn't. He wanted to be on his own.' When the scene was completed, Cushing went to his dressing room leaving everyone shocked and saddened.

The Ghoul did not deserve Cushing's 100% commitment. It is a boring film with tired directing and a lack of suspense. The characters are unlikeable and the climax is too busy for anyone to care.

While he evokes audience sympathy, Cushing's performance is not a joy to watch. He never played another bereaved character again, so one can assume his work on *The Ghoul* helped him get some of his pent-up grief out of his system.

The Ghoul was released in England in June 1975, but never got Stateside distribution, although the film did well in Europe with Cushing winning the Best Actor award at the *International Festival of Science Fiction and Terror* at Sitges, Spain in October 1976.

Undaunted, Kevin Francis' next film was *Legend Of The Werewolf*, retaining the services of Peter Cushing, Freddie Francis and Anthony Hinds, along with a stronger supporting cast of Ron Moody, Hugh

Griffiths and Roy Castle. Production began at Pinewood Studios on 19 August 1974.

Legend Of The Werewolf was a welcome return to the humorous eccentrics of *Horror Express* and *From Beyond The Grave* with Cushing delivering a fun performance as Professor Paul Cataflanque, a jaunty, sardonic pathologist investigating a series of werewolf attacks in Paris, while happily munching on his sandwiches in the morgue where he works. 'I played what today would be called a police pathologist, with quite a sense of humour. A man doing this kind of job dealing with murder and death would probably need a little light relief every now and then.'

The Professor is an interesting character. He has scant regard for authority figures and looks happy among the dead. It's a winning turn and the character is worthy of his own TV series, which perhaps should have been the direction Tyburn should have taken in view of the situation within the British film industry.

Legend Of The Werewolf is a laboured effort that suffers from a threadbare production and an unconvincing period setting. It is still more fun to watch than *The Ghoul* and it is nice to see Cushing enjoying himself once more.

Legend Of The Werewolf was released in October 1975, but once again it was denied distribution in the USA. It did well in Europe and Kevin Francis' next Cushing vehicle, *The Satanists*, an adaptation of Denis Wheatley's 1960 novel *The Satanist*, was due to be shot at Pinewood Studios in March 1975. Unable to secure American distribution for *The Ghoul* and *Legend Of The Werewolf*, all of Tyburn's proposed horror projects were dropped and filming of *The Satanists* was cancelled at the last minute.

Legend Of The Werewolf was Cushing's final starring role in a British gothic chiller, and while it isn't great, it is enjoyable. Cushing was seriously considered to play the Criminologist in *The Rocky Horror Picture Show* (1975) where he could have further expanded his comic talents. Vincent Price was also considered, but the role eventually went to Charles Gray.

Cushing's next film role would be his only American made chiller.

28: Shock Waves (1976)

Cushing in *Shock Waves*.

At the start of 1975, Cushing remained busy, if less prolific, as the downturn of British film production continued. 'Over the last few years, most of my films have been made abroad. I hate travelling, but you have to go where the work is today.'

Brief TV appearances in *Film 74*, *Horizon* and the religious programme *What Was He Like?* kept him busy, along with a return to science fiction in an episode of *Space 1999*, 'Missing Link', where he played a 508-year-old scientist called Raan, sporting a long gown, a metallic gold painted face and a strange wig under a weird hat. Hardly his best look but he still rises above the silly premise.

Even an interesting theatre role came his way courtesy of Michael Carreras, who wanted to bring Hammer horror to the stage.

To have Cushing on board would have been a huge boost for Carreras, but the actor was reluctant to take part and the idea was quickly abandoned: Carreras could no longer rely on his star.

Cushing also received an offer to play the Great Detective in a Broadway production of *The Crucifer Of Blood*, his first since *The Seventh Trumpet*, but once again he declined. 'The part of Sherlock Holmes was originally offered to me, but I'm afraid the theatre is a thing of the past as

28: Shock Waves (1976)

far as I'm concerned.'

Instead, Cushing flew to Biscayne Bay, Florida, at the beginning of June 1975 to work on an ambitious low budget chiller directed by first-timer Ken Wiederhorn called *Death Corpse*.

Wiederhorn and his business partner Reuben Trane were former students at Columbia University in New York. Their first venture into filmmaking won them an Academy Award for *Best Dramatic Student Film* in 1973. With a successful film behind them, the duo embarked on their first feature. 'We wanted to make a commercial project,' said Trane. 'We had no interest in doing a personal film.'

Wiederhorn and Trane raised a $300,000 budget to make a horror film, which is what the backers wanted. According to Wiederhorn, 'They heard that horror movies have a better chance of making their money back than any other genre.'

The next step was to develop a unique horror concept. 'We started spit-balling ideas,' said Wiederhorn. 'What's scary? Since we were going to be filming in Florida, we thought, water can be scary. Then I came across this book called *The Morning Of The Magicians* [1960, by Louis Pauwels and Jacques Bergier] which lays out a theory that the Third Reich was heavily into magic, so we thought, Nazis always work!'

Night Of The Living Dead (1968) established the zombie as a frightening menace, and with Nazis forever associated with evil in countless war films, Wiederhorn turned his Nazis into the undead, and for added menace, this creepy army could function underwater.

Feeling that the presence of a name actor would enhance the film's box office prospects, Wiederhorn and Trane turned to producer Richard Gordon for advice.

Gordon had previously used Cushing in *Island Of Terror* and was happy to help the fledgling producers. Cushing was also happy to help out. 'I knew it was a new and young company, and I felt if my name could help them at all it would be a good thing to do. I might have made a mistake doing *Death Corpse*, but I don't think it shall do me any harm and it certainly won't do that company any harm.'

Wiederhorn scoured a double coup by also securing the services of American horror star John Carradine. 'We had John Carradine for five days,' said Train, 'and then we had Peter Cushing for five days, at two separate times.

'John Carradine was paid $1000 a day,' he added. 'We sound dirt cheap, but back then it was real money, and Peter Cushing for $25,000, to be paid up front into his English bank account, and first-class air travel from London, hotel accommodation, plus a driver.'

The supporting cast was largely unknown, the most famous actor being Luke Halpin, a former child star best known for playing Sandy in the TV series *Flipper*. By the time he did *Death Corpse*, Halpin never matured into adult roles and eventually retired from acting to work as a stuntman.

Playing the female lead was Brooke Adams, who went on to enjoy a reasonably successful film and TV career, which included *Invasion Of The Body Snatchers* (1978) and *The Dead Zone* (1983). She was working as a waitress when she was offered the role in *Death Corpse*.

Renamed *Shock Waves*, the film was shot on 16mm film and then blown up to 35mm, giving the movie a grainy look that works surprisingly well. Florida locations included Miami and West Palm Beach, with the swamp scenes shot near Miami's Crandon Swamp. The Nazi freighter where the zombies reside is the wreck of the *SS Sapona*, a cargo steamer that ran aground near Bimini in the western Bahamas during a hurricane in 1926.

A group of friends are vacationing on a seedy yacht, captained by John Carradine, who in real life commanded a coastguard frigate during the war. After experiencing strange weather conditions, the yacht collides with a disused freighter not far from an island.

With the yacht damaged, the crew and passengers make their way to the island for repairs, but all they find is an abandoned hotel with the only resident being an old hermit (Peter Cushing).

The hermit is a former SS commander who was once in charge of a new breed of German soldier. During World War 2, these zombie-like troops were designed by scientists to survive in all battle conditions, without the need of food or rest, or even the use of weapons. 'We created the perfect solider,' says the Commandant, 'from cheap hoodlums and thugs and a good number of pathological murderers and sadists.'

The soldiers under his command were designed for underwater conditions but due to their increasingly violent behaviour, and with the war coming to an end, the freighter carrying the soldiers was sunk, only to emerge later from the watery depths. The Nazi zombies have also made their way to the island.

Among the inexperienced film crew was Fred Olen Ray, now a successful director of low budget horror and action movies. 'It was shot in Florida. I was a stills photographer, gofer. I did a lot of things. I did whatever I could to get to the film because I was so desperate to work on it.'

'I found out about it from a makeup man named Doug Hobart. Back then there was no film industry in Florida, so I called him and said, "isn't there anything going on?" And he said, "Oh, nothing but that Peter Cushing/John Carradine movie they're making." I said, "Oh, my God!" these two were my heroes! Doug had passed on the makeup job, but he interviewed on my behalf and pleaded with the producer to give me work. And he agreed, provided I worked for free, which was okay with me, Because I had a regular job that I was on hiatus from, I couldn't stay for the whole show. Shooting took about five weeks, and I was there for two, but I was there the entire time Cushing and Carradine were there, and that was a real treat because no one else on the film was a real fan of those guys. The producers basically hired them because they were making a horror film, and they knew those guys were big horror film names.

'Peter wasn't well known by the rest of the cast and crew,' he added, 'and he initially kept to himself. Things got off to a bad start when he broke a tooth on the plane, and he was afraid he would hold up the shoot. While most stars spend a lot of time asking others to do things for them, he spent much of his time fixing coffee for the crew and helping the ladies through the swamp. During breaks I would ask him questions which he would graciously answer, but he preferred talking about his late wife. The filming was done under very difficult conditions, like crabs crawling up the camera legs.'

Although there wasn't much press coverage during the shoot, one of the zombies was played by journalist Jay Maeder, who was writing for the *Miami Herald*. Maeder went for to the audition under the impression that this was a possible scam, and ended up getting a part. He wrote an article about his experience on the film entitled *I was a Zombie*. During filming, he never told anyone on the set that he was a reporter. Maeder went onto to publicise the film extensively in the *Miami Herald*.

Despite the obvious low budget, *Shock Waves* is an unusual and stylish movie. The underwater scenes, brilliantly photographed by Irving Page, show the undead soldiers walking on the seabed with a certain otherworldly quality. *Shock Waves* isn't perfect, but it does its job, and with a slightly larger budget, could have been a classic film instead of a cult one.

Wiederhorn makes the most of the bare bones budget, and manages to turn the few zombies he had into a small army. 'It looks like fifty zombies,' said Train, 'but we only had six.' Wiederhorn wisely kept the zombie extras away from the cast to give added scares.

Even though it wastes the dream teaming of Cushing and Carradine who never met during the production, their presence gives *Shock Waves* a touch of class with Carradine bringing enough salty humour and seafaring wisdom to his cameo as the gruff old captain.

Cushing's role is also a cameo, but he too makes the most of it with a first-rate performance. His first appearance confronting his uninvited guests adds quiet but menacing dignity to his SS Commander. 'Cushing came up with an interesting accent,' recalled Wiederhorn, 'which made him sound German every 5th sentence.

'The thing you have to say about Cushing' he added, 'is that he does bring a sense of gravitas to the scene. He has a wonderful screen presence that works in every movie he's in, good, bad or indifferent.'

'Watching Peter's performance,' said Ray, 'is like watching the film actually happening. He told me that he modelled himself on Louis Hayward.'

It was also one of Cushing's scruffiest roles. Always the most elegant of dressers, Cushing wears a ragged safari suit complimented by a dirty neckerchief and a convincing facial scar, courtesy of makeup artist Alan Ormsby. 'He had the finest skin I've ever seen anywhere,' recalled Ormsby.

He's also quite athletic, spending his time running around the island and wading through the water looking for his soldiers, before meeting a watery end. A scene where Cushing's wet body is found in the hotel by the tourists never made the final cut.

The supporting cast do well with Brooke Adams and Luke Halpin being noteworthy. Both actors enjoyed working with Cushing. 'He's brilliant,' said Halpin, 'he really knows how to make a scene work.'

'Peter was very eccentric,' recalled Adams. 'He always wore a glove on one hand, I'm not sure. I think it was one hand. He was so old world and eccentric.'

Shock Waves received its Stateside release in Los Angeles on 21 September 1977. It came to the UK the following year under the title *Almost Human*, and then received a cult following when it was released on video by Vipco in the 80s.

There were few reviews of the film at the time of its release, but the contemporary evaluation has been positive. Tom Milne of the *Monthly Film Bulletin* commented that the zombie Nazis looked 'agreeably sinister when they first emerge from the bottom of the sea with dripping hair, hideously scarred faces and uniform dark glasses', but the film's 'inadequate budget is all too evident. Both script and direction tend to settle for simple repetition: a sizeable chunk of the footage is devoted to assorted characters stumbling through swampy shallows out of which, naturally, zombies emerge with sinister intent.'

Mike Long of *DVD Talk* wasn't impressed, 'Horror fans looking for a zombie gorefest will be quite disappointed by *Shock Waves*, but those who want a subtle and unique experience may enjoy this quirky low-budget film.'

Oktay Ege Kozak, also writing for *DVD Talk*, felt, '*Shock Waves* is a cheap, uninteresting, and entirely too forgettable genre effort from the 70s, a decade that otherwise revitalised horror cinema.'

More concerned with atmosphere than with shocks,' wrote Patrick Bromley of *DVD Verdict*, 'it avoids a number of what would become the cliches of the genre; the flip side of that coin is that it delivers little of what we want from a zombie film.' Patrick Naugle, also writing for *DVD Verdict* found *Shock Waves*, 'repetitious and boring.'

Returning to England, Cushing featured in Kevin Connor's *Trial By*

28: Shock Waves (1976)

Combat (1976) with an appearance as Sir Edward Gifford, founder of a medieval re-enactment group known as the Knights of Avalon.

The guest role is misleading because Cushing is killed off before the credits roll by his second-in-command Donald Pleasence, who takes his cosplay a little too seriously by kidnapping known criminals to take part in their medieval antics and killing them with his own elaborate sense of vigilante justice. Sir Edward stumbles on one of their 'executions' and gets quickly dispatched.

Cushing's only other appearance consists of a series of flashbacks where Sir Edward teaches his son (David Birney) the importance of chivalry but succeeds in causing their estrangement. That is the extent of his performance and while he plays it well, his participation is a waste of his talents. *Trial By Combat* was released in September 1976 and came to US shores the following year under the lurid title of *Dirty Knight's Work*.

After a few television appearances, Cushing surprised everyone by making a final return to the stage.

Cushing was a fan of the 1975 TV drama series *Edward The Seventh* starring Timothy West and was especially taken by West's leading lady. 'Miss Helen Ryan took the part of Queen Alexandra and played the royal parsonage as if she lived and breathed and had her being during that period of our island's history. I was deeply impressed by this remarkable recreation and wrote her a fan letter.'

This was a good move because Ryan's husband, Guy Slater, was organising a repertory season at the Horseshoe Theatre in their hometown of Basingstoke. This piqued Cushing's interest in going back to theatre once more.

'I had not been on the stage for ten years, back in 1965 at the Garrick, when I played Sir Hector Benbow-Bart MFH in *Thark*, that glorious play by Ben Travers, and was anxious to try myself out again "on the boards" after such a long gap. And so many films. So, I wrote once more, this time to Miss Ryan's husband, asking if it would be possible to open the season with *The Heiress*, a play by Ruth and Augustus Goetz, based on *Washington Square* by Henry James, with myself as Dr Austin Sloper. Helen and Guy applauded the idea.'

The Heiress opened on 21 October 1975 and played to a full house until 1 November. Despite his fears about acting on the stage again, Cushing found it a happy experience.

'Peter was wonderful,' said Helen Ryan, 'super in the play, but he was terribly nervous. The play opened at 7.30 and Peter would be at the theatre three hours beforehand to check his props and his costume.'

Despite the personal success, *The Heiress* didn't mark a permanent return to the theatre. Cushing admitted the constant repetition of a stage role every night would never give him the satisfaction of a film role, and that the reason he did *The Heiress* was out of loyalty to Helen Ryan.

Cushing returned to America as a guest of honour at *New York's Famous Monsters of Filmland*. The convention was organised by noted fan and collector Forrest J Ackerman, and joining Cushing were Michael Carreras and Ingrid Pitt. Cushing also made a rare American TV appearance when he went to New York to promote the event on Tom Snyder's programme *Tomorrow*.

Michael Carreras wanted to adapt the comic strip *Vampirella* (1969 to the present day) to the big screen with John Hough pencilled in as director. Cushing and Ingrid Pitt were there to support Carreras, but like most Hammer projects at the time, nothing came of it.

Ingrid Pitt had happy memories meeting up with Cushing during the event. 'I remember coming in from Argentina for a horror convention Marvel Comics had put on in New York. Michael Carreras of Hammer Films was there with Peter. It was a massive affair. Thousands of people crowded into the ballroom where a dais was set up and each of us had to make a speech and hold a question-and-answer session. It wasn't until I'd finished and heard how quietly self-effacing Peter was that I realised how crass and over the top my performance had been. It was wonderful the way he treated everyone, answered their questions with such gentleness and patience that he got a standing ovation.'

It begs the question as to why Cushing never pursued film roles in America following his time on *Shock Waves*. Travel overseas had improved considerably since his first trip to the States, and he remained popular with American fans. He could have also seen his many friends living in Los Angeles like Christopher Lee, Vincent Price, Hazel Court, Patrick MacNee and Veronica Carlson, and could have reconnected with Ida Lupino, Louis Hayward and John Ireland. Re-establishing these friendships might have helped him overcome his bouts of homesickness.

Instead, Cushing continued the globetrotting by flying to Greece for a new horror film produced by Getty Pictures and Poseidon Films.

29: The Devil's Men (1976)

Cushing in *The Devil's Men*.

Also known as *Land Of The Minotaur* (for its shorter – 89 minute – American release), *The Devil's Men* follows the same lines as *Shock Waves* by being a departure from the usual gothic chillers Cushing was associated with. Unlike *Shock Waves*, this effort is dreadful.

The film begins with a group of tourists visiting a Greek island. While exploring an archaeological dig, several are abducted by a satanic cult and sacrificed to their ancient minotaur god. The leader of the coven is Baron Corofax (Cushing), a Romanian exile from the Carpathian Mountains and the island's most influential figure.

For years the islanders have worshipped their god without any interference from the outside world, until the tourists' arrival poses a threat to their way of life. The disappearances attract the attention of eccentric Irish priest Father Roche (Donald Pleasence), who enlists the help of an old American friend, private detective Milo Kaye (Kostas Karagiorgis) and archaeology student Laurie Gordon (Luan Peters), whose sister is one of the missing tourists.

Under the working titles of *The Devil's People* and *Demon*, it was the brainchild of Frixos Constantine, a producer wanting to establish a Greek film industry to rival Hollywood. Making an Anglo-Greek co-production with money from the Gettys Pictures Corp, shooting began in November 1975 with a $650,000 budget. Donald Pleasence was initially cast as Baron Corofax but opted to play the priest to break away from playing bad guys. Cushing was then added to the cast, and the actors went on location for a week.

Directed by Kostas Karagiannis, *The Devil's Men* is a chaotic mess. The flat photography makes the Greek landscape extremely grim, and Arthur Rowe's nondescript script suffers from poor plotting, dreadful dialogue and non-existent character development. Even Brian Eno's soundtrack is surprisingly awful.

Decked out in ridiculous red robes, Cushing's very English villain is out of place on a Greek island (he drives a Rolls-Royce and wears Saville Row tweeds). Looking bored throughout, he walks through the movie with no conviction at all, a clear indication that he was ready to give up the horror genre.

Adding humour to the proceedings, Donald Pleasence fairs better, but even he's fighting a losing battle. Luan Peters, who should have been a strong character, does little more than scream and walk around nude. At least she fares better than Kostas Karagiorgis, a pointless nonentity hired by Roche, but he does next to nothing.

The Devil's Men is let down by a ridiculous climax where the long awaited minotaur turns out to be a small fire breathing stone statue. When Roche utters a Christian exorcism ritual that results in Corofax and his followers exploding, one wishes he had done it at the start of the movie and saved the audience from suffering through 95 minutes of tedium.

The Devil's Men received a limited release, although it made its money back with a box office gross of $1,020,000. Critical evaluation was negative with only positive review coming from *Fangoria*'s chief editor Chris Alexander. 'Make no mistake, it's a lowbrow exploitation film, but it's one that's filtered through a very stylised art house sensibility. Don't be swayed by the negative mainstream reviews and general fanboy silence.' Alexander also praised 'the suffocating ambiance and dreamlike atmosphere and Brian Eno's electronic score.'

29: The Devil's Men (1976)

John Stanley of the *San Francisco Chronicle* was unimpressed, feeling that it wasted Cushing and Pleasence. 'A film without logic or characterisation and its location photography is without distinction. The movie is far beneath the talents of both actors and hopefully one assumes they accepted the assignments solely to enjoy an extended holiday in Greece.'

Screen International found it a 'garbled tale,' but added that, 'Peter Cushing adds a touch of elegant evil.' The *Los Angeles Times* stated that, 'The movie is distinguished by the presence of two seasoned actors, Donald Pleasence and Peter Cushing, starring as obvious opposite symbols of good and evil. The direction of [Kostas Karagiannis] is staid, failing to provide an atmosphere of terror in spite of scary and sadistic moments. Location shots of ancient Greek ruins are picturesque, but the village itself lacks a specific locale.' *Cinefantastique* found the film 'weird', but added that, 'Cushing fends for himself (and rather well) in his first totally unsympathetic role in years.'

Cushing returned to England for a new Amicus production, due to start on 20 January 1976. With British horror going into decline, Milton Subotsky and Max Rosenberg changed direction by producing the dinosaur flick *The Land That Time Forgot* (1975). The box office success allowed Amicus to produce further movies based on the Edgar Rice Burroughs novels. Their next effort would be *At The Earth's Core* (1976) with Doug McClure and director Kevin Connor returning.

After his depressing Greek excursion, Peter Cushing landed the comic role of a lifetime as Dr Abner Perry, who could be described as an unofficial Doctor Who. The dotty scientist invents an earth burrowing machine called the Iron Mole. With the assistance of American financier and friend David Innes (Doug McClure), the duo burrow into a Welsh hilltop, taking them to the centre of the Earth, which turns out to be a primitive underground civilisation known as Pellucidar.

Perry and Innes are captured by the Sagoths, a tribe of half-human creatures who are minions to the frightening bird creatures called the Mahars. The humans who inhabit Pellucidar are used as slaves for the Mahars. The duo befriends Princess Dia (Caroline Munro) and they quickly unite the neighbouring tribes to fight back against the Mahars and the Sagoths.

Made on a low budget, this studio bound effort has a cramped air about it. The Pellucidar sets look skimpy, and the monsters are obviously stuntman in rubber suits. These faults didn't matter because *At The Earth's Core* is pure entertainment for kids and adults alike.

Peter Cushing gives an enjoyably over-the-top performance; he's also at his most athletic, running around Pellucidar with McClure with the energy of a much younger man.

The corny one-liners he had to utter are an absolute hoot. 'They're so excitable, like all foreigners,' is classic Cushing when he describes the Sagoths. There's also a variation on his *Horror Express* quote, when he confronts a dreaded Mahar. 'You cannot mesmerise me, I'm British!' Most of the jokes were courtesy of Cushing, who admitted, 'The script was 90% action, so most of the dialogue had to be invented as we went along.'

It's so refreshing to see Cushing enjoying himself, and this was obvious among the cast, especially Caroline Munro, who had previously seen a melancholy Cushing on *Dracula AD 1972*. 'He really enjoyed the movie because it was a departure from his normal roles. Peter is a very sweet and sensitive man. He's very quiet and unspoiled, so unlike a star. I defy anybody who's met him to say a bad word about him.'

It was a feeling shared by Doug McClure. 'I never worked with anyone like him in my life. By the time you finish a film with Peter, you find you have a lot of feeling for him. You can't walk away from him very easily. He's a brilliant actor. His range of comedy is unbelievable.'

Although critical evaluation was negative, *At The Earth's Core* became the 18th most profitable British film at the box office, following its premiere at the Marble Arch Odeon on 15 July 1976.

Cushing returned to familiar ground after Brian Clemens and Albert Fennell arranged a deal with a French backer to resurrect *The Avengers*. *The New Avengers* saw the return of Patrick MacNee as John Steed, but being a little older for the action scenes, Gareth Hunt was brought in to handle the punch-ups, while Steed's 'Girl Friday', Purdey, was played by Joanna Lumley.

'The Eagle's Nest' was the first episode of the series and filmed on the Isle of Skye. Cushing returns to familiar Frankenstein territory as Dr Von Claus, who reanimates a frog during a science conference. He is then kidnapped by a group of monks and taken to a remote Scottish island, initially to help resurrect one of their members who is currently in a coma.

To the scientist's horror, the monks and the islanders are all descendants from a German military unit stranded there during the war and the monk in question is Adolf Hitler. It's up to Steed and his colleagues to sort it out before it's too late.

'The Eagle's Nest' was a great start to the series but while there were some decent episodes, the show lacked the panache of the original, and funding problems prompted a move to Canada to complete the series.

Cushing gives a fine performance, but the melancholia had returned. 'It was sad to see how fragile Peter was,' observed Brian Clemens. 'He told me he was just treading time until he could join his wife.'

At the end of April 1976, Cushing embarked on his next film project, one that became an important part of cinema history.

30: Star Wars (1977)

Cushing with director George Lucas and Carrie Fisher in *Star Wars*.

A long time ago, in a galaxy far, far way.

The slogan speaks for itself, the beginning of an enormously successful franchise consisting of sequels, prequels, stand-alones, books, comics, TV shows – live and animated – and toys. *Star Wars* (1977) started it all, and Peter Cushing was a part of it.

The impact of *Star Wars* was phenomenal and for Cushing, it not only proved an incredible boost to his film career, it ushered in a new generation of fans unfamiliar with his previous work.

Filming began in March 1976 with location work in Tunisia, and interiors shot at Elstree Studio. Cushing was added to the cast four weeks into production. Lucas originally wanted him to play Obi-Wan Kenobi with the Grand Moff Tarkin role going to Alec Guinness. After meeting both actors, the director decided to swap roles as he felt Cushing's lean features suited the villain, and the actor enthusiastically accepted.

'Peter Cushing is a very good actor,' said Lucas. 'He's got an image that is in a way quite beneath him, but he is adored and idolised by young people and by people who go and see a certain type of movie. I feel he'll be fondly remembered for the next 350 years at least.'

Star Wars was released in May 1977 to a massive box office. Tarkin may be the commander of the notorious Death Star, but his second-in-command remains the cinema's greatest villain: Sith lord Darth Vader (Dave Prowse, with James Earl Jones providing the voice). David Miller was correct in his observation of the relationship between the two characters, 'By an occasional haunted glance, however, Cushing is able to imply that Vader holds the real power, and Tarkin is uneasy in his presence. Thus, both characters are made more frightening.'

Cushing worked on *Star Wars* for a week and all his scenes were with David Prowse and Carrie Fisher, who he mentored during production. According to Prowse, 'The interesting thing about Peter was he had a lot to do with Carrie Fisher. It was Fisher's first major film, and he went out of his way to show her the ropes. When there would be some dialogue between them, he'd turn around and say, "Look Carrie, if I stand here, I'm going to get my shadow on you and you're not going to be seen in a very good light etc. So, what I'll do, I'll move around so I'm in the shadow and you're in the light."' This made Tarkin a darker, more shadowy (and eviller) figure, while Princess Leia retained her brightness, emphasising her as the symbol of good.

There is one famous story that has become legendary among fans. 'I have enormous feet – wide size 12 – which can present problems,' said Cushing, 'and we met out at Waterloo when *Star Wars* was being equipped. I wore what looked like an Edwardian chauffer's outfit, complete with knee-length boots. Usually, these items are made to my measurements, but on this occasion, "Time's winged chariot" caught up with us and perforce, I had to make do with a pair from stock.'

The boots were too small for Cushing. 'When I crammed on the size 9 boots I could hardly walk.

'After the first day's work, I could not bear it no longer, so I approached the director, George Lucas. "Dear fellow," I said, "I'm not asking for close-ups, but do you think you could shoot me from the waist up from now on?" He consented kindly and was allowed to stomp about looking very cross as Grand Moff Tarkin for the rest of the picture in carpet slippers.'

Don Henderson, who played General Tazzi remembers the slippers. 'For some odd reason his jackboots were missing from his sinister costume for that film, and all the boots they could find for him were too small. He ended up stomping about in a totally black costume wearing a pair of ladies' bedroom slippers, brilliant blue in colour, with wobbling pink pom-poms on them, just out of camera range. Each take ended in mega giggles, and keeping a straight face during the takes was a massive exercise in self-control. No matter how we tried not to look at Peter's feet, his colourful bedroom slippers could be seen always, out of the corners of one's eyes! A bit like acting opposite a naked lady and trying not to look at her nude breasts.'

Tarkin met his match against the rebel forces led by Luke Skywalker and Han Solo. 'I was blown to smithereens by those two intrepid young

30: Star Wars (1977)

lads Mark Hamill and Harrison Ford, who managed to blow up my little *pied-a-terre*, a modest DIY affair about twice the size of Jupiter called, appropriately enough, The Death Star. A pity this happened to me really, because it meant I couldn't very well take part in any of those subsequent outer-space adventures.'

Star Wars was a great personal success for Peter Cushing, but despite the amazing impact, the expected career boost never materialised.

Shortly after completing *Star Wars* Cushing flew to Hollywood on 11 May 1976 to star in his first American made-for-TV film for ABC Television, and his role made an interesting addition to the Sherlock Holmes part of his career.

The Great Houdini (1976) is a biopic about legendary escape artist Harry Houdini, played by Paul Michael Glaser, with Sally Struthers as Houdini's wife Bess and Ruth Gordon as his mother. The roster of guest stars included Bill Bixby, Adrienne Barbeau, Wilfred Hyde-White, Clive Revill, Maureen O'Sullivan and Nina Foch.

Cushing was cast as Sir Arthur Conan Doyle, which gives him the unique distinction of playing both Sherlock Holmes and his creator.

Cushing worked on *The Great Houdini* for four days. Arriving at Fox Studios on 12 May, he joined the cast and crew celebrating Wilfred Hyde-White's birthday (Cushing cut the cake for his colleague). The following day, he joined Hyde-White and Clive Revill for a scene where he is introduced to Houdini prior to the artist performing his latest escape to the surprise and delight of his guests. In dramatic terms this marked the beginning of the friendship between Houdini and Conan Doyle.

The Great Houdini went over budget, resulting in Cushing's scenes being rushed and filming continuing until midnight. The actor didn't complain and even found time for a question and answer session with his American fan club although he felt his performance would suffer as a result.

The second half of the film focuses on Houdini's self-appointed role of exposing spiritualists and mediums as frauds following his mother's death, a situation that would eventually clash with Conan Doyle's spiritual beliefs.

This leads to an excellent scene where a concerned Sir Arthur and his wife (Maureen O'Sullivan) try to dissuade Houdini from his obsessive one-man campaign.

The Conan Doyles invite Houdini to their hotel room where Lady Conan Doyle acts as a medium. She receives a warning message from Houdini's mother watched over by a concerned Sir Arthur, while Houdini views it all with amused tolerance.

When the message is conveyed, an unmoved Houdini thanks the Conan Doyles for their kindness, but tells them that they have wasted their time.

'You and Arthur want to believe so badly that you can talk to your son who was killed in the war,' Houdini tells his friends. 'Surely you know what the subconscious can do to the mind? You want it so bad it seems possible. Me, I'm convinced. Even honest people can't get through. Nobody can. We're stuck here on this side and there is no *Other Side*.'

Undeterred, Conan Doyle tries to convince Houdini otherwise. 'Alright, don't believe, but for God's sake listen to her warning. I've been through this. Three of my friends have died and the warnings weren't this clear. Call me fake if you like but call me your friend too. Don't take the risk, Harry. Stop your atheistic campaign.'

Houdini's reply sours the friendship. 'What happened to that man who wrote Sherlock Holmes; has your brain turned to mush?'

Conan Doyle finally snaps, giving Cushing a chance to display his steely presence. 'Get out! You have insulted me. You have insulted my wife and more than that you have insulted the Almighty himself!'

It is an excellent scene, superbly acted by Cushing and Glaser, and the highlight of an interesting, but dull film.

Back in England, Cushing guested on the popular children's show *Jim'll Fix It*, fronted by Jimmy Savile. For this bank holiday edition, two boys wrote to Savile asking if they could play monsters and scare their hero, Peter Cushing. The kids were made up and Cushing was scared accordingly. Some years later, Savile hosted an episode where elderly viewers could write to him with their wish. Cushing wrote to Savile asking if a rose could be cultivated to honour his wife.

With the various child abuse scandals making headlines after Savile's death, the series, along with all his other endeavours became off-limits. Had he known the truth about Savile, Cushing would never have participated in either show.

31: Battleflag (1977)

During the autumn of 1976 Cushing reunited with Vincent Price for a new BBC radio drama.

Developed by *Doctor Who* script editor Robert Holmes, *Aliens In The Mind* was set in Scotland where a genetic mutation on the island of Luig evolves into powerful telepathic aliens. Price plays brash American bohemian scientist Professor Curtis Lark while Cushing is prim British brain surgeon Dr John Cornelius. In addition to dealing with all this paranormal activity, Cornelius is teaching his free-spirited colleague the finer points of British life. The series proved very popular when it was screened in January 1977.

Cushing's options were surprisingly limited following *Star Wars*. 'As the British film industry continued to decline,' said David Miller, 'Cushing increasingly found that he had to travel more and more to find work – only one of his next seven films was made in England.'

There were several films that Cushing turned down for different reasons, among them Peter Walker's religious slashfest *The House Of Mortal Sin* (1977). Walker wanted Cushing to play sexually perverted priest Father Meldrum, but his agent wasn't happy about his client's involvement in an exploitation movie. The role went to the equally distinctive looking Anthony Sharp.

Another effort would have reunited Cushing with Doug McClure and Kevin Connor for the independently produced *Warlords Of Atlantis* (1978). Cushing was scheduled to play the leader of Atlantis, but conflicting schedules with another film prevented him from taking part. He was replaced by Daniel Massey.

The most famous film that got turned down was *Halloween* (1978), a groundbreaking low budget horror film directed by John Carpenter. 'In the spring of 1978, I began to cast *Halloween*. My first choice was Peter Cushing as Dr Sam Loomis, this avenging psychiatrist on a desperate mission to stop Michael Myers, the demonic mental patient on a rampage in his hometown of Haddenfield.

'This was the year after *Star Wars* had been released. We were a tiny little low budget movie. I was a nobody with a lot of dreams. We offered the script to Cushing and were immediately turned down. Cushing's agent at the time sounded as if he had a permanent sneer on his face as he phoned in the rejection. "Mr Cushing wouldn't deem to appear in such a low budget enterprise" was the jist of the conversation. Now he was a big star from *Star Wars*, "They're going to make movie about him!"'

Carpenter was philosophical about the decision. 'I was terribly disappointed, but decided, right or wrongly, that this was the agent talking and not Cushing himself. I never found out.'

Carpenter then offered Christopher Lee the role, and he too turned it down, later admitting it was a big mistake. Donald Pleasence finally took it on, launching his horror career. There's no reason to assume that *Halloween* would have been as successful if Cushing had played Dr Loomis, and while it is unlikely he would have done the sequels, success would have taken his career to new dimensions, including bigger budget films for Carpenter.

Cushing's post *Star Wars* career began in Spain in October 1976, travelling to the Toledo Province for the First World War drama *Die Standarte* (AKA *Battleflag*), an Austria-Spanish-West German co-production directed by Ottokar Runze.

Berlin born Runze worked in a variety of capacities within the German film industry before becoming a full-time producer and screenwriter. His first venture into directing was the award winning *Der Lord Von Brambeck* (1974). He followed it up with *In The Name Of The People* (1974), which won him the Silver Bear at the *25th Berlin International Film Festival*, and *A Lost Life* (1975).

Financed by several studios, including Runze, *Battleflag* looked like the perfect high-profile film for Cushing. Adapted from Alexander Lernet-Holenia's 1934 novel *The Standard* and set in Belgrade towards the end of the Great War, it had previously been filmed as *Mein Leben fur Maria Isabella* (1935). Further location work also took place in Vienna, Austria.

Battleflag boasted a strong international cast that included Hammer veterans Simon Ward and Jon Finch. Other notable names taking part were Maria Perschy, Siegfried Rauch, David Robb, Wolfgang Preiss, Lil Dagover and Robert Hoffman.

With many of the European actors being proficient in English. Runze was aiming towards the international market and *Battleflag* being a major production, expectations were extremely high.

Peter Cushing plays Baron Von Hackenberg, a military officer of the old school in what was an extended cameo. Seen mainly on horseback and looking resplendent in his grey uniform, he doesn't do much else. Von Hackenberg is a reserve officer who carries a lot of influence in Vienna. Sporting a beard, smoking a cigarette and surrounded by dogs, he spends his time carefully observing the front-line action without taking part.

Arriving 40 minutes into the film, Cushing has an excellent scene when he exposes the regiment's standard bearer as a lowly gypsy posing as a count. Von Hackenberg then gives the standard to young army officer Menis (Simon Ward).

From then on Menis guards the standard with his life, even when it is stolen by enemy forces invading Belgrade. Menis tries to retrieve it so he can bring it back to Vienna, resulting in the needless deaths of the men under his command.

Ward first met Cushing on the set of *Frankenstein Must Be Destroyed* (1969). Almost ten years had passed when they reunited for *Battleflag*, which proved a difficult shoot for the actor. 'Apart from guest appearances by Peter Cushing and Jon Finch, I was the only English-speaking actor in the cast. It was a very odd experience, because it was shot in three languages, and I never worked on a production like it before. In the film, there was all this German and all this Spanish going on and as I cannot speak a word of either language, it was rather difficult to know what to do.'

Despite the limited screen time, Cushing turns in an interesting performance, showing his usual gravitas behind his aristocratic bearing to great effect, but it hardly ranks as one of his best efforts.

Battleflag received a special screening at the Cannes Film Festival, but it wasn't well received. According to *Variety*, 'A great deal of money was invested in Ottokar Runze's *Battleflag* with the aim of capturing a commercial market at home and abroad. But this tale of the Austria-Hungarian monarchy and a young cadet officer believing in the limited tradition of the Austrian Empire loses credibility as it goes along, particularly in so far as the love story and action sequences are concerned. Chances are poor for the box office return unless the picture is recut to save embarrassment for the awkward script and thesp rules. The film is properly lensed and has some lovely location scenes. The condemnation of duty for its own sake also has relevance. A few strong cameo roles by famous actresses and actors help.'

The poor response at Cannes resulted in no distribution deal. *Battleflag* received a European release on 18 May 1977, but nothing in the US and the film quickly sank without trace.

Lost for many years, *Battleflag* resurfaced on British television during the 90s. It is an earnest attempt to make a good film, and Runze's direction is serviceable. The acting is solid, the action scenes are well executed, and there is a sense of place and period thanks to the costumes and Peter Scharff's excellent sets, but the film makes dull viewing thanks to Herbert Asmodi's underdeveloped script.

Cushing's next assignment had him travelling to Canada for his final horror anthology.

32: The Uncanny (1977)

Ray Milland and Cushing in *The Uncanny*.

Cushing's first post-*Star Wars* horror film was his last for some time. It was also his final feature to be shot across the Atlantic.

Nowadays Canada is used for location work for many notable films and TV shows, but back in the seventies the country's independent film industry was hardly booming despite strenuous efforts by the Canadian government to promote its potential, although the National Film Board of Canada remained a major influence in terms of documentary filmmaking.

It was up to low budget auteur David Cronenberg to stimulate a belated interest with the home grown chillers *Rabid* (1974) and *Shivers* (1976), and with the release of Bob Clark's *Black Christmas* (1976), a potential horror market looked promising. The Canadian government then made an interesting, if half-hearted attempt to escape Hollywood domination by encouraging local filmmakers and bringing in overseas investment by passing the Quebec Cinema Act in 1975. Included in the agreement were the UK, Italy, Germany, Israel and France.

After leaving Amicus in 1975, Milton Subotsky saw co-productions with Canada as the way forward when he tried to re-establish himself as an independent producer.

Moving to Canada in 1976, Subotsky formed Tor Productions with Canadian producer Claude Heroux. He then arranged a co-production deal with Cinevido of Canada for a screen adaptation of his short story omnibus *Beware The Cat*.

According to Subotsky, 'I was asked to do an anthology based on my stories. We changed the idea to three and not five stories and the title became B-R-R. The third story was to be a comedy. Rene Dupont made a deal. I got a co-producing credit and editing rights, so I moved to Montreal to work on the cast. Vincent Price turned me down. So did Peter Cushing and Christopher Lee. Cushing relinquished when he found out it was one of my pictures. He hadn't realised.'

Retitled *The Uncanny* (1977), production began at the city's Panavision Studios on 16 November 1976. Budgeted at $1.1 million, the four-week shoot included location work in Senneville and Quebec. Additional filming took place at Pinewood Studios followed by post-production and editing work.

Directed by Denis Heroux and adapted to the screen by Michel Parry, *The Uncanny* tells the grim story of writer Wilbur Gray (Cushing). A specialist on ghosts, UFOs and other weird phenomenon. The almost fearful Gray is convinced that cats are in league with Satan and will take over the world. He brings his new manuscript to the home of his sceptical, cat loving publisher Frank Richards (Ray Milland) and relates three creepy tales where the cats were responsible for the deaths of the protagonist featured in each story.

The first tale is set in London in 1912 where an eccentric old lady (Joan Greenwood) changes her will to leave everything to her cats instead of her layabout nephew (Simon Williams). His lover and the old girl's maid (Susan Penhaligon) plot to kill her and destroy the new will, only for the cats to take care of them both in grisly fashion.

The second story is set in modern Quebec. An orphaned girl (Katrina Holden) and her pet cat are sent to live with her dead mother's family. The poor girl must deal with her spoilt and hateful cousin (Chloe Franks) who tries to have the cat removed. Like her mother, the girl practises black magic, and uses sorcery to exact a well-deserved revenge on her cousin.

The final tale is set in 1930's Hollywood where the celebrated horror star Valentine De'Ath (Donald Pleasence) stages the 'accidental death' of his wife during the production of his latest chiller and has his airhead mistress (Samantha Eggar) replace her. In Edgar Allan Poe fashion, the couple fall foul of his wife's hated cat.

The film ends with Wilbur leaving his manuscript with Richards and heading off home under the watchful eyes of a group of felines who have followed him from the start. Richards' own cat uses telepathy to make him burn the manuscript while the moggies outside pounce on poor Wilbur.

Cushing's time in Canada brought back memories of his early years. Staying at the Ritz Carlton in Montreal, the actor was interviewed by journalist Dane Lanken from *The Gazette*. 'The last time I was in Montreal,' he told Lanken, 'I was staying around the corner at the YMCA.'

32: The Uncanny (1977)

Subotsky encountered serious problems during post-production and blamed it on Denis Heroux. 'The worst mess-up was my film *The Uncanny*. That was done in Canada, and it was directed by the co-producer's brother, who is really a producer and not a good director. He's a big producer in Canada now. I went to Canada to edit the film or there wouldn't have been a picture.

'Nothing matched, we could only make one cut! They hadn't edge-numbered. I fired the editor and hired Michael Guay. The whole thing was an appalling mess. I worked on the third story and the framework and found later that Heroux had re-edited and was proud of what he'd done! It was a miracle we got a final print.'

Cinematographer Harry Waxman also threatened to quit the production, complaining about the way some of the cats were treated.

The Uncanny works better on paper than on film, for the simple reason that cats are not in the least bit scary. It's not a bad film and despite Subotsky's protestations about Denis Heroux's abilities as a director, the film has some great atmospheric moments.

The first tale is reasonably effective thanks to an excellent performance by Joan Greenwood, but the second is terrible, badly made and boasting awful special effects and non-descript acting.

The third segment is more fun thanks to a hilariously hammy turn from Donald Pleasence. It's an engaging performance that enlivens an otherwise average story.

The linking tale remains the film's highlight thanks to Cushing's manic performance. Looking even shabbier than he did in *Shock Waves*, the nerve wracked Cushing is at breaking point as the down-at-heels Wilbur. He works well with Ray Milland, whose quietly underplayed performance compliments Cushing's neurotic intensity.

Cushing never spoke about his time working with Milland, who was an important part of Hollywood in the forties, something that frustrated Marcus Brooks, founder of *The Peter Cushing Appreciation Society*. 'Of all the many cases of casting in the work of Peter Cushing, the time together on set with Ray Milland and Cushing is one I wish we knew more about. It's true Peter only had a few days in Canada working on *The Uncanny*, but these two giants of the big screen had such a CV of work and experiences. It is a great shame that in both of Peter's autobiographies, there is little that goes into the day-to-day work on his films, nothing on the detail of what the experience was actually like. So many people, real artists, so few named or recalled.'

The Uncanny was released in Canada through Cinevideo on 26 August 1977, with Rank Productions releasing it in the UK on 4 April 1978. Critical reaction was negative with only *House of Hammer* magazine having something positive to say, 'What a relief to see a good old fashioned horror film again. *The Uncanny*, one can say, is good, clean, nasty fun.'

Others were not so happy, with *Screen International* calling it, 'A run-of-the-mill mixture of straight and camped up horrors that read better than they play. There are no surprises, and it's unlikely to endear the film to cat lovers.' *Variety* was even less impressed, adding that, 'There's nothing to recommend this one beyond its cheapness.' Leslie Halliwell found *The Uncanny* a 'Below-par horror compendium with crude effects failing to bolster a sagging script.'

Time Out were scathing. 'Truly terrible trio of tales, all based on the false premise that, since a shot of an ordinary domestic cat is already fairly scary, then shots of several hundred cats must be very frightening indeed. Yet the animals come out of it better than the poor actors, forced to do their best with such dusty Amicus anthology type plots as the bedridden aunt with the cats and the changed will; the child with the cat and the occult power (using the girl from The *House That Dripped Blood*, but here dubbed by what sounds like a middle-aged Canadian); and the self-parodying horror film star and starlet (Pleasence and Eggar, making you wish you were watching *Dr Crippen* [1963] instead) who own a cat. The stories are linked by cat-crazy Cushing and purring Milland, as a sad pair of back taxpayers as you could wish to see.'

The Uncanny performed poorly at the box office. In view of Cushing's newfound status thanks to *Star Wars*, the choice of film roles were becoming increasingly suspect.

The globetrotting phase continued the following year with a trip to Australia as presenter and narrator for an eight-part documentary series called *A Land Looking West*.

1977 brought two film assignments that clashed, and the one he went for took him to West Germany.

33: Hitler's Son (1978)

Cushing in *Hitler's Son*.

Hitler's Son (1978) is an unwatchable mess, making one wonder why Cushing accepted the assignment.

This unfunny effort was the brainchild of German writer Burkhard Driest, who saw the comic potential of parodying Hitler following the cult success of Mel Brooks' *The Producers* (1968). Driest was no stranger to notoriety, being imprisoned for armed robbery: his time behind bars became the subject of his semi-biographical film *Die Verrohung des Franz Blum* (1974). Also acting as producer, Driest had an uphill struggle obtaining finance. 'Everybody turned the film down. Not one of these money guys was prepared to finance a film which made fun of Hitler. They were repelled by the idea. So, because of the difficulties we faced, we eventually travelled abroad and got it privately financed.'

Driest secured a $5 million budget via an Anglo-German co-production deal with Navos Film Productions. Rod Amateau, who had an extensive career on American TV was brought in as director, with German writer Lukas Heller co-writing the final screenplay with Driest. Under the working title of *Return To Munich*, shooting commenced at Arri Studios in Munich in September 1977 with location work in Bavaria.

Cushing had been scheduled to appear in another film to be shot in England. 'I am making a guest appearance in a film entitled *Seven Cities To Atlantis*. My part is Atraxon, Imperator of the supreme council.' Renamed *Warlords Of Atlantis*, it clashed with his trip to Munich to begin work on *Hitler's Son*, and so *Warlords Of Atlantis* lost out.

The premise of *Hitler's Son* is unbelievable. As the script tells it, towards the end of the war, Hitler and his mistress Eva Braun conceived a child, and the boy, christened Wilhelm, or Willie (Bud Cort), was raised by a former SS officer (Peter Capell) in a desolate mountain area not far from Munich.

News of Willie's existence comes to the attention of another former Nazi, Heinrich Hauser (Cushing), leader of the German fascist group N.E.I.N (Never Encourage Intellectual Nonsense – oh please!) who sees the potential of Willie leading their movement.

Willie is an illiterate, uneducated, childlike woodcarver who lives a reclusive life in a log cabin. Even when he finds out about his father's identity from his dying guardian, the infamous surname means nothing because he has no knowledge of the outside world. Arriving in Munich, he loses his birth certificate and ends up in an asylum.

Haussner rescues Willie from the asylum and teaches him his father's mannerisms, right down to styling his hair and moustache. Willie's childlike innocence is at odds with Haussner's goal for world domination.

Production wrapped in January 1978 with the final cut taking place in Munich and post synching work completed at Elstree. *Films and Filming* published a two-piece spread on the film in their May edition, but Cushing was absent from the photos published in the magazine.

'Our film is directed against Prussian spirit,' said Driest. 'So, although I think the English-speaking countries will enjoy a comedy about Hitler's son, it's very doubtful that the Germans will.'

Hitler's Son was due for release in May 1978, but nothing came of it. A second screening took place in January 1979 pending possible distribution in the UK, and once again, the response was non-existent. As *Hitler's Son* wasn't released outside Germany, a country that wasn't going to respond positively to a comedy that crossed the line in bad taste, the film disappeared into obscurity.

One wonders what went wrong. Charlie Chaplin got it right with *The Great Dictator* (1940), as did Mel Brooks with *The Producers*, yet Driest managed to get it completely wrong despite the talent involved, including Oscar winning art director Herbert Strabel.

Hitler's Son is available on *YouTube*, but on viewing the film, it is highly unlikely that Brooks or Chaplin could have saved this garbage. Unattractively photographed, the film neither works as a satire or as slapstick. Judging by the cringeworthy moments, it looks like the director

33: Hitler's Son (1978)

made it up as he went along.

The film boasts an excellent but ill at ease cast, with Bud Cort looking as baffled as the intended audience. It's sad to recall that the actor once starred in *Harold And Maude* (1971), and *Hitler's Son* wasn't a great career move for him. Cort had high hopes that the film would do well but got quickly disenchanted by the continued interference by the producers, who constantly changed an already confused script.

The film's comedic element could be the only reason Cushing agreed to play another Nazi character. Looking healthier than he had been in a long while, he gives a hilariously broad performance, demonstrating his athleticism to comic effect. The scene where he knocks over several display cans in a corner shop is vintage Laurel and Hardy. Once again, Cushing shows what he can do with little at his disposal.

Cushing is well partnered with Hollywood heavy Leo Gordon (replacing Aldo Ray at the last minute). Gordon also rises above the material with a surprisingly sympathetic performance. One can assume he took on this assignment to subsidise his more interesting career as a novelist and screenwriter. Gordon's wife Lynn Cartwright also appears in the film along with Anton Diffring.

Since *Hitler's Son* vanished immediately after its release, critical evaluation was non-existent other than a few negative reviews on *IMDB* and *YouTube*.

If *Hitler's Son* was bad, Cushing's next film abroad was even worse.

34: A Touch Of The Sun (1978)

Cushing (centre) in *A Touch Of The Sun*.

It's inevitable for an actor of Cushing's calibre to star in some bad movies, and *A Touch Of The Sun*, was the nadir of his long career.

Shooting took place in July 1978 and Cushing wasn't first choice to play Commissioner Potts, a long forgotten British colonial governor, who had no idea that World War II had ended, didn't know Winston Churchill had died, and was still under the impression that the independent African state of Akasuba remained under British rule. John Mills was offered the role before it went to Terry-Thomas, who dropped out due to his poor health. When Cushing took on the assignment, he grew impressive side-whiskers for added authenticity.

Filming began in Zambia, with location work taking place at the Victoria Falls, the Kafue River and the local countryside around the town of Lusaka. Assigned to direct was Peter Curran, who had helmed some undistinguished British films in the early seventies. Budgeted at £1.5 million, *A Touch Of The Sun* boasts an impressive cast of Oliver Reed, Keenan Wynn, Wilfred Hyde-White, and Melvin Hayes.

One assumes the bulk of the budget went on Oliver Reed's bar bill, and it wouldn't be surprising if Peter Cushing and Melvyn Hayes joined him for several drinks and reminisced about the good films they had made for Hammer.

The plot concerns an American space capsule crashing in Akasuba, which is then captured by the state's dictator Emperor Sumooba (Edwin Manda) who demands a ransom for $25 million from the US government for its safe return. With the help of the British government, bungling Captain Nelson (Reed) is sent there to retrieve the capsule, which has a solar-powered ray that is capable of mass destruction.

Nelson enlists the help of Commissioner Potts, and complicating matters further, there's a camp Tarzan figure (Melvin Hayes) who thinks he's Ginger Rogers, a not-so-subtle reference to Hayes' soldier 'Gloria' Beaumont in the BBC wartime sitcom *It Ain't Half Hot Mum*.

With khaki shorts and pith helmet, Potts is a man out of step with the times, and when Nelson tells him about the space probe, he quickly points out to his colleague that he has read far too much H G Wells.

But Potts is a streetwise character, and a bit of a rascal, who embraces the modern age with surprising confidence, seizing every opportunity to take financial advantage of the situation, charging Nelson $1000 for using the local Zawa tribesmen as bearers for the mission.

For what it's worth, Cushing is hilarious. With his facial reactions incuding baffled, bewildered and downright confused. His finest comic moment is when he sees the native bearers wearing colourful smoking jackets and drinking cocktails. 'I think I'm going mad!' he exclaims. 'Stark staring mad! First the war's over. Then Winston's dead, then invisible sun walls. Now all my bearers think they're Noël Coward!'

Being the first international co-production to be shot in Zambia, there was a lot of local press publicity surrounding *A Touch Of The Sun*, with Cushing being described as, 'an international star of *Star Wars*, *Frankenstein* and *Sherlock Holmes* fame.'

The *Zambia Daily Mail* was enthusiastic about the new movie with the headline *Top Film Star Jets In*, adding that 'Peter Cushing of *Star Wars* and *Dracula* fame arrived in Lusaka yesterday to join international film stars Oliver Reed, Keenan Wynn and Sylvaine Charlet in *A Touch Of The Sun*, a film which is currently being shot in the country. The 65-year-old actor who has had 42 years of acting experience, arrived looking as cheerful as ever and visibly unaffected by the Zambian weather.'

According to another piece entitled *Cushing in Central Africa*, 'Peter Cushing is a retiring personality whose monstrous deeds on the big screen in the *Frankenstein* films are hard to reconcile with the fragile looking gentleman of 65 who is inclined to describe himself as an old age pensioner from the tiny English seaside village of Whitstable in Kent.'

'Between takes, Cushing sits quietly along in his own sea of tranquillity and people constantly drift up to talk to this popular though retiring person. Someone says he is looking slightly tanned after a week in Zambia. "I'm afraid not, it's only a little makeup," he smiles.

'The quiet Zambian temperament appeals to Cushing, a courteous and unassuming man who finds the local people gentle, sympathetic and more inclined to be content without the luxuries of life than their European counterparts.'

A Touch Of The Sun wrapped on 20 August 1978, and a screening of the rough-cut took place at the Cannes Film Festival in May 1979. To celebrate Zambia's 14th year of independence, the film premiered in Lusaka on 24 October 1979.

The official screening took place on 13 September 1979 prior to its general release through 20th Century Fox. However, the film never saw the light of day outside Africa and subsequently disappeared without trace.

The film resurfaced years later on British TV under the title *No Secrets*, and its plainly obvious to the viewer that it is an appalling, badly made mess that is both unfunny and embarrassing.

Apart from an amusing performance from Cushing, the acting is dreadful. A miscast Oliver Reed mugs away with an awful American accent and a drunken look that seems completely justified under the circumstances.

Sylvaine Charlet's acting is limited to two things – clothes on and clothes off! She appears naked in several scenes, usually coming out of the shower or bath, and making a telephone call. It looks like these scenes were a last-minute addition to spice things up and overlook her nondescript acting.

Because of its limited release, critical evaluation is reduced to irate comments on *IMDB*. The only official review came from Leslie Halliwell, who described *A Touch Of The Sun* as, 'An unbelievably atrocious movie: a crude mix of dim-witted script, bad acting, and heavy-handed, mistimed comedy.'

Returning to England, Cushing made a cameo appearance in *Arabian Adventure* (1979). Working once more with Kevin Connor, this *Thief Of Bagdad/Sinbad* inspired adventure has Christopher Lee playing the villainous Alquazar the Wizard while Cushing has a tiny appearance as deposed leader Wazir al Wuzara.

Playing the handsome Prince Hasan was Oliver Tobias. He shares an amusing dungeon scene with Cushing (retaining his whiskers from *A Touch Of The Sun*), and when Hasan makes his escape to search for the Rose of Eli in order to defeat Alquazar, the Wazir stays in the dungeon, missing out on all the fun. He should have followed Hasan on his adventure and developed a similar comedy rapport that he had with Doug McClure in *At The Earth's Core*.

Arabian Adventure lacks the panache of *The Thief Of Bagdad* (1949). The ideas are there, but the old style is sadly lacking. There is plenty for youngsters to enjoy, and it boasts an interesting cast of Milo O'Shea, Capucine, Mickey Rooney, Suzanne Danielle and a pre-TV stardom Emma Samms. The film was released in July 1979 to an indifferent critical and commercial response.

After making his last appearance on *The Morecambe And Wise Show* in October 1978, and finally getting his money, Cushing narrated the short film *The Detour* (1978). With no further work in 1979, he quietly moved into semi-retirement.

The new decade took him back to Spain for two more films, ending the globetrotting phase of his career on a low note.

35: Mystery On Monster Island (1980)

Cushing in *Mystery On Monster Island*.

Horror roles still pursued Cushing, one of which came from Milton Subotsky, who was producing a kids' horror film called *The Monster Club* (1980).

'I offered Peter the part of Chetwynd-Hayes,' recalled Subotsky. 'But he turned it down saying he didn't like the script. I offered him the part of the innkeeper, but he turned me down. I then offered him a guest spot, but he turned me down. He turned down three roles because he didn't like the script. I don't know. I guess he thought it was a gruesome horror film and not one for the kids.' The part eventually went to John Carradine.

Another horror role followed in June 1980, and this time it was from Hammer, now little more than a name synonymous with a once famous genre.

Roy Skeggs and Brian Lawrence were now in charge, and to capitalise on the name, they moved into TV with the series *The Hammer House Of Horror*.

Sadly, the show owed more to the modern day Amicus approach, than the traditional Hammer Gothic. All the episodes were shot in Buckinghamshire and in a modern-day setting. They featured no monsters,

35: Mystery On Monster Island (1980)

and all had downbeat endings. Not surprisingly, many fans had scant regard for the series.

'The Silent Scream' is probably the most fondly remembered episode. It stars Peter Cushing, who gives a nicely malevolent performance as a pet shop owner, initially believed to be a concentration camp survivor but in reality is a former Nazi who still carries out his brutal experiments within the confines of his shop. Although reluctant to play another deposed Nazi after *Shock Waves* and *Hitler's Son*, Cushing accepted the role out of loyalty to Hammer.

Playing opposite Cushing was Brian Cox. 'My particular episode of *Hammer House Of Horror* starred Peter Cushing so, lucky me, I got to work with one of the cinema's great gentlemen, a man who could boast of having worked with Laurel and Hardy among many others. "I don't like the word horror," he told me. He was a vegetarian and always wore gloves. "I don't even think of them as horror films. To me they are just fantasies."'

Sadly the story being told in 'The Silent Scream' is slow and Alan Gibson's direction is static, which detracts from the great performances.

Another interesting horror role came courtesy of zombie meister Lucio Fulci, who offered Cushing the starring role in *The Black Cat* (1980).

It's impossible to imagine Cushing in a Fulci film, considering the director's gore-hound reputation. At least he didn't have to travel to Italy as the production took place in England. Cushing received the script in May with shooting due to start in August.

Cushing meticulously went through the script making his usual notes, amendments and costume requirements, but eventually declined the role. Patrick Magee took his place.

The Black Cat also clashed with a more interesting production that began in July 1980. *The Hallmark Hall Of Fame* produced a TV adaptation of Charles Dickens' *A Tale Of Two Cities* (1980) starring Chris Sarandon in the dual role of Charles Darnay and Sydney Carton, with Alice Krige, Billie Whitelaw, Kenneth More, Flora Robson, Barry Morse and Robert Urquhart making up an excellent cast. The six-week shoot began at Shepperton Studios with location work in Paris

Cushing plays the pivotal role of Bastille inmate Dr Manette, unjustly imprisoned but eventually freed by his daughter only to be dragged into the French Revolution when his son-in-law Charles Darney is arrested because of his association with the vile Marquis St Evremonde.

Although well-made and decently acted, the film didn't get a positive response from the intended American audiences. It was better received in England even though it suffered in comparison to an excellent BBC adaptation that was broadcast the same year. It is a shame that Cushing's last great performance went unnoticed.

Cushing's next assignment took him back to Spain, and to more familiar ground with a fantasy film aimed at younger audiences. *Misterio en la isla de los monstrous*, or *Mystery On Monster Island* (1980).

Based on Jules Verne's 1882 novel *The Robinson Crusoe School*, *Mystery On Monster Island* is the second of two Verne novels adapted to the screen by Spanish filmmaker Juan Piquer Simón, the previous one being *Where Time Began* (1976), an adaptation of 1864's *Journey To The Centre Of The Earth* starring Kenneth More and Euro horror favourite Jack Taylor.

Replacing original choice James Stewart, Cushing plays shipping magnate William Kolderup, America's richest industrialist. It is little more than a cameo despite top billing alongside Terence Stamp. When his restless nephew Jeff (Ian Serra) gets cold feet about marrying Meg (Ana Obregön), because he wants to experience life and adventure, his uncle sends him on a cruise. Accompanying him on the journey is his pompous teacher Professor Artelect (David Hatton).

Kolderup has more sinister motives for his nephew after he outbids the mysterious Taskinar (Stamp) on the sale of an island being auctioned in San Francisco for $5 million. Taskinar has his own reasons for buying the island: it has a large deposit of gold.

Jeff and Artelect also have their own problems when the ship catches fire! With the crew dead, the duo then make their way to an island populated by a variety of monsters.

They also come across Carefinatu (Gasphar Ipua) a native who escaped from a cannibal tribe, and Dominque (Blanca Estrada), a fellow castaway who has lived on the island for several years but keeps her hair and makeup intact! Things are further complicated by the arrival of Taskinar and his pirate crew in search of the hidden treasure. As it turns out, this is the island that Kolderup bought at auction, resulting in an unsatisfactory twist ending.

Mystery On Monster Island was shot on location in Puerto Rico and the Canary Islands. Being set in the 19th Century, the Victorian costumes and the San Francisco sets were convincing enough, clearly a good budget was allocated for the 18-week shoot.

Juan Piquer Simón enjoyed working with Cushing and was impressed by his versatility. 'What surprised me was the tremendously professional approach of Peter Cushing during the making of *Monster Island*. I was really amazed. As a person he was a true gentleman, so charming and kind. He was, a genuine living legend, and as advanced in years, as he was, his enthusiasm during the shoot was unbelievable. I remember, he told us that he believed in reincarnation, and that he wanted to die so that he could join his wife, who had died some time before. I recalled this story years later and used it as the beginning of (my film) *Cthulhu Mansion* (1991).'

35: Mystery On Monster Island (1980)

Although it is a vast improvement on his previous films, *Mystery On Monster Island* isn't great. Cushing and Stamp only appear at the beginning and the end of the film. Both are in fine form, with Stamp exuding the right amount of charismatic evil and Cushing making Kolderup an interesting and ambiguous figure.

The film is let down by ropey special effects and fake looking monsters. The silly twist reveals that Kolderup organised the whole island charade for his nephew's benefit. The inhabitants that Jeff and Artelect meet are hired actors, and the monsters were created by a toymaker, so they were fake all along. Only Taskinar and his pirates weren't part of the make-believe. In the wake of *Star Wars*, cinema audiences cried out for awesome special effects, which *Mystery On Monster Island* lacks.

The other fault is the duff performances from the main leads. Ian Serra is bland and David Hatton is more annoying than amusing as he constantly screams and whimpers. It would have been far more interesting to see Cushing in the role. Had the film been made ten or five years earlier, it could have been an effective Amicus monster vehicle for Cushing and Doug McClure.

The most glaring fault was the shameful waste of Spanish horror legend Paul Naschy, who appears briefly at the beginning of the film as a pirate and gets killed off immediately. 'I was a "special guest" star,' he recalled, 'and Peter didn't have much screen time either, but Piquer knew the marquee value of the names Terence Stamp, Peter Cushing and me.'

Mystery On Monster Island was released in America in April 1981, and quickly disappeared. *Variety* described the film as an 'Entertaining action-filled treatment of the Jules Vern yarn,' further adding that, 'it's good clean fun, and should appeal to a wide range of audiences.' Tony Crawley of *Starburst* was not enthusiastic. 'Now the bad news, Jean Piquer is directing a new movie. He'd have difficulty directing traffic as evidenced in ruining Jules Verne in his tawdry version of *Journey To The Centre Of The Earth* with Kenneth More.'

Mystery On Monster Island isn't a worthless film. It is beautifully photographed and makes excellent use of the locations. Cushing's contribution, though small, is impressive and worth watching, which is more than can be said for his final Spanish assignment.

36: Black Jack (1981)

Cushing in *Black Jack*.

Cushing's second Spanish film remains his most obscure effort, and one that vanished without trace until it recently resurfaced on *YouTube*. Judging by the negative comments from viewers, *Asalto al casino* AKA *Black Jack* (1981) should have remained locked away for good.

Making a heist movie is a welcome departure for Cushing, and as wealthy, aristocratic horse breeder Sir Thomas Bedford (replacing Donald Pleasence), he instigates the robbery of one of Spain's biggest casinos.

The casino is situated in Santander on the northern coast of Spain and the gang, headed by Tony Fuentes, pose as a group of musicians working for a famous singer performing at the casino. However, the authorities are aware of the situation and things are further complicated by a hostage situation involving a former Nazi.

This French-Spanish co-production was the brainchild of producer/director/writer Max H Boulois who also plays the role of Dynamite Duck, the rap singer who falls foul of the gang's heist. Playing his manager is former Bond girl Claudine Auger. Despite her billing, she has little to do and shares no scenes with Cushing.

Cushing has three scenes in total. His first is at his English stud farm where he briefs Fuentes on the heist, illustrating the faults in the security system compared to Las Vegas. He then turns up halfway through the film at one of the Casino's gaming tables, looking very distinguished in formal black tie, and finally at the end, after the heist ends in disaster, when he sails away in his yacht.

The interesting cast include Mexican cult favourite Hugo Stiglitz as the detective on the case, George Riguad, who worked with Cushing on *Horror Express*, and bizarrely, British actor Brian Murphy, forever George Roper in the TV sitcom *George and Mildred*. He didn't share any scenes with Cushing but was given star treatment by the producers. 'I was rushed over to Spain to be included in the film because *George and Mildred* was a huge success in Spain and it was thought at the time that to get a hold of Murphy was a great coup! As to what the story was about, I had little idea, but the money was excellent – and they wined and dined me. I suspect I was cheaper than Alec Guinness.' Sadly, Murphy was just there for comic relief and had nothing to do with the heist.

Working as assistant director was Francisco Gordillo, who had fond memories of Cushing. 'Peter Cushing worked on that film for three days. I remember between scenes, Peter and I were talking, with the aid of an interpreter, because Peter only knew a few words in Spanish, but we had quite a lengthy conversation about the *Cinefantastastico* genre that he had done a lot of great work in. It's a funny thing that in the space of that one conversation we became so friendly. Peter told me he would like to work with me again on a new film I was then trying to get off the ground *El cepo* (1982). I felt flattered by that because Peter didn't know me at all.' Cushing's role in that film was eventually taken by Jack Taylor.

Black Jack wrapped towards the end of 1980 and was screened at the Cannes Film Festival in May 1981 to attract overseas distribution, but nothing came of it. Nor did it receive a release in Spain.

'*Black Jack* didn't have much luck,' Gordillo added. 'As far as I know it was never shown theatrically. I don't know what happened to it.'

One can see why *Black Jack* languished in obscurity for so long, the film is dreadful! Looking more like a home movie, thanks to the grotty cinematography, it is a badly made, confusing mess that makes no sense and wastes a decent cast who battle valiantly against a dreadful script and appalling music. Cushing gives a good account of himself, and his scenes add some impact, but there's little more to be said about his performance.

Critical evaluation is restricted to negative *IMDB* and *YouTube* reviews so the less said about the film the better.

Black Jack marked the end to Cushing's globetrotting career. As the 80s progressed, health issues eventually led to his retirement.

37: The Final Years

Cushing in *Top Secret*, pastiching a photograph from *The Skull* (see page 137).

It was during May 1982 that Cushing experienced serious health problems. 'My left eye became swollen to about three times its normal size. Not a pretty sight, and extremely painful. As the eruption occurred on a public holiday, I didn't want to pester overworked doctors, and thinking it was just an oversized stye, I bathed the offending protuberance with Optrex, and lay down on the couch, hoping it would go away after a rest.'

His housekeeper later found him unconscious. 'She thought I was on my deathbed, so she immediately rang the health centre.'

Cushing was diagnosed with prostate cancer, and the doctors gave him 18 months to live. 'They held little hope of my recovery, although I wasn't made fully aware of how serious my condition was until sometime later.'

Cushing successfully fought off the cancer and lived another 13 years. 'To their utter amazement, I confounded medical science, and with no operative treatment, made almost a complete recovery. I nearly lost my eye, but it was saved, leaving me with slight double-vision.'

Cushing then moved into the home of his secretary Joyce Broughton and her husband Bernard. 'He hated hospitals and desperately wanted to come home,' she recalled, 'but the specialist said he could not go home alone so he came to live with us in Hartley. Suddenly he was thrown into a household with two teenage girls, cats, dogs and many friends around. I don't know how the poor man coped after living a quiet and orderly life then coming almost to a madhouse with telephones ringing, different music in different rooms, boyfriends, girlfriends always around. But he was marvellous, and he began to slowly enjoy life a little more.' Eventually, the Broughtons moved to Whitstable to be near him.

Cushing returned to work with his final horror film, *House Of The Long Shadows* (1982), which marked a long overdue teaming with Vincent Price, Christopher Lee and John Carradine.

Directed by Peter Walker, production began in August 1982, and from the start the actors enjoyed their time together. 'We've all worked together before,' said Vincent Price, 'but never as a foursome. It was a sort of joyful class reunion.'

Also appearing in the movie was Desi Arnaz Jr. 'I grew up watching Peter Cushing as the hero in the *Dracula* movies where he represented the force of good winning over evil. When I finally met him during the filming, he exemplified goodness in that he was very polite, had a good sense of humour, and was very supportive of me. Another aspect of his character that I will always admire is this – he never wasted words, but when he did speak it was always something worth listening to. I liked him very much and am thankful to work with and learn from him.'

While Price and Lee traded on their familiar personas, Cushing never had a specific horror image. What made the actor unique was his ability to tackle any role with total conviction. Usually cast as a heroic character it's refreshing to see him playing a cowardly figure who drinks far too much hot punch to cope with the guilt of his actions. Always an instinctive actor, a bout of bronchitis during the making of the film gave him the idea of mispronouncing his 'R's to comic effect.

'If I had known,' said screenwriter Michael Armstrong, 'I would have written him more dialogue with the letter R.'

Although fun to make with the horror icons in excellent form, poor marketing by producers Menahem Golen and Yoram Globus, meant *House Of The Long Shadows* sank at the box office. The film doesn't work as a serious chiller or a spoof of the genre and fails to achieve any prominence other than wasting the talents of these great men, who have little to do but play to their outstanding reputations.

Cushing remained with Golen and Globus for *Sword Of The Valiant* (1982), a medieval fantasy that began production in September 1982. Location took place in Ireland and France with Cushing's scenes shot in Wales. The film boasted an amazing cast of Sean Connery, Trevor Howard, Leigh Lawson, Lila Kedrova and Douglas Wilmer.

Directed by Stephen Weeks, *Sword Of The Valiant* is a remake of his film *Gawain And The Green Knight* (1971). It tells of a young squire (a wooden Miles O'Keefe) in King Arthur's court who takes on a challenge provided by the mysterious Green Knight (an over-the-top Connery).

Cushing has a few scenes as Gaspar Seneschal, military advisor to King Fortinbras (John Rhys Davies) and his depraved son Oswald (Ronald Lacey), but all he does is twitter away in the background. He does it very well, and he looks great in costume, but that's about it.

Cushing's next film was another cameo, and a hilarious one at that. *Top Secret* (1983) is a screwball comedy from the mad minds of Jim Abrahams, David Zucker and Jerry Zucker, the people behind *Airplane* (1980) and *The Naked Gun* (1988).

Top Secret spoofs the spy/war genre with comical aplomb. It features scene-stealing turns from Omar Sharif, Michael Gough, Jeremy Kemp and Peter Cushing, all happy to send themselves up with some classic comic moments that makes the film impossible not to laugh at.

Cushing has one extremely well executed scene as a Swedish bookshop proprietor who happens to be a resistance contact for the main leads enjoyably played by newcomers Val Kilmer and Lucy Gutteridge.

The Proprietor rises from behind his counter with a magnifying glass to his eye. When he lowers the glass, the massive eye is still huge. This is followed by Cushing and his young co-stars walking and talking backwards!

'We had to do the whole scene in one take' he recalled. 'We had to do everything backwards. We had to walk backwards. If a book was thrown up, it was really thrown down. I knew that this magnifying glass was going to be there at the end of every take we did. And it terrified me!'

Cushing's next effort was an episode of *Tales Of The Unexpected*, which was shot in May 1983. Entitled 'The Vorpal Blade', the episode featured the frail actor as another former Nazi recounting his university days. Not the best episode in the long running series, but Cushing gives a subtle and poignant performance reflecting regret and lost love.

Cushing followed it up with a final trip to Hollywood where he reunited with Alan Gibson for the made-for-television biopic, *Helen Keller: The Miracle Continues* (1983), with Marie Winningham as Helen Keller and Blythe Danner as her mentor Ann Sullivan. Cushing has a fun cameo as Helen's lecturer Professor Charles Copeland, who is responsible for getting his student a commission to write for a magazine. It's a nicely played turn, but the film makes bland viewing.

In 1984, Cushing returned to Sherlock Holmes for another TV movie produced by Kevin Francis.

To accommodate Cushing's age, Francis went for an original story where Holmes and Watson come out of retirement to investigate another mystery. The duo would be up against foreign spies and the possibility of war between Great Britain and Germany.

The Mask Of Death has a strong Hammer flavour with a script by Anthony Hinds and Roy Ward Baker brought out of retirement to direct. The supporting cast included Sir John Mills as Dr Watson, Anne Baxter (as Irene Adler), Ray Milland, Anton Differing and Gordon Jackson.

Shot at Twickenham Studios in August 1984, *The Mask Of Death* is uninspiring thanks to a slow, convoluted plot. Period costumes and sets are well done, but Roy Ward Baker's direction is tired and uninvolving.

Remaining as sharp and intuitive as ever, Cushing looks frail, especially when compared to the still healthy-looking John Mills. The only person who was frailer than Cushing was Ray Milland, who was recovering from a stroke. That aside, it remains a fitting tribute to Cushing's interpretation of one of his most famous characters.

The Mask Of Death was popular enough for a follow-up, this time an adaptation of Conan Doyle's story *The Abbot's Cry*. Kevin Francis also envisaged a potential TV series starring Cushing and John Mills.

Plans to film *The Abbot's Cry* were scheduled for 1986, but Cushing's health made it impossible for him to continue. 'I don't think Peter was well enough to do it,' lamented John Mills. 'I seem to remember. I know we talked about it a lot on the telephone.'

A few years earlier Cushing had the opportunity to work with Jeremy Brett, who made Holmes his own in the popular TV series. Cushing was offered the role of Merridew the clergyman in a feature length adaptation of *The Sussex Vampire* but turned it down after being knocked off his bicycle by a couple of dogs while cycling to Tankerton.

This resulted in a lengthy stay in hospital with a damaged hip. 'I'm just not up to travelling to Manchester and doing location shooting now, especially with my troublesome hip.' The role was taken by Maurice Denham.

At the beginning of 1985, Cushing starred in his final cinematic feature, a sort of semi-fantasy about the famous British World War 1 flying ace Captain James Bigglesworth AKA Biggles. For *Biggles – Adventures In Time* (1985), the WW1 ace (Neil Dickson) is involved in a time travelling story with his modern day 'time twin', played by Alex Hyde-White.

Cushing plays retired Air Commodore William Raymond, who previously served with Biggles on the Western Front. A mysterious and eccentric figure, Raymond's home is situated at Tower Bridge, and is very much a character out of step with the modern world. He takes tea at 4 o'clock and has a portrait of Queen Victoria in his den. Looking extremely frail, Cushing still invests the same level of commitment that never let him down during his long career.

Alex Hyde-White had nothing but praise for his co-star. 'Peter's professional courtesy and respect for the craft of acting has no parallel as far as I can tell, He speaks with modesty of his many accomplishments and his rich and varied life. He treats everyone he meets with the joy of discovery that he keeps firmly in his grasp at all times.'

Biggles – Adventures In Time was honoured with a royal charity premiere on 22 May 1986, with Prince Charles and Princess Diana in attendance. A gentleman to his fingertips, Cushing broke royal protocol by kissing the Princess' hand.

Biggles – Adventures In Time is a misfire on every level. The time-travel idea doesn't gel with the Great War; it would have been better to have Biggles going on an *Indiana Jones* inspired mission. John Hough's direction is competent, and the lead actors are amiably weak. It is Cushing who keeps one watching even though the viewers are more disturbed by his frailty.

Cushing eventually in 1987 gave fans what they wanted, his autobiography, which he decided to publish when old friend John Mills threatened never to work with him again.

Called simply *Peter Cushing: An Autobiography*, it is an enjoyable read. Cushing gives little away about his Hollywood years, his work with Hammer and his various travels across the world, disappointing his fans. His decision to take his life story no further than January 1971 when Helen passed, left everyone frustrated because he still had a life and career after that.

Cushing's response was to publish *Past Forgettings* in 1988. Once again it is an enjoyable read, with some lovely anecdotes, but it still leaves fans disappointed by the lack of information about his Hollywood years and the many films he worked on. The definitive book on Cushing's life and career was *Peter Cushing: A Life In Film*, written by David Miller and published in 2013.

Now in demand for book signing tours, he did several radio and TV

37: The Final Years

interviews and celebrated his career at the National Film Theatre. He took part in the *Everyman* programme 'The True Story of Frankenstein' and for *Omnibus*, 'Hammer – The Studio That Dripped Blood', where Cushing joined Christopher Lee, Ingrid Pitt and others in sharing their experiences with the studio.

Cushing had been offered two film roles, but on 1 June 1987, he announced his retirement. His health made it impossible for him to continue as an actor, although he remained in the public eye.

Jeffrey Richards of the *Daily Telegraph* paid tribute to Cushing when he wrote, 'It is high time that his achievement in British cinema was publicly recognised. A knighthood would not be an inappropriate reward for a man who has become one of the best loved and most widely respected of British film actors.'

The knighthood never happened, but on 22 March 1989, Cushing, steadying himself on a walking stick, went to Buckingham Palace to be invested with the OBE by Queen Elizabeth II for his services to the British Film Industry. Ever the modest gentleman, he was overwhelmed by the investiture.

The celebration of his life continued when Kevin Francis produced the 90-minute documentary *Peter Cushing: A One-Way Ticket to Hollywood*. Broadcast by Channel 4 in June 1989, Cushing was interviewed by writer Dick Vosburgh. Interspersed by photos and film clips, Cushing is delightfully engaging, clearly showing there was still life left in the old boy.

And it was *This Is Your Life* for Cushing when Michael Aspel presented him with the 'Big Red Book'. Broadcast in February 1990, Cushing was aware of what was happening, but remained overwhelmed by the presence of old friends Peter Gray, John Mills, Caroline Munro, Joanna Lumley, Ernie Wise (still haggling over money) and a video link from Christopher Lee.

The celebrations continued with another TV appearance in *The Human Factor*, the episode entitled 'For the Love of Helen', sees him speaking about his life, his faith, his artwork and his battle with cancer.

Towards the end of 1990, Cushing made his acting swansong on BBC Radio with *The Human Conflict*, playing a RAF pilot trying to restore the reputation of Air Chief Marshall Hugh Dowding (voiced by Alan Dobie) Such was his admiration for Dowding, Cushing and Dobie did the show for nothing and because of his poor health, it was recorded at his home.

The town of Whitstable paid tribute to their much-loved celebrity with a sea-viewing platform named Cushing's View. Overwhelmed by the act of kindness by the residence, he donated a garden bench from his home, which bore a plaque saying, 'Presented by Helen and Peter Cushing'. 'I'm an incurable romantic, and there's only room for two on my bench.'

Around his 81st birthday, Cushing published the semi-comic novel *The Bois Saga*, which was compared to the work of Irish writer James Joyce: one wonders why his didn't pursue a literary career sooner.

May 1994 was Cushing's final professional engagement when he returned to the nostalgia circuit narrating an American television documentary produced by Ted Newsome called *Flesh and Blood: The Hammer Heritage of Horror*. His fellow narrator was Christopher Lee.

The recording took place in Canterbury and Cushing clearly looked ill, the cancer that remained dormant for so long recurred with only Christopher Lee and Joyce Broughton being aware of the situation. 'Peter and I were together for the narration of the Hammer archive video, *Flesh and Blood*,' recalled Lee. 'There was something a little bit different about Peter, waiting for the end.'

Cushing enjoyed working on the documentary, laughing and joking with his old friend. 'His mind was as sharp as ever,' said Lee, 'but obviously he was very frail, having endured illness for so long.' During a break in filming, Lee arranged for a private screening of old Warner Bros and Tom and Jerry cartoons. When filming wrapped, the exertions kept Cushing in bed for two days.

The documentary was screened in two parts on British television in August 1994. During the screening of the first part, Cushing had been transferred to the Pilgrim's Hospice. By the time the second part was screened, he finally succumbed to cancer on 11 August 1994.

'He couldn't wait to join her,' Lee commented sadly. 'Only now is he happy.'

'The news left horror fans with a profound sense of loss,' said Jonathan Rigby, 'accurately reflecting Cushing's status as the finest actor ever to lend his name to horror cinema.' Bruce Lanier Wright agreed with the sentiment when said Cushing's death, 'sparked an outpouring of affection and respect equalled only by that for Vincent Price, who had left us about a year earlier.'

Tributes from friends and colleagues were unanimous, but it was Christopher Lee who remained deeply affected by his passing. 'He really was the gentlest and most generous of men. It could be said of him that he died because he was too good for this world.'

'Peter had expressed his wish for a low-key funeral,' said Joyce Broughton. 'The town was absolutely packed with many thousands of townsfolk, friends and visitors.'

The funeral brought Whitstable to a standstill. According to David Miller,' The funeral procession, led by the frock-coated Mr Terry Davis carrying one of the actor's walking sticks, first visited Cushing's View which was decked with flowers, then stopped outside Cushing's favourite restaurant, the Tudor Tea Rooms in Harbour Street, which was closed for

37: The Final Years

the day as a mark of respect. Whitstable residents, many of whom followed the cortege on foot paid tribute.' It marked quite a tribute for such a modest man.

On 12 January 1995, a memorial service was held in Cushing's memory at St Paul's in Convent Garden, with Christopher Lee, Ingrid Pitt, Joanna Lumley, Ron Moody and Paul Eddington in attendance. 'It was beautiful,' said Joyce Broughton, 'and attended by many of the profession and of course, his fans. Addresses were given by Kevin Francis, Christopher Lee, Ron Moody and his dear friend for many years, James Bree. Rosie Ashe, who had sung at his 80th birthday party, sang the same song to a packed, rapt congregation.'

Tim Burton paid his own tribute to Cushing in his gothic chiller *Sleepy Hollow* (1999). Fellow fan Johnny Depp said his portrayal of Ichabod Crane was intended to resemble one of Cushing's Hammer horror performances.

Peter Cushing's legacy remains enduring to friends, fans and admirers, and an unusual tribute was made to that legacy thanks to George Lucas.

Cushing with Christopher Lee in one of their last photographs together.

Epilogue: Rogue One (2016)

A CGI Peter Cushing in *Rogue One: A Star Wars Story*.

Rogue One: A Star Wars Story (2016) is an interesting, but darker addition to the famous franchise that charts the life and times of the Skywalker family.

Thanks to the wonders of CGI, certain minor characters from *Star Wars* were brought back for brief appearances, one of which was Grand Moff Tarkin.

The film takes place just prior to the beginning of the original *Star Wars* film. As many of the scenes take place inside the Death Star, it was unlikely that Tarkin couldn't be mentioned in name only. Rather than replace Cushing with another actor, Lucasfilm created a likeness of the character, which sparked a great deal of controversy.

The special effects department digitally recreated an image of Cushing and superimposed it on Guy Henry, who played Tarkin. Many fans who watched the film expected, 'a cough, a spit and a fire when ready,' but Tarkin has a reasonable amount of screentime, nearly as much as Cushing had in the original film.

The use of special effects to resurrect a long dead actor was called into question by critics and fans concerned about ethics. Lucasfilm obtained permission from the estate and Joyce Broughton was heavily involved in the production side of it. She admitted during the London premiere of

Rogue One that she was 'dazzled' and 'taken aback' at the sight of Cushing on the big screen once more.

In 2024, Kevin Francis sued Lucasfilm through his film company Tyburn Film Productions and also brought claims against *Rogue One* producer Lunak Heavy Industries, the late executors of Cushing's estate, and Cushing's agency Associated International Management. Francis claimed he needed to give authorisation for any recreation of Cushing's image following an agreement made between him and the actor in 1993, one year before his death.

Lucasfilm claimed it didn't think it needed permission to recreate Cushing's image due to his original contract for *Star Wars* and the nature of the special effects. It also paid around $37,000 to Cushing's estate after being contacted by his agent about the recreation. As of writing, the case has yet to be settled.

Controversial or not, to see Cushing again, even in CGI form is thrilling, and reflects how important he was to the franchise.

Peter Cushing had an incredible 50-year career, and the globetrotting he did provides an interesting aspect of his amazing legacy to cinema.

Bibliography

Baker, Roy Ward: *The Director's Cut*
Brosnan, John: *The Horror People*
Bryce, Alan: *Amicus, The Studio That Dripped Blood*
Connolly, John: *Horror Express*
Cox, Brian: *Putting the Rabbit into the Hat*
Cushing, Peter: *Past Forgettings*
Cushing, Peter: *Peter Cushing: An Autobiography*
Del Vecchio, Deborah and Johnson, Tom: *Hammer Films, An Exhaustive Filmography*
Del Vecchio, Deborah and Johnson, Tom: *Peter Cushing, The Gentleman of Horror and his 91 Films*
Frank, Alan: *The Horror Film Handbook*
Haining, Peter: *Peter Cushing's Movie Monsters*
Halliwell, Leslie: *The Dead That Walked*
Hamilton, John: *Beast in the Cellar*
Hearn, Marcus: *Hammer Glamour*
Hearn, Marcus and Barnes, Alan: *The Hammer Story*
Humphries, Justin: *The Dr Phibes Companion*
Iveson, Mark: *Cursed Horror Stars*
Iveson, Mark: *Vincent Price: The British Connection*
Kinsey, Wayne: *Hammer Films, The Bray Studio Years*
Kinsey, Wayne: *Hammer Films, The Elstree Studio Years*
Lee, Christopher: *Lord of Misrule*
Lindsey, Cynthia: *Dear Boris*
McCarty, John: *The Sleaze Merchants*
McKay, Seymour: *A Thing of Unspeakable Horror*
Meikle, Denis: *A History of Horrors*
Meikle, Denis: *Vincent Price, The Art of Fear*
Miller, David: *Peter Cushing: A Life in Films*
Miller, Mark A: *Christopher Lee and Peter Cushing and Horror Cinema*
Ogilvy, Ian: *Once a Saint*
Peary, Danny: *Cult Movie Stars*
Pitt, Ingrid: *Life's a Scream*
Pykett, Derek: *Michael Ripper Unmasked*
Rigby, Jonathan: *Christopher Lee: The Authorised Screen History*
Rigby, Jonathan: *English Gothic*
Rigby, Jonathan: *Euro Gothic*
Sachs, Bruce and Wall, Russell: *Greasepaint and Gore, The Hammer Monsters of Roy Ashton*
Sangster, Jimmy: *Inside Hammer*
Sothcott, Jonathan: *The Cult Films of Christopher Lee*

Title Index

1984	101-102, 107	Cornelius	18
49th Parallel, The	72	Corruption	143-144, 148
A Chump at Oxford	35-36, 38-40	Creature, The	101-102
A Fourth for Bridge	82	Creeping Flesh, The	169, 173, 175-176
A Land Looking West	226		
A Social Success	93	Curious Dr Robson, The	82
A Tale of Two Cities	235	Curse of Frankenstein, The	107-108, 110, 118
A Touch of the Sun	230-232		
Abominable Snowman, The	101	Daleks' Invasion Earth 2150 A.D.	138
Alexander the Great	103, 105-106, 115	Damascus Blade, The	87
		Dark Potential, The	80
Aliens in the Mind	219	Destination Unknown	80
And Now the Screaming Starts	177-178	Detour, The	233
Anthony and Anna	20	Devil's Agent, The	121
Anthony and Cleopatra	88, 92	Devil's Men, The	211-213
Antigone	86	Dick Whittington	19, 21
Arabian Adventure	232	Dr Phibes Rises Again	162
Asmodee	93	Dr Terror's House of Horrors	125, 141
Astonished Heart, The	82	Dr Who and the Daleks	9, 138
Asylum	175-176	Dracula	110-111, 117, 136, 180, 231, 241
At the Earth's Core	213-214, 232		
Avengers, The	143, 214	Dracula AD 1972	158-160, 179, 214
Battleflag	219-222		
Beast Must Die, The	183-184	Dreams	52-53
Beau Brummell (Radio)	86	Eden's End	89-90
Beau Brummell (TV)	93	End of the Affair, The	97-98, 101
Bees on the Boatdeck, The		Evil of Frankenstein, The	205, 140
Biggles – Adventures in Time	244	Face of Love, The	93
Biography	69	Face of Theresa, The	83
Black Cat, The	235	Fear in the Night	161-162
Black Jack	238-239	Fifth Column, The	80
Black Knight, The	94-97, 101	Flesh and Blood: The Hammer Heritage of Horror	246
Blood Beast Terror, The	144-145		
Blood From the Mummy's Tomb	154-155	Flesh and the Fiends, The	116
		Frankenstein and the Monster from Hell	178
Born Yesterday	83		
Brides of Dracula, The	117, 121, 200	Frankenstein Created Woman	140
Browning Version, The	102	Frankenstein Must Be Destroyed	147-148, 202, 220
Caesar and Cleopatra	88		
Captain Clegg	123	Fresh Fields	22
Cash on Demand	122, 180	From Beyond the Grave	182-183, 203
Caves of Steel, The	124	Fumed Oak	69, 82
Claudia	70	Fury at Smuggler's Bay	13, 122, 180
Cone of Silence	117	Gaslight	110

Gay Invalid, The	87	Memoirs of Mendelssohn	80
Ghost Train, The	69, 73	Midshipman, The	20
Ghoul, The	201-203	Moment of Truth	102
Gorgon, The	125	Monica	139
Grandpa Family, The	68	Monkey Business	22
Great Houdini, The	217	Morecambe and Wise Show, The	151, 154, 180, 233
Greeks had a Word for It, The	22	Morning Star, The	80
Hamlet (1948)	83-84, 143	Moulin Rouge	90-92
Hammer House of Horror, The	234-235	Mummy, The	116
Happy Few	81	Mystery on Monster Island, The	234-237
Hay Fever	20	Naked Edge, The	121
Heiress, The	209-210	New Avengers, The	214
Helen Keller: The Miracle Continues	43	Night Must Fall	69
Hellfire Club, The	121	Night of the Big Heat	142-143
Hidden Master, The	52-53	Nothing But the Night	176-177, 179
Hitler's Son	227-229, 235	Number Three	93
Horror Express	161-173, 203, 214, 239	One More Time	150
Hound of the Baskervilles, The	116	Orley's Farm	82
House of the Long Shadows	241-242	Orson Welles' Great Mysteries	178
House That Dripped Blood, The	153, 226	Outward Bound	68
		Passing Parade	52-53, 64
Howards of Virginia, The	58-60, 62-63	Petrified Forest, The	69
Human Conflict, The	245	Plan, The	124
I, Monster	153-154	Potash and Permutter	20
If This Be Error	93	Pound on Demand	69
Incense for the Damned	148-149	Price of Fear, The	182
Island of Terror	139, 142, 205	Pride and Prejudice	91
It Pays to Advertise	20	Private Lives	76, 81
It Speaks for Itself	83	Proposal, The	86
John Paul Jones	113-117	Red Umbrella, The	17
Laddie	55-58	Revenge of Frankenstein	110, 125
Lady Precious Stream	21	Richard III	84-86
Land of the Minotaur	(see *The Devil's Men*)	Richard of Bordeaux	102
		Rivals, The	12, 81-82
Lay of Horatius, The	80	Rogue One: A Star Wars Story	248-249
Legend of the 7 Golden Vampires, The	185, 188, 92-195	Satanic Rites of Dracula, The	179-180
		School for Scandal, The	84-86
Legend of the Werewolf	202-203	Scream and Scream Again	149
Love From a Stranger	44	Seagull, The	82
Macbeth	69	Seventh Trumpet, The	66, 70-71, 204
Madhouse	181-182, 200	Shatter	195-198
Magic Fire	99-101	She	126-129, 131-136
Man at Six, The	20		
Man in the Iron Mask, The	27-31, 33, 35-36, 42, 61, 104	Shock Waves	204, 206-208, 210-211, 225, 235
Man Who Finally Died, The	124	Silver Whistle, The	110
Mask of Death, The	243	Skin of Our Teeth, The	84-86

Title Index

Skull, The	137-138, 240
Soldier and the Lady, The	93
Some May Live	142
Son of Hitler	(see *Hitler's Son*)
Sound of Murder, The	116-117
Space 1999	204
Spread of the Eagle, The	124
Star Wars	215-217, 220, 223, 226, 231, 237, 248-249
Suspect, The	116
Sword of Sherwood Forest, The	118-121, 123, 125
Sword of the Valiant	242
Tales from the Crypt	156, 158-159, 165, 180
Tales of the Unexpected	242
Tender Dracula	199-201, 203
Tendre Dracula ou les confession d'un buveur de sang	(see *Tender Dracula*)
Thark	138, 141, 209
They Call Me Mr Shatter	(see *Shatter*)
They Dare Not Love	61-63, 65
This is Your Life	180, 245
This Was a Woman	(see *The Dark Potential*)
Three Musketeers, The	180
Time Without Pity	106
Top Secret	240, 242
Torch-Bearers, The	17
Torture Garden	141
Tovarich	93
Trial by Combat	209
Twenty Questions	86
Twins of Evil, The	155, 158
Uncanny, The	223-226
Uncle Harry	110
Vampire Lovers, The	151-152, 187
Vigil in the Night	42-43, 45-47, 51, 57, 68, 180
Violent Playground	111-112
War and Peace	79
We All Help	73
We Were Dancing	82
Wedding Ring, The	92-93, 143
When We Are Married	91
While the Sun Shines	81, 83
Winslow Boy, The	110
Winter Sunshine	21
Women in War	49-51, 58
Zoo Gang, The	158, 180

Name Index

Arnaz Jr, Desi 241
Ashton, Maude (Aunt) 12
Aynesworth, Allan 16-17
Badel, Alan 99-101
Bates, Ralph 152, 161, 187
Beck, Violet Helen (Wife) 44, 65, 76-82, 84, 87-88, 91-93, 95, 101-102, 104, 115-116, 136, 139, 146 ,150-155, 157-158, 161-163, 167, 180, 187, 202, 207, 214, 236, 244-245
Bloom, Claire 103-105
Brooks, Marcus 44, 225
Brosnan, John 62-63, 66
Broughton, Joyce 155, 241, 246-248
Burton, Richard 103-106, 111
Cairns-James, James 17
Carreras, James 107, 110, 126-127, 144, 147-148, 185
Carreras, Michael 126-128, 133, 155, 158-159, 185-186
Cavens, Fred 32
Coleman, Peter 20-21
Coote, Robert 41, 43
Copeland, Elizabeth 44
Craft, Joan 78
Cribbins, Bernard 128-131, 133, 135-136, 138
Cushing, Albert (Uncle Bertie) 12-13, 86
Cushing, David (Brother) 11-16, 75-76, 155
Cushing, George Edward (Father) 11-13, 15-16, 23, 25, 92
Cushing, Helen (Wife) (see Beck, Violet Helen)
Cushing, Henry William (Grandfather) 12
Chiang, David 187-189, 194

Collins, Joan 80, 156, 161
Day, Robert 128-133, 135-136
Del Vecchio, Deborah 40, 44, 59, 96, 98, 101, 104, 106, 111, 114, 121, 142, 187
Doran, John 130-131
Eddington, Paul 124, 247
Evans, Edith 81-82
Fisher, Carrie 215-216
Fisher, Terence 110, 119-121, 125, 136, 139-140, 142, 147-149, 152, 178
Ford, Harrison 134, 217
Francis, Freddie 125, 137, 141, 156, 158, 165, 173, 175, 201-202
Francis, Kevin 201-203, 243, 245, 247, 249
Franklyn, William 122, 179-180
Fraser, Bill 17-21
Fraser, John 13, 122
Goodkind, Larney 25
Gray, Peter 21-23, 41, 82, 245
Haley, Wilton 23, 25
Hardy, Oliver 35-39, 176, 229, 235
Harris, Len 119, 122
Hayward, Louis 29-31, 33-35, 40-42, 44, 47-48, 64, 66, 208, 210
Helpmann, Robert 92-93, 143
Henderson, Don 216
Herriot, Wilton (Step Uncle) 12
Hudd, Roy 145
Ireland, John 68, 210
Kerr, Deborah 97-98, 121
King, Nellie Maria (Mother) 11, 13-16, 22-23, 25, 72, 76
Ladd, Alan 94-97

254

Name Index

Laurel, Stan   35-39, 176, 229, 235
Lee, Christopher   13, 15, 84, 92, 106-111, 121, 123, 125, 128-129, 132, 134-135, 138-139, 141-143, 149-150, 153-155, 158-164, 166-181, 187, 193-194, 210, 220, 224, 232, 241, 245-247
Ling, Peter (stage name)   16
Lombard, Carole   43-44, 46-47, 82, 143
Lucas, George   215-216, 247
Lumley, Joanna   179-180, 214, 245, 247
Lupino, Ida   31, 35, 40, 42, 44-45, 51, 64-66, 100, 210
MacNee, Patrick   92-93, 143, 148, 210, 214
Miller, David   31, 59-60, 64, 67, 69-71, 79, 85-86, 88, 95, 97, 101, 104, 114, 134, 162, 216, 220, 244, 246
Miller, Mark   64-65, 77, 84, 121, 127-128, 132, 163, 166, 176
Mills, John   97, 158, 230, 243-245
Mix, Tom   14, 21-24, 32
Moody, Ron   202, 247
Morley, Robert   24, 26
Munro, Caroline   213-214, 245

Nesbitt, John   52-53
Parker, Al   79, 83, 93
Pitt, Ingrid   151-152, 210, 245, 247
Price, Vincent   9, 149, 155, 162, 180-182, 200, 203, 210, 219, 224, 241, 246
Prowse, David   215-216
Pyne, Natasha   181
Quarry, Robert   162, 181-182
Ray, Fred Olen   206-207
Redington, Ann   79
Roach, Hal   35-38
Sangster, Jimmy   108-110, 117, 152, 161
Schildkraut, Joseph   29-30, 33
Sinden, Donald   95
Small, Edward   25, 27-29, 31
Stevens, George   43, 46-47, 51, 56
Squire, Ronald   12, 81, 176
Tosh, Donald   146-147
Whale, James   28-33, 51, 61-64, 107
Wise, Ernie   151, 154, 180, 233, 245
Wise, Pauline   119
Zeliff, Marjorie   25

About The Author

Mark Iveson is the author of *Cursed Horror Stars* and *Vincent Price The British Connection* both published by Telos. Gateshead born Mark spent his early years in London before returning to the North-East where he currently works as a civil servant for the Department for Work and Pensions.

A lifelong horror fan, Mark has been an admirer of Peter Cushing since childhood. He is also a fan of science fiction, British film comedy and James Bond.

After writing articles and reviews for *Up Front*, *Bite Me* and *The Geneva Times*, Mark became a principle writer for the movie webmag *Shadowlocked*. Recently, he has written for the celebrated horror magazine *We Belong Dead*, and has contributed to several books produced by the magazine.

Mark's other passion is music. He is the former bassist for the North East rock band *Old Man Goat* and currently runs a buskers night at the Associates Club in Gateshead.

Since the publication of his books, Mark has done several book talks across the North-East and attended several events as a guest speaker. He is regularly involved with the *Whitley Bay Film Festival* and the *Morpeth Book Festival*. Most recently, he was guest at the *2022 Sci-Fi Weekender*, where he interviewed the popular actress Madeline Smith. He also interviewed author Jo Lyons at the 2024 *Morpeth Book Festival*.

Mark attends the Swanwick Writers' Retreat at the Hayes Conference Centre in Swanwick, Derbyshire, a great inspiration to his writing career.

Other Film Titles From Telos Publishing

Taboo Breakers
Calum Waddell

Hulk
Tony Lee

Still the Beast is Feeding: Fifty Years of Rocky Horror
Rob Bagnall and Phil Barden

The Making of Casino Royale (1967)
Michael Richardson

Cursed Horror Stars
Vincent Price: The British Connection
Mark Iveson

A Vault of Horror (80 Great British Horror Movies From 1956 – 1974)
Return to the Vault of Horror (58 Great British Horror Movies From 1956 – 1978)
Keith Topping

Time is Luck: The Cinema of Michael Mann
James Slaymaker

Flying Fists: Guide to Western Martial Arts Films of the 1970s
John Beckett

Rubber Sharks and Wooden Acting: The Ultimate Bad Movie Guide
Far From Holmes: An Irreverent Guide To All The Sherlock Holmes You Really Don't Want To Watch Yourself
Nico Vaughan

Infogothic: An Unauthorised Graphic Guide to Hammer Horror
Alastair Hughes

It Lives Again: Horror Movies in the New Millennium
Axelle Carolyn

All available online from
www.telos.co.uk

www.ingramcontent.com/pod-product-compliance
Lightning Source LLC
Chambersburg PA
CBHW060503090426
42735CB00011B/2089